# At The Water's Edge

By the same author

*The White Island* (1972)
*The Seeing Eye* (1979)
*Seal Cull* (1979)
*Ill Fares the Land* (1994)
*One for Sorrow* (1994)
*Song of the Rolling Earth* (2003)
*Nature's Child* (2004)

# At
# The
# Water's
# Edge

## A Personal Quest for Wildness

# JOHN LISTER-KAYE

CANONGATE

Edinburgh · London · New York · Melbourne

Published by Canongate Books in 2010

1

Copyright © John Lister-Kaye, 2010

The moral right of the author has been asserted

First published in Great Britain in 2010 by Canongate Books Ltd,
14 High Street, Edinburgh EH1 1TE

www.meetatthegate.com

For Acknowledgements, please see page 309

'Crow' and 'An Otter' by Ted Hughes. From *Collected Poems* © The Estate of
Ted Hughes and reproduced by permission of Faber and Faber Ltd.

Every effort has been made to trace copyright holders and obtain their
permission for the use of copyright material. The publisher apologises for
any errors or omissions and would be grateful if notified of any corrections
that should be incorporated in future reprints or editions of this book.

*British Library Cataloguing-in-Publication Data*
A catalogue record for this book is available on
request from the British Library

ISBN 978 1 84767 404 3

Typeset in Monotype Dante by Palimpsest Book Production Ltd,
Grangemouth, Stirlingshire

Printed in the UK by CPI William Clowes Beccles NR34 7TL

This book has been printed on FSC certified paper.

for
Magnus Magnusson
in gratitude


'Wealth dies, kinsmen die, a man himself must likewise die. But one thing I know which never dies – world-fame, if justly earned.'

*– Odin, in 'Hávamál' ('Words of the High One'),*
*from the Sæmundar Edda (Old Icelandic mythological poems)*

'Every once in a while we all need to get out, to give ourselves up to a favourite wild landscape, to explore and experience and to wonder. We should do this in every season and all weathers, by day and by night. We should touch and smell and listen. We should absorb moonlight on water, feel the wind in our hair, and discover the other creatures with which we share the world. We should be forcing ourselves to reconnect with wild nature and our origins. We need to do this before it's too late.'

*Dr Jeff Watson, scientist and conservationist,*
*1952–2007*

# Contents

# Preface

*January 9th*  The frost's sunlit sparkle that opened our year was quickly banished by a shroud of grey. The nights have been raw and the days burdened with icy drizzle. For a week we have shivered in the damp of winter chill. I have left my desk and my fireside only reluctantly, briefly venturing out for my Jack Russell terriers, Ruff and Tumble, and always without conviction. Even they have been happy to scuttle back indoors. But today is different. At last a troubled sun has shouldered through, with bright lances of green striping the river fields, drawing me to my study window. Mist hangs over the river but the sun's courage is calling me out. It's not quite ten o'clock.

I left the dogs curled in their kitchen basket, pulled on my old jacket, my boots, hat and gloves, grabbed my binoculars and stick and set out on the circular walk I have done more times than I can count. I turned up the Avenue between the tall trunks of ancient limes and horse chestnuts, kicking the drifts of leaves across the path just for the reassuring swishing sound they make.

My walk takes me gently uphill, northwards with the sun at my back towards high, rocky crags and then turning to face the lurching clouds of the Atlantic west by following the Avenue's parallel lines of lofty trees, precisely planted by Victorian landscape gardeners. Now, more than a century later, in the reassuring way that nature always does in the end, the trees have broken free. The old drive they lined where carriage wheels once crunched on raked gravel is long disused, lost beneath a blanket of leaf mould, and their stretching, moss-sleeved arms have mingled overhead, forming a tunnel of bosky shade. Only the rigid spacing of the trunks reveals their hand.

In the lower branches of one of the limes a spider's web caught my eye. It arched from twig to twig in a mist of fine lace. It was strikingly beautiful, so much so that I stopped to look more closely at the intricacy of the design. It was studded with beads of dew. The weak, low-angled sunlight gleamed from tiny prisms, incidentally distilled from the night's cold air, an unnecessary adornment tipped in for good measure. The spider herself was invisible. She had withdrawn to a bark crevice, where she waited, with one foreleg fingering the pulse of a silken cord to alert her when her trap was sprung. I couldn't resist jiggling the web with a straw, imitating a moth struggling in its tacky mesh. She was fooled, but only for a second. She rushed out to rope her victim round and deliver the poisoned bite to paralyse her prey. Halfway to my straw she realised her mistake, stopped, seemed to think for a second and then returned to her lair. I smiled. That spider was smart. I knew I couldn't fool her twice.

That net was a killing machine – I knew that well enough – but that's not all I saw, nor what I chose to write in my journal. What had stopped me was the beauty of the morning caught in the dewy eye of her device. I was witness to its delicacy, its symmetry and its inspirational cartwheel design. It was this beauty that possessed me and made me stand and stare. It possessed me not in a purely poetic sense, blinding me to everything else, but in the practical perfection of its own intricate existence. A spider's web doesn't *need* to be beautiful to work, but the presence of such radiance is a constantly recurring natural melody I have noted over and over again, almost always there, underscoring the drama of the moment.

Wherever I look in nature I find myself confronted by the paradox of sublime design and grim function, almost as though one is mocking the other – a deadly game, sometimes so violent and brutish that it takes my breath away – the stabbing bill of the heron, the peregrine's dazzling stoop, the otter's underwater grace in pursuit of a fish. And then the beauty floods back in as though some grander plan than evolution fits it all together with added value, that extra aesthetic ingredient, the work of some unnamed genius quite incapable of creating anything shoddy or brash. So I walk, and I watch, and listen, and slowly I learn.

Back at my desk I wrote this brief entry for the day's walk. It's a habit. I always try to write down what I have seen and perceived to be the truth, a journal of these secret and personal thoughts and undertakings. It's not a diary, nor in any sense a scientific record – but I have noted down those things that have caught my attention and hauled me off, incidents and happenings that I have wanted to remember and revisit, and which have helped me engage with the land and the animals and plants that share this patch of upland delight with me, the place I have come to know as home, theirs and mine.

Flicking back through these pages and volumes, I find a perpetually repeating theme. It is the timeless paradox of beauty and the beast inextricably tangled with the impact of man. It is the indescribable and often inexplicable beauty of nature and the overarching sense of wonder it carries with it, always drawn into sharp contrast by her utterly ruthless laws and the terrible truth of mankind's peaceless domination of his and their environment.

Slowly, as the decades have slid by, I have become intimate with my circular walk in a way few of us can hope to achieve in the hurly-burly of modern life. I never cease to be grateful that my work has permitted this level of involvement with the natural world. It doesn't matter what day or what season it is, my walk is an addiction and an escape. I'm taking off towards a loch – my loch encircled by wild and sensuous woods. I don't mean *my* as in my car or my coat, or as decreed by a deed in some lawyer's dusty safe, but *mine* in the sense that no one can ever steal or deny; a private, unassailable *mine*, the *mine* of hopes and dreams.

On a good day if I walk briskly I can do the whole circuit – up the burn, round the loch, across the bog, through the woods and back to the house again – in under an hour. But those days are only good from the perspective of wind in my hair and a spring in my step; good for heart and lungs. They usually mean my mind is somewhere else, transported, clogged with trivia and unable properly to take in where I am and what else is with me – walking for walking's sake. Later, they become the bad days. When I sit to write my journal I can find nothing to say.

Other days are quite different. I only get to the end of the Avenue or to the bridge over the burn, or perhaps halfway round the loch before I realise I have run out of time and must turn back. I have sauntered and dawdled. The walking has been hijacked by some insect or bird I have seen or heard, by a strange footprint or maybe a rustle in the grass, something that freezes me to the spot – something that has caused me to fade into the undergrowth where I can transmogrify into the observer, not the observed. Too often shortage of time has meant I've had to tear myself away, only to regret it later. These are the days that fill my journal, that return to me again and again, resurfacing from my deep subconscious, where they lodged like pleasure-charged pockets of narcotic, days that have sent me back down the path with fresh images to hoard away, new riddles to crack.

I have lived here, on this little glen-side patch of the northern central Highlands of Scotland, for thirty years, man and boy, for I was a hot-headed and incautious youth when first I bought these few acres of rough land and made them my home and my work. It was an impulsive move, but one I have never regretted. I fell in love with the place then and that primal attraction has never waned, although, as in a good marriage, we have grown comfortable together as I have come to know and understand its ways.

All good farmers get to know the dynamics of their land: the wet and the dry ground, where the sun or the winds scorch thin earth, the hollows where frost lies all day and how the invisible drainage runs. They will know where the cattle stand with their backs to the driving rain and where the sheep hunker down against a dry-stone wall; where the rushes constantly invade the grass and where every summer the stinging nettles and creeping thistles reappear however many times they are weeded out. So it is with a naturalist, although perhaps the cast of dramatis personae is longer and the plot a little more complicated, demanding both a predilection for nosiness and a well-developed capacity for dawdling.

I walk when the mood takes me. In summer it is sometimes absurdly early in the morning when the first birdsong tugs me from my bed, sometimes at lunchtime to take a welcome leg-stretch from sitting at a desk and sometimes a break from the dull routines of more dreary work, and occasionally as a closing thought in the long, elastic and emotion-tingling dusk Highlanders have dubbed 'the gloaming'. There are no rules. It is just an unplanned convenient amble and a way of keeping in touch with what lives and moves around me.

The path takes me across field edges, along an old farm track and, most importantly, beside the burn. This spills from the loch and runs down the fringe of the woods to the fields. Its friendly gossip brings a smile to my cheeks and its moods come and go with the clouds; the burn always has something to say. Long ago its flow powered a sawmill and the cobbled lade is still present for part of its course. I am lucky that my trail passes through so many different habitats, something that has happened more by chance than design as the route has established itself over the years, although a desire to feed my own curiosity has undoubtedly revealed its hand.

I have scant equipment. An old felt hat and a once-waterproof jacket, stout shoes and a long stick called a crummack to lean on (from the Gaelic *cromag*, a shepherd's crook, but with a wide curve for hooking a sheep by the neck, not the tight, conventional crosier shape for catching a leg), and, of course, my faithful Swarovski binoculars. Good binoculars are to a field naturalist as a set of spanners is to a mechanic, a stethoscope to a doctor. They must be clear, sharp and an effortlessly natural extension to the eyes and the hand. They are a vital, silent route to where you want to be. Bad binoculars are a distraction, an affront to the watcher and the watched, a hindrance that should be tossed away; better without any at all.

I have worn the same old khaki jacket for years, now tatty and torn, but soft and friendly and, above all, silent. Jackets that rustle are made and worn by people who think human, not wild. There was a time when I would have worn only tweed, but wonderful though tweed still is, its weight when wet and the length of time needed to dry it have pushed it aside in favour of modern convenience fabrics. My aim is to blend, not stand out; to be accepted, not to alarm.

I believe in routine and familiarity, those two. Nothing that lives on this land can fail to be aware of my scent and my regular and hopefully benign presence. Those are the keys I rely on to open nature's doors, to help me slough off some of the universal plume of dread that sheds from all humans like bad smoke. In winter I sometimes wear workman's leather gloves – cold is an unnecessary distraction and, besides, I cannot write with frozen fingers. In summer, if the midges on the moorland are intolerable, in my pocket

I carry a veil to wear over my face; Highland midges can be irksome to the point of despair. On my belt I have a knife, and always, always, always my notebook and two pens in my pocket.

I go alone. Wildness favours the solitary. Company is good, but there are other times and better places for human companionship. And that's it; anything else is superfluous clutter that will detract, not enhance. And expectations? No, none of those. There is a trump card in the expectation game that nature loves to play.

This, then, is a sharing of thoughts and images rekindled from my journal, drawn from the rock and the wind, the snow and the rain, the trees and the birdsong and the blush of wild flowers that have welcomed every spring. Turning its pages and dipping in, I realise it has taken me over thirty years to cover little more than a mile.

John Lister-Kaye
House of Aigas

# I

# The Lie of the Land

Nature knows nothing of landscape. For nature scenery is the natural habitat, while our landscape is the habitat manipulated by man for his own uses. If either man or the habitat changes then so inevitably must the landscape.

– Nan Fairbrother, *New Lives, New Landscapes*

The word 'glen' is sensuous. Like 'mountain', with which it is irredeemably paired, it stirs the spirit. When, quite unthinking, the word pops into my sentence as it's always bound to when I'm talking about my home, I see strangers' eyes brighten; eyebrows lift as though some inner book has been opened at a well-loved passage. That's what Highland glens have always done: stir spirits and arouse passions in a country that spawned the word from its own language. In the Gaelic tongue *gleann* is a mountain valley, almost always with a river, a burn or a loch. It gives itself away.

All Scottish glens were carved by ice; the yawning, glacial troughs left as bare as a canvas for nature to paint afresh, scoured and desolate. For several thousand years after the ice melted away nature took over; it laid down primitive soils and, welcoming all comers, ultimately created great forests of pine, birch and oak. Stone Age, and later Bronze and Iron

Age man hunted through a land rich in game where wolves howled at the stars and brown bears foraged for bilberries in the beneficent shade of the forest. Bronze Age farmers were the first to create clearings for their crops. Cultivation and the teeth of their grazing animals ensured the trees could not return.

When, fifteen hundred years ago, Celtic tribes from Ireland known by the Romans as the *Scottii* came rampaging into this land they called Caledonia, running the prevailing winds across the sixteen miles of petulant sea between Antrim and the Mull of Kintyre, their furious and warring invasion was certain to award it a new name – the land of the Scots. The Gaelic-speaking *Scottii* created a desolation and a deception of their own; the mountains became strongholds from which to raid and counter-raid, pillage and burn. From turf and boulders they constructed lowly hovels for their families and formidable stone towers and keeps rose up for their chieftains; on the flood plains they nurtured their meagre crops. In summer they looked to the high grazing of the mountains and moors for their cattle, sheep and goats, a transhumance which, unwittingly, was gradually creating a landscape of open vistas and bare hills. All those centuries ago mankind was busy taming this land, shaping it to his immediate needs, the needs we all share, for food, security and a home, without any inkling of the long-term conse-quences of his actions. With a relentless urgency to extract a living from the fragile soils, the forest wilderness was pushed back and another land began to emerge, a land that is immeasurably changed, but which still clings to that essential quality of wildness today.

My home sits in a bowl with one side broken away. As the glacier melted back, so the steep side of the valley washed out along a fault line, the friable conglomerate rock collapsing and flushing away to the sea. This hollow awards us shelter and a cascade of gravel terraces – now upland pasture – absent elsewhere in the glen. This geomorphological and glacio-fluvial legacy enabled people to farm the land long before the wild Gaels came barracking in and took over. It was the Bronze Age farmers who first created permanent settlements here, forging the lie, as they broke into our precious Highland soils some five thousand years ago – the lie that is deeply rooted in the romantic mythology of the Highlands, that the moors and hills are naturally bare and have always been that way.

Long before the first smoke curled from the thatched roofs of those early settlements, the glacier sculpted its U-shaped trough which gouges back into the mountains to the south and west for twenty miles. No ice creaks out of those high corries now, but every winter and spring the rain and melting mountain snows keep the brown spate waters of the river pulsing through, a seasonal flare of elemental spleen far beyond the control of mankind, and now the glen's most uplifting feature.

This half-tamed land of sheep pasture and forest is foothill country solemnly lifting to a spine of mountains beyond the immediate horizon, a luminous presence felt but unseen until much higher up. The valley sides are steep and rocky, swerving upwards to a cloud edge a thousand feet above sea level. Birch trees cling on between crags and scree slopes too dry and loose for roots. From afar the trees merge to a cloud of pastel softness, but when, breathless, you clamber up the rocks to their feet the sky has levered them apart and invited a spiny scrub of gorse and broom to share their thin mineral soils.

Far above the glen high, boggy moorland soothes the eye back into the mountains. On a clear winter day from the hill behind my home I can see the Affric Mountains' snowy peaks framing my wider world, alluring and mysterious, promising the adventure of real wildness beyond – a view and a promise always accompanied by a singing heart and an ascending spiral of the spirit.

This famous landscape of craggy peaks and purple moors is gripped in passionate affection by the Gaelic Highlanders – 'Ye bonny banks and braes' – revered and celebrated in folklore, ballad and verse, and loved by free spirits the world over. Yet the notion of wilderness this landscape evokes is the lie – the deep-rooted and fundamental deception that nature alone has shaped this land. To many visitors it is an unpalatable truth that, for all its uplifting qualities and romantic associations, it is man who has imposed his will on this desolate upland scenery by systematically removing the forests and exhausting the frail fertility of its soils.

To the east, across the river – the far rim of the bowl – woodland and dark conifer plantation on a high ridge of moraine bars the way to the sea and another world, a world to which inured glen dwellers like me do not really belong. Only five miles away the Beauly River is tidal. An east wind brings the tang of salt flats and the broad firth beyond like a ghost of the herring and sprats once so abundant in these coastal waters, a bounty that drew many people to settle there. On the Black Isle, the island that isn't an island, trapped between the Cromarty and the Beauly firths, pink sandstone towns and former fishing villages cluster the shore of a much more fertile coastal plain which, for many centuries, sent Highland folk to their beds with full bellies. Their narrow streets and picturesque fishermen's cottages lining the shore also belie the stark and largely ignored truth that those inshore waters can no longer sustain the folk for whom these villages were built. Now they house holidaymakers, commuters to Inverness and the retired.

Across the Beauly Firth, some fifteen miles away, the Highland capital is now a bustling city, said at the turn of the millennium to be one of the most rapidly expanding communities in Europe. Beyond the horizon its amber lights glow on dark nights as if the forest is on fire. Horizons are what contain us every day. If you live in a bowl you sleep with dim horizons of darkness and rise with new light from beyond in the dawn. You dream in their cupped hands.

I have always wanted to live with wildness. In another age I fancy I might have chosen to be a pioneer settler on the very frontier of real wilderness. Oh! To have felt the earth tremble beneath those massed millions of buffalo hooves thundering across the American plains, and to have heard the night howls of the thousands of wolves in constant pursuit. Oh! To have known the unknown – like Meriwether Lewis and William Clark – a grizzly bear or an Indian camp around the next twist in the creek.

At times the Highland hills come close to the wilderness they seem to evoke, alluring echoes of their wilder, not so very distant past. I have never regretted migrating north from my English ancestral homeland. In the context of wider Britain this muscular upland landscape still elicits the notion of true wildness; is still physically and emotionally demanding in ways we have forgotten across most of the rest of the country. Its rocks and its moors and its excoriating seven-month winters purge the soul like hyssop. We take them for granted at our peril.

The road that winds up the wooded rim heading out, away from the glen, leads within a few miles to the tangled world of city life – housing estates, shops, supermarkets, cars and warehouses. I go there when I have to, only grudgingly acknowledging my dependence. When I leave Inverness heading for home, I pass quickly through a farmed landscape of wide, arable fields of pasture, crops and plough, and the euphemistic, contrived greenness which, with the complacency of drab urbanisation, we have come to accept as the countryside norm. A downward somersault of the heart pursues me across a farmscape of mechanically levelled spaces cleared by growth economics, and now shared mostly by rooks and pigeons – the man-manipulated relics of a far more diverse and abundant wildlife that frequented these lands long ago. Buzzards and hooded crows wheel over pheasants squashed at the roadside. Here I feel out of place and burdened, despondent for country lives locked into the orthodoxy of political systems and tractor cabs, suppressed by dull routine and duller necessity.

But once I cross the old, three-arched, sandstone bridge over the Beauly River the glen road lifts and weaves and narrows, expelling my gloom. After a few miles the birch-woods and the river take over; houses vanish, squeezed out by steepening valley sides and pressing trees. Arable farms dwindle away and become honest crofts, the once subsistence smallholdings of a native people who have lived out the turbulent choreodrama of this land for a thousand years, the reading of whose history is almost as cathartic an experience as the task of breaking and cultivating their tiny upland fields. That word 'glen' – that particular defining quality of Highland-ness – has somehow sneaked in and taken the landscape over, an unmistakable and palpable quality of separateness and latent wildness that awards it its special place in the consciousness of all Highland people.

What I love about glen land is its very rough-and-unreadiness, its sense of nature unbowed, its patrician intransigence, still struggling, damned if it's going to be reined in, and offering nothing to humans but back-breaking toil. Yet for all this, my mood soars with the wheeling buzzards to the steep valley slopes and the hills beyond. Those who have always lived here, the glen's dwindling residuum of native Highlanders, seem to reflect the land's resistance; they are also patrician and unflinching, clinging to these unrelenting metamorphic rocks with a poetic tribalism celebrated across the globe.

Above the flood plain and the steep valley sides the soils are acidic, dark and wet, the best they can manage from the rocks and the glacial till, the ubiquitous boulder clay that was clumsily smeared across the moors by the departing ice. With a nonchalant nod of the head towards the skyline, this land is euphemistically known by its crofting incumbents as the 'high ground', by which is meant poor-quality seasonal grazing of heather, coarse grasses and peat bog. Only the

river flats have alluvium, and their productivity is persistently threatened by flash floods from melting snow in the
mountains.

Everything up here in the hills is clean and resonant, like
fine glass – the rocks, the air, the snow and the stinging rain.
In sunlight the glen glistens and sparkles with the mica and
quartz of its metamorphic schists and from its omnipresent
water tumbling from the hills. The crash of falling water is
never far away. It's as though in a last stand for independ-
ence nature is fighting off the lie and the whirlwind of
romantic deception; you feel that it's had enough, clenched
its teeth and refused to cooperate any longer with the
advance of man's ambitions.

Such uncompromising country has always given sanctuary
to wildlife, although man has long plotted against it. The
wolf, the bear, the lynx, the wild boar and the beaver were
all vanquished long ago, and their habitats of woods,
wetlands and forests systematically removed with them,
but, encouraged for sport, the red deer have thrived. Their
furtive presence speaks plainly from the hatch-work of paths
criss-crossing from moorland brown to valley green. Such
relative rarities as the red squirrel, the pine marten and the
wildcat still cling on, although all three have struggled to
make it through the twentieth century and still face many
threats. Yet roe deer, foxes, badgers and otters are commonplace and in the high hills golden eagles thrive on the
inevitable harsh-winter fatalities from the surfeit of sheep
and deer that have dominated this land for so long. Thank-
fully the woods are never empty of birds.

To the north there are no roads, save one track for

extracting commercial lumber. In this direction the bowl's curving side is curtained by spruce and pine; a managed plantation forest where the only relief is occasional rocky escarpments breaking through halberds of military green. And to the west, lifting above ever rougher and wetter pasture, the crimped valley light explodes across a smothering of blanket peat where a sea of heather and bog is lost in the milky haze of higher hills and clouds.

This landscape is unexceptional for this part of the Highlands. Our glen could have many names. How I came to live here is a tale already told in *Song of the Rolling Earth*, but these hills and fields and the wooded slopes I walk almost every day, the river and the burn and the wild creatures they harbour have been such a central part of my life for so long that writing about them is irresistible, a *force majeure* that has elevated the keeping of a journal – a personal record of the land and its wildlife in my time – from the status of a chore into a joy.

The loch is only eight acres in size. Its water is dark with peat. It is roughly heart-shaped, with one or two bays and sedgy marshes; an earth dam sixty yards long flattens the point of the heart. The burn from a smaller natural lochan flowing out across a rock sill was dammed in the late nineteenth century as a water supply, more than doubling the size and depth of the loch. Tucked neatly into its own hollow, the loch is its own secret, hiding from the visible world. It nestles there on the edge of human intervention: above it the wind sings across uninhabited moorland, wild woods of downy birch, eared willow and Scots pine, rowan and aspen, goat willow and wych elm, juniper, gorse and broom crowd in to its banks, and below the dam the manipulated quilting of forest and field is where people have always lived. Over the years I have created a circular trail around the loch. In places the water laps at the path's edge, which then veers off into the woods, winding over bogs and heathery knolls, only to be lured in again at a little bay or a marsh as though the walker has been drawn back, unhappy to be out of sight of the water for long. In summer water lilies burst from a surface of green plates; in winter my loch brims with pure sky.

On the loch's northern shore stands a timber fishing hut I built many years ago, called the 'Illicit Still', and where I sometimes sit to write. 'The day was squinting bright and ear-tinglingly cold', I would later enter in my journal.

*February 16th*   In the afternoon I took off up the hill to the loch. I needed to stretch my legs and I wanted to check the snow for tracks. Straightaway I found the trail of a fox that had used my path while sauntering through. The single-file line of his unhurried paws wove a border of Celtic symbolism up the middle of the track that you could read like a text. That pleased me. I like the thought that the route I take is acceptable to the deer and the badgers, the foxes and pine martens around my home. Whether I meet them or not, I draw satisfaction from their presence. I followed this fox straight to the loch. He had meandered along, pausing here and there; he had left the path to check out something in the bushes and returned again a little further on. I could see where he had stood as still as a gravestone, ears cocked, the heat of his pads burning deeper into the snow, listening to mouse or vole rustlings in the undergrowth, assessing, biding his time for the pounce, then abandoning it and padding on up the path.

The loch was frozen and that was where our paths parted. He carried on across the ice; I wasn't prepared to risk it. So I turned aside and went to the fishing hut. It has an old chair and a bunk and a stove, nothing special, just enough for back-woods comfort, somewhere I often come to think and write. I lit the stove and sank into the armchair beside it and kicked off my boots. I sat looking out at the white world outside and the frozen loch, waiting for the warmth to percolate through to my toes. Slowly I realised I wasn't alone.

A woodmouse, *Apodemus*, was eyeing me up from the woodpile stacked on the far side of the stove. 'Hullo,' I said quietly. I have always loved woodmice. They have style, real élan, and are as golden as hamsters, with huge, shining eyes and ears and a long, flowing tail that wafts behind them like a thread in the wind, never touching the ground. (They used to be called long-tailed fieldmice). They outclass the house mouse in every way. This particular mouse was not in conver-sational mood, and he disappeared back into the woodpile. But he wasn't alone. As I sat quietly for the next hour I heard constant rustlings inside the old sofa beside my chair, more in the roof. There were many more than three bad mice. It was a winter invasion and they were very pleased with the accommodation.

There is a *realpolitik* about nature I have always admired. A ruthless opportunism simmers within every organism. There is nothing cuddly or cute out there, nothing sentimental or romantic, nothing generous or forgiving, nothing magnanimous or altruistic. Just sheer functionality honed to perfection, perpetually thrust forward by single-minded sexual hedonism and the narcissistic selfishness required for survival. Every species is driven by need for a home, for food and for the universal urge to procreate. To wild nature mankind's lofty notions are as meaningless as his grand pretensions. They are as sounding brass or a tinkling cymbal, superfluous flights of fancy, there to be grabbed and exploited to the full. I built a fishing hut and a lochside hideaway for my own purposes and those of my family. The woodmice saw only a convenient, dry sanctuary from predation and an excellent place to rear their young. It was as though they had said, 'Thank you very much, that will suit us nicely.'

The sun was sinking. A golden gleam had caught the pines on the far side of the loch and tiger-striped the ice. Soon the woodmice would venture out for food and take their chances with tawny owls and foxes and the pine martens with which they share this little patch of wildness. For now this place was theirs. I had a home of my own and it was time to go.

## 2

# Spring at Last

The tree which moves some to tears of joy is in the Eyes of others only a Green thing that stands in the way. Some see Nature all Ridicule and Deformity . . . and some scarce see Nature at all. But to the Eyes of the Man of Imagination, Nature is Imagination itself.

   – William Blake. A letter to Dr Trusler, 23rd August 1799

*May 1st*   Spring comes late to this neck of the Highland woods, but when it finally arrives it does so with virtuoso panache – and an irresistible surge of passion and activity, like a dam bursting. Up at the little loch, where I have gone to think and work, I sit leaning against an old pine tree with my notebook on my knees. I am sitting on a folded square of thick blue polythene membrane I have carried around for years, a bit of damp-proofing left over from a building job. The ground is still moist from six months of sodden winter although the early morning air is fine and the sun, up and out since 5.00 a.m., is generous. This *is* spring, there's no doubt of that; the light is yellow; today the sun's gift is of both song and dance.

April in the Highlands is firmly gripped by winter's long tendrils. It toys with spring and then draws back. Snow and the bleat of new-born lambs are April's signature. I heave a sigh of relief when the month passes. May is defiant; it breaks free like a half-trained puppy, running away from the north wind and the rain, ducking the sleet squalls and raising its shout for the sun and the springing grass. Buds and bird-song belong to April, the only poetic concessions it makes between flights of caprice and outbursts of spleen. But leaf is May's great gift, tentative at first, egged on by the anxious early flowers of wood anemone, violet and wood sorrel, then building to a climax with a rush of orchids, fixing the moment, no going back from here. My birthday is early in May; every year I gauge the spring's progress by the extent of new leaf on that day.

Even if I didn't know it had just turned May, if I had somehow just awoken from a deep coma to find myself bewildered and totally blind, my first unmistakable impression would be of spring. It assaults you. It rides the breeze that teases the surface of the loch and whispers in the willow's new, unfurling leaves at its edge. You can taste its tangy intoxication on the air. Irrepressible birdsong envelops you as in Caliban's haunting dream: 'sounds and sweet airs, that give delight and hurt not . . .' and '. . . a thousand twangling instruments will hum about mine ears . . . that, when I waked, I cried to dream again'.

Despite my polythene square, spring is surging up at me from below. Green shoots are piercing the tufts of winter-bleached grass and worm casts have oozed to the surface like toothpaste, as though the very soil is sick of being stuck below ground. Nature is shaking out her skirts after a coma of her own for six long months. In the pines and birches around me blackbirds, song thrushes, great tits and coal tits, wrens, dunnocks and chaffinches, and willow warblers just in from Africa are fluting, trilling, sawing and hammering out their rousing refrains of life and duty. They are grabbing the moment as if their lives depend upon it, which, come to think of it, they almost certainly do. It's infectious. Whatever the day is arousing in my red blood corpuscles is surging in theirs too.

But here's the rub, the first of the great barriers between wildness and the human state, of which I have to keep reminding myself lest I get carried away. For them, the birds, insects, mammals – any sentient organism out there – no conscious thought process exists: this is no chance encounter with a bright spring day as it is for me, in which I can revel and wax lyrical if the mood takes me; for them it is programmed in, a climacteric of expectation and urgency they have all prepared for and are utterly dependent upon, every last one of them. For all the inherent poesy of the birds' melodious accomplishment, the spiralling muses of Keats, Wordsworth and Ted Hughes are a million miles away from where nature grinds its uncompromising corn. The birds are at it in earnest – a deadly, heaving, rugger-scrum earnest, because their lives and futures depend upon it. Their hormones are surging with the turning year, responding to the call of the lengthening days, bursting out into sunshine, revelling – all of that – and dragging me with them, but there is no unison here, no shared compunction between human and the wild, none at all. They are apart and mindless and prescribed. We would do well to remember that. Every individual organism is out there settling old scores, fixing space for themselves and their future alone. Pheromones are teeming and lifting off into champagne air: breasts are swelling, opinions changing, adopting new stances. To me, the lofty observer who can walk away from all this if I choose, it seems that forces have combined to insist upon – to demand – this spontaneous exultation to the turning year.

There have been, of course, all the clichéd envoys of spring with a capital S – the daffodils, the cherry blossom, the birdsong, the rush of early nesters, the return of the ospreys from West Africa, and, as a grand orgiastic climax to it all, the great churning and croaking congregation of toads in the loch, pushing and shoving, thronging, clasping, ovulating, ejaculating and, with fixed amphibian grins, coldly revelling in it all. And it would be quite wrong to suggest that at these latitudes (north of Moscow) nothing at all happens in March and April. Day on day the temperature has been rising, teasing upwards, two steps forward one step back, and all tantalisingly slowly. But even if the toads and the birds do know what's happening, the weather is confused and uncertain. Between bursts of over-optimistic sunshine snow piles in and angry rain and sleet squalls seem to chase us right back to February. But what the capricious weather patterns can't interfere with is the sun.

The great god Sol is creeping up on us, each dawn a fraction higher, stretching every day longer and longer, reaching out for grander ambitions. By the end of April we are enjoying fourteen hours of daylight, against the meagre ten we had back at the beginning of March. The season's tug is winning a nuclear war. The land is soaking up solar energy like dew in a desert. It is being absorbed, sucked in and relished by the plant world's chlorophyll, kick-starting the rush of leaves into violent action once again. May gives us first fresh leaf and it gives us green. That is why I don't allow myself to get excited about spring until the first of May, when all that leaf *is* sudden, sudden, sudden – all change. One minute the world is a tracery studded with buds, the next time you look a viridescent pastel haze has suffused the land in every direction. It's a bad moment to go away. When you come back you're in a different land.

Across the other side of the loch, in the marsh, mallard are chasing their own destiny through the shallows. I can hear them and see them – at least, I can hear frantic quacking and see the flurrying among the rushes. Every now and again a skirmish of wings rises a few feet into the air and drops down again, out of sight. I feel sorry for the females. It is a duck's lot to be hounded by two or three drakes at once. If I were to creep up, as one easily could – so intent are they upon this pressing affair that I could get very close – I would see the poor duck ignominiously shoved below the surface by each swain who grips the feathers on the back of her neck in his bill and treads her back with his bright orange webs while his frantic tail spreads to a broad white fan. In his passion he entirely smothers her. No sooner is he spent than another ardent drake leaps on with all the subtlety of a playground bully and roughly shoves her under all over again. Ducks have been known to drown this way.

I have come to the loch today to write my journal precisely because it is such an uplifting morning. I don't normally. My routine is to take rough notes as it pleases me and return to my desk after a walk and write it up at some idle moment of the day when pressing things are done. But after the long winter there are forces inside desperate to get out when the day is seductive and anodyne like today. Winter walks have been fine – good, bracing, ear-tingling sorties, often more to do with gloves and scarves and steaming breath than with observation of wildlife and any focused attempt to feel at one with the natural world. Back then the feel-good factor came afterwards, a 'well-I-did-it' glow of achievement only experienced when I was back at the fireside, quite different from this 'what-a-hell-of-a-place-to-sit-and-work' sensation that's overwhelming me today.

There are other reasons for being here right now. Some years the Highland spring can last for only a few days. May is still capable of snow showers, although they won't stay – 'lambing storms', my crofter neighbours call them, with that terse and comprehending cynicism that so often defines their byre and baler-twine brand of wisdom, garnered over centuries of hard-won pragmatism – sending everything scurrying for cover again for as long as they last. And then June can suddenly soar to lofty temperatures on static anti-cyclonic highs that dawdle through long days of mackerel-feathered, cirro-stratus blue. Searing through thin, dry air the UV is merciless, bringing a first ruddy blush to the pallid cheeks of winter. Before we know it, summer is firing in.

These bug-free early days must be grabbed. The Highland midge, that scourge of humid days to come, is as yet still a maggoty little larva hiding in its millions in the peaty ooze of the marsh. But the earth is absorbent; the warmth of the sun is piercing and probing deep into the soil and the damp, winter-killed vegetation. The great reawakening, silent and invisible, is mustering its armies twenty-four hours a day. Soon the insect harvest will erupt in all its rampant, multifarious forms, from the exquisitely refined, like the first speckled wood butterflies that any day now will delicately lift from the path beneath my feet, to the execrable great diving beetle, the scourge of the loch's edge, whose calliper-mandibled larva lurks among the rotting stems of last year's water lilies, waiting for what must be its high point of the season. When the toad and frog tadpoles fatten and wiggle free from their natal plasma, this dragon of the murky shallows embarks upon a feeding frenzy, seizing tadpole after tadpole in ferocious, hypodermic jaws, injecting them with a cocktail of pernicious digestive acids which, in the space of a few minutes, without ever letting go, dissolve the tadpoles' insides to a protein soup so that the larva can suck them dry.

From the peaty sludge in the loch's deeps, from the soggy sedge blanket of the marsh, in the root-caves of trees, beneath the rufous bark flakes of pines, deep within dead logs and decaying fence posts, snug inside soft moss cushions and the surface inches of the soil, under rocks and stones, a horde of creeping, flying, crawling and slithering wildlife is fingering the solar pulse. Armoured legs are creaking, suckers are opening and closing, wing veins are pumping up, jaws are hungrily flexing and twitching antennae are tentatively reaching out, probing the possibilities of the future.

These are precious days of warmth and excitement, days a naturalist cannot afford to miss. If I have to go away I can't wait to get home again, hurrying up the loch path to check out the incalculable, unsleeping and effervescent metamorphosis of spring. Dawns cry out for attendance, dusks are just as alluring. I struggle to know which to exploit, often giving in to both. To sit quietly beside the loch at either end of these rapturous spring days delivers a soul-exalting equanimity I have never achieved anywhere else in the world.

Deep underground, milk-full badger cubs, as blind as moles, are curled up in their mother's long belly-fur. At sunset she will emerge to stretch and scratch and when she comes to find the peanuts I have put out for her I shall be able to see her hollow sides and her full udders touching the ground. The bitch otter is suckling four cubs in a cavernous holt under alder roots down by the river. Back in February this year at the far end of the loch I watched her sinuous play-fighting with a powerful pale-throated dog otter, rolling and diving and chasing each other across the marsh in the frantic build-up to receptivity. The hedgehogs, too, have produced their soft-spined litter in rocky dens. Roe does have tiptoed into thickets of dense gorse and broom and dropped their twin fawns in the long grass, where they will lie, scentless and motionless, for the first week of life utterly dependent upon their flecked camouflage like almonds sprinkled on a cake. Their mother will return to suckle perhaps only twice or three times a day, desperate not to give their presence away to prowling foxes that would make short work of new-born fawns. The proud weasel has whelped in her mossy nest deep inside the stone wall and on the wooded hill above the loch the vixen is thinking of bringing her rowdy cubs above ground.

In the top of an old pine not half a mile from the loch the ospreys have laid eggs – all I can see is the glaring amber eye set in the mocha-crested head of the incubating female. On the cliff at the gorge the peregrine falcon is hunkered down on her eggs so tight that I can barely make her out. We know from local archives that peregrines have nested at this site for close on two hundred years, but because the vertical face is so perfect for peregrines it is a reasonable assumption that it has been occupied for many millennia, stretching back to the post-glacial age before man first topped the ridge and saw this glen stretching before him like the promised land. I like to think back down those centuries and of all the thousands of peregrine falcons that have hatched on these rock ledges. It is an ancient dissonance: nature's long perspectives set against man's frantic, short-term bleatings. Visiting the eyrie in spring is a time-eliding experience that brings me down to earth with a bump. A little patience will reward me with the sight of the tiercel flashing in the sun, bringing in a kill, the metallic screams of his approach lifting the falcon off her eggs and rising effortlessly on flicking wings to accept his offering in mid-air.

As rough-hewn as the rocks of the cliff, a pair of ravens lurking just round the corner have two troll-like chicks: fat, noisy and appropriately satanic. In the disused quarry below the loch, with wings as silent as snow, the barn owls have a nest in a crevice once used by rowdy jackdaws, who have now moved out and taken up residence in the dark caverns of a boulder field high above the quarry's rim, from where their merry, bickering chatter echoes across the valley like women at a jumble sale. And down at the house a pair of pied wagtails have loyally returned to nest in the garage roof, every move warily impaled on the jet, unblinking eye of a mistle thrush who has engineered her muddy cup into the fork of a Douglas fir.

Many of these events are predictable; the same or similar sites used year upon year, decade upon decade. After so many years of familiarity the season's scenes and sequences seem to repeat like floral patterns on wallpaper, warm and comforting so that I am relieved to see them back again after the long winter. If our peregrines miss a year I worry, wondering what mishap has kept them away. Instinctively I find myself checking out all the well-used sites on my walk, and in the process I always find a few others, like the robin that I discovered this morning in a ridiculously exposed position in an old yew stump only two feet above the ground, the hen so smoothed into her moss and horse-hair cup that only the glint in her eye gave her away. It will be a miracle if the pine martens don't find her.

My page is crowded with notes. Just now there is no time to think of purpose or meaning, to ponder the creation or the unfathomable web of interdependence that somehow manages to hold it all together. There are long winter days for all that. For now I must be out and seeing, jotting and scribbling, hoarding gems for later delight. I am just happy that spring is here at last.

# 3

# Dreams in a Jar

Those who dream by night in the dusty recesses of their minds wake in the day to find that it was vanity; but the dreamers of the day are dangerous men, for they may act their dream with open eyes, to make it possible.

– T.E. Lawrence, *Seven Pillars of Wisdom*

Long ago I used to think that dust dancing in a sunbeam was a direct product of the sun, that these motes of weightlessness streaming into my childhood bedroom were particles of the sun itself, and that the brilliant stripe slicing across my pillow, searing me into squinting awareness, was intended for me alone. Awakening and forcing my eyes to adjust, I imagined that those sunbeams were a downward draught of bright air silently blowing my way, delivering their gleaming flecks from some unimaginable solar smelter. They burned and then vanished, like sparks. I tried to capture them in a jam jar, shutting them in with a firm twist of the lid. Then I would rush them under the bedclothes to see if they still shone.

It never occurred to me that dust was everywhere. If sunlight was just bright light, I reasoned, why, then, did it have sun-dust with it? The light bulb didn't issue a visible fallout, nor did the precious little torch I had been given for my sixth Christmas. I was convinced that whatever I had in my jam jar was real – a gift of pure sun. I became a heliophile, a secret sunbeam worshipper. They infiltrated my dreams.

If I braved myself to face the window and opened my eyes, even for a split second, and then ducked beneath the blankets I found that I could take the whole window with me, the frame, its astragals and square encasement, branded, no matter how tight I screwed up my eyes, upon the soft pixel-palate of my consciousness. 'Why me?' I mused. And what could be the meaning of this fierce reveille? Was I hallowed? Had I been singled out for one of those epiphanies I had seen in graphic illustrations, Holy Ghost descending in a shaft of brilliance, which were liberally sprinkled into children's bibles of those days? It seemed I had.

Nipping down the passage to my sister's room confirmed this beyond doubt. She lay in gloom. There were no heliographic signals of any kind, divine or otherwise, illuminating her room. No, the sun was signalling to me and me alone, and it was private. It had picked me out and I was in no mood to share its favours. I kept my jam jar hidden in my sock draw. When pressed by my mother for what, precisely, it contained, I ducked the issue, knowing instinctively that grown-ups wouldn't understand.

*May 10th* 'Remember that you come to each day anew,' chides the existentialist philosopher Martin Buber, 'and hallow the everyday. All real living is meeting.' That's where I am; a new day to hallow and some real living to be done. I've taken this walk a thousand times, but even after all these years every stride adopts new form, lit anew by shafts of virgin light, another priceless joust with Providence, fresh garlands to be won. On a hallowed day like today I can step out of the present and feel the future roaring at me, seeking me out, careering in to greet me, one more self-propelled plunge into the great ocean of unknowledge in which we all blindly swim.

Desk work dictates that today's walk has to be in the middle of the day, so I'm breaking free too, springing away to the Avenue with the mischievous gladness of real escape. It's hard to hallow the day when the phone is ringing. But now I'm out, hungry for some living and meeting.

The sun is high and mine all over again. From 93 million miles away it seems to have a gravitational pull of its own. I feel I'm being hustled along by the glow of the year's turning. It has spent the morning elbowing through clouds to reward my truancy with a dome of hard, metallic blue. Leaves are translucent, so that once among the limes and chestnuts I stride through a viridescent haze, wading among tiger-stripes of brilliance, breathing deeply. This is it – living again; this is why I come. I'm heading out, hallowing. Every stretched pace is a triumph of living, of just being a sun-struck mote dancing above the awesome planet revolving beneath my feet.

Great tits are insisting. The shrill 'Teacher! Teacher! Teacher!' repeats over and over again, refusing to let go. Others answer distantly, all staking claims. The waistcoat of a cock bird, as bright as a buttercup, is split wide by the black stripe which heaves and parts as he throats his pride. His purpose is infectious; today his tiny presence on this Earth is as huge and strident as my own.

There are a few more certainties in life than Mark Twain's 'death and taxes', even in our uncertain world. They are the sparks of recognition riding the sunbeams' current, the flecks of familiarity that hold us all together and tell us who we are. I know this bird has a mate and at this moment she is snuggled into her ring of moss and felted down feathers, deep inside a nest box nailed to one of the limes. She is fluffed out in her dim hollow, baring her 90°F brood patches to the five ovals of her future, pressed close. Song resonates above her, new life stirs below. I push on, still anxious that I could be called back.

At the wooden bridge over the burn I begin to unwind. I lean on the handrail and bathe in stillness. This is what Yeats meant by 'peace comes dropping slow'. You can't rush it; breathe deeply. I'm emptying down, draining dross like bathwater. The burn murmurs confidingly, like inconsequential chatter with an old friend. Wrinkled ripples shine and burble behind the birdsong like a melody constantly repeating. I'm out of hailing distance and, more importantly, no one knows I'm here. I feel like Huck Finn: the bridge is my raft, the burn my 'big ol' Mississippi . . . ain't freedom purdy'.

The sun is strong here and I feel the urge to sit. The grass is friendly – winter's lifeless mat impaled by bright new growth – yet chill to the touch. The year's first gnats dance over the pool. Cock chaffinches are bellowing in the willows and birches. A wren trills deliciously. Far away, high over the moorland, a curlew floats its sad notes into the breeze. I need a moment to work out what's going on here.

I close my eyes and turn my face to the sun's radiance and the world becomes pink. It's easy to see why so many pagan cultures threw themselves before it and trembled with fear at the dark gasp of an eclipse. In seconds I am drowsy with the sun's deception; lying back is irresistible.

Just what *is* happening does not bring comfort. Everything around me is grabbing its chance for renewal. In that sense spring is a celebration, a triumph of survival of the long winter. But a survival for what? Where are we all headed under this exuberant star we call Sol? The revelations of physics and the assurance that the sun is 93 million miles away, that it is halfway through its calculated life cycle and will one day run out of heat, plunging us all into ice and gas, reveal no more answers than my jam jar. The knowledge that the glow on my face is a magnificent nuclear engine driving life on Earth, delivering energy through space via photons captured by the very green plants I am sitting on and the result of unthinkable nuclear reactions at the sun's core, consuming 5 million tonnes of matter every second and releasing $3.9 \times 10^{26}$ watts of energy, hasn't helped me a jot. I'm still in deep shadow, and I know it.

And survival at what price, and for whom? It's not by birth and rebirth alone that we survive, but also by the relentless scythe of the Reaper. We inch our way forward over the piled corpses of the dead. No amount of romantic imagery or poetic licence can balm either the fact or the pain. They were right, those pagans, to worship the sun in dread. These warming rays, these beams that seem to ruffle the very essence of the air, that load the great tits' and chaffinches' breasts with jubilation, are where it all begins. Deceptive and unimaginable though it may be, the sun's energy – so vast that we can express it only in a mathematical formula – is systematically sending us out to kill. It is the power source that kick-starts the whole girning, churning conundrum of life into violent alert. We are, every one of us, its slaves and its utterly merciless militia.

I well remember doing photosynthesis back whenever it was so long ago. It gripped me; it seemed such a fiendishly good idea. Beam down the solar energy, fire up the chlorophyll to hang onto the light, suck in the carbon dioxide and water and – Hey Presto! A bag of sugar emerges at the other end. With a wag of the finger and a shake of his bald pate, Tommy Wallace insisted of us languid adolescents never to overlook that this could happen *only* in the presence of *protoplasm* in *living* cells. Ah yes, of course, *life* – living and meeting. That's you and me. And what, dear, kind, generous-spirited, eye-twinkling, pipe-sucking Director of Biology, is life? What is it that sparks back and forth in this wonder gel we've named protoplasm? And what is it for? Just what is it, precisely, that makes you *you* and me *me*? In his book *The Immense Journey*, Loren Eiseley seems to sum it up:

> Through how many dimensions and how many media will life have to pass? Down how many roads among the stars must man propel himself in search of the final secret? The journey is difficult, immense and at times impossible, yet that will not deter some of us from attempting it. We cannot know all that has happened in the past, or the reason for all of these events,

any more than we can with surety discern what lies ahead. We have joined the caravan, you might say, at a certain point; we will travel as far as we can, but we cannot in one lifetime see all that we would like to see or learn all that we hunger to know.

Had I possessed the wit and the courage, aged thirteen, to press the point, I fear that I would have been disappointed. There were no answers in his biology department (despite having it endlessly banged into us that *bios logos* meant the 'reasoning of life'), nor were they in his long shelves of books gathering dust beneath the lab windows; not even, I suspect, inside that wise old head. The answers I sought were then and are to this day back in my jam jar – dreams and sunbeams mingling.

Back in 1953 (only six years before I discovered the joys of photosynthesis) Stanley Miller hit lucky. The young Stan, of whom I have a photograph in front of me on my desk, is dutifully dressed in a collar and tie and an immaculate white lab coat. He looks serious, with trim '50s short back and sides and horn-rimmed glasses. He seems to be posing: holding up a flask at the University of Chicago, where he conducted his groundbreaking experiment. He looks a little nervous, which is hardly surprising since at the raw age of twenty-three he had just been catapulted into the global forefront of organic science. Nervous or not, he is every inch the chemistry student. I get the impression he's never been shopping in his life, that he has an over-protective mother, folds his pyjamas every morning and persistently ducked out of games at school.

He is standing in front of a grid of retorts from which hangs a tangle of apparatus: a flask and a pressure vessel, pipes, valves, U-tubes and cables. This is the young man who set the science world a-buzzing with what the world's press headlined as 'Finally ringing the death knell on Creationism' – a final blow added to the still-haemorrhaging wound of iconoclasm inflicted by Darwin and the Evolutionists back in the 1860s. Miller had, they proclaimed, handed science the unequivocal proof for the origin of life on Earth. The question was inevitable. At a seminar presenting his results to rows of famous faces in the internationally acclaimed and predominantly sceptical audience of scientists, he was asked if he thought this was how life started. Miller's professor, Harold Urey, leapt to his student's defence. 'If God didn't do it this way, then he surely missed a trick!'

What the young graduate student had actually done was nothing of the sort – he hadn't proved a thing. But he had managed to simulate in his flasks and vessels the primitive conditions that probably existed on Earth about 3,000 million years ago, roughly when life might first have emerged.

The Earth is about 5,000 million years old; for the first 2,000 million it was too hot and all the oxygen was tied up in rust – bonded into oxides with other elements such as iron and silicon, which form much of the Earth's crust. The atmosphere consisted principally of four gases: methane, ammonia, hydrogen and water vapour from volcanic eruptions. Then along comes the irreversible influence of the sun.

Somehow, somewhere, all those billions of years ago, in some anonymous mist of eye-stinging, nauseous vapour swirling through the Earth's electrically crackling atmosphere, lightning, together with ultraviolet and gamma radiation from the sun, bombarded those four gases until they metamorphosed, brewing themselves into a stew of amino acids. *Bang!* (or perhaps it was *Fizz!*) – the first building blocks of proteins had arrived on our planet.

Stanley L. Miller rigged up his pipes, tubes and electrodes with the water flask, pressure vessels and a cooling jacket, sealing the vital ingredients within a bell jar. He sucked out the air, creating a sterile vacuum. Then he pumped in the mix of gases and boiled up the water in the flask so that steam circulated throughout. Once he was satisfied that they were all in place in the sparking chamber he gave it a kick of home-made lightning.

He ran it for a week. The solution in the flask turned yellow-brown and an oily tar formed on the walls of the sparking vessel. As the water cooled he found that fifteen different amino acids had condensed out in the U-tube. This was laboratory-induced prebiotic synthesis.

The experiment was opened to peer review with publication in *Science* – one of the leading journals of the scientific world – on May 15th 1953. It was an experiment, no more than that – a shot in the almost-dark of inspired guesswork. It had not proved how life *did* start, but it did demonstrate how life *could* have started. Later, Melvin Calvin did much the same thing using gamma radiation, shunting Miller's work a quantum leap further forward. As well as a mix of amino acids, Calvin's experiment produced simple sugars, and some of the purines needed for nucleic acids. Nineteen fifty-three was an extraordinarily productive year in the world of organic chemistry. Only a few months later Watson and Crick would publish their double-helix model of DNA.

If, in fact, these primitive organic molecules were synthesised in the atmosphere, it is likely they were washed down to Earth by rains, which in time accumulated in oceans and lakes – life's natal soup. By some unfathomable twist of chemistry these tiny molecules – now blue-green algae or bacteria-like organisms – discovered how to replicate each other (asexual reproduction) and nourish themselves by grazing on the others around them. Some stole a march – did better than the rest. Competition was born. It was probably competition that forced some of them to abandon chemosynthesis (munching other molecules for energy), and turn to sunlight – photosynthesis – instead. That was the really smart move. Now we had single-cell organisms pumping out free atmospheric oxygen – so far absent from our story – and the beginnings of a balanced ecosystem. One lot of primitive organisms was capable of synthesising organic food from inorganic materials and providing the oxygen for the rest, which hungrily consumed it and emitted carbon dioxide for the first lot to feed on – the very beginning of the cycle of interdependence of all living things, of which we are an essential part.

So there you have it – the progenitors of the plant kingdom busy feeding the progenitors of the animal kingdom. Let Darwin have his say and before you can mutter 'deoxyribonucleic acid' you have asexual and sexual reproduction operating side by side, both primed with variant mutations (thanks to radiation from the sun) and all replicating and out-competing themselves as fast as they can. Suddenly there are sharks and whales in oceans brimming with plankton, iguanas clambering over rocks, mountains wrapping themselves in jungle, kiwis not bothering to fly, dung beetles rolling globes of their own, albatrosses circumnavigating the oceans of the world and Red Indians chasing buffalo over cliffs. Here we all are, from the amoeba to Einstein, munching each other in glorious sunlight for all we are worth. God, meanwhile, whoever he may be and wherever he lives and moves and has his being, and whether he engineered the whole thing or not, has somehow been left in the shade.

The grass I am lying on is heading in two directions at once. The pallid stalks of winter are going to ground. The forces of decay are already breaking them down, microbes are jostling for their sugars, bacteria are ravenously ingesting, saprophytic mould and slime fungi are pitching in with the slow, mechanical infiltration of their fibres. In a few weeks the old mat will be gone, no longer distinguishable as grass, just a mushy, khaki mulch rapidly decomposing its way to becoming soil, loaded with humic microbes, providing nutrients for its own roots. The new shoots of photosynthesis are heading up, worshipping the sun, dizzy with light and carbon dioxide.

A shadow crosses my closed eyes. For the briefest flicker something has passed between me and the sun. I am instantly awake. I know I'm no longer alone. My eyes ease open, feeling the drag of my irises urgently and involuntarily stopping down. Squinting, I glance to the right and left. The sky above me is enamelled with brilliance, but the chaffinches are no longer singing. Even the busy wren has stilled her trill. Slowly I pull up onto one elbow.

Twenty yards to my left a line of electricity distribution poles crosses a field. My eye is drawn to the apex of the nearest pole. There, shining in newly burnished copper, is a kestrel. He is small, smaller than a pigeon and neat with it in a dressy way, but he gleams with all the presence of a prince. I can feel him. My skin tingles. His shadow snapped me out of my daydream and now his aura is hauling me in on a rope. For once he hasn't seen me. Normally you can't fool birds of prey. Their eyesight is so fierce, so finely tuned, so instantly absorbent to every twitch of life that our feeble efforts at concealment are a worthless gesture.

I raise my binoculars and scour the profile of his blunt little face. He is brand new under a hood of blue slate. His primaries are blades of black, crossed behind his back like a schoolmaster's hands. The grey tail is long and dipped in black ink, except at the very tip, where a crescent of copper shines through. The nares are a golden glimmer crowning the arc of the neat, downward-tucked bill; yellow rings encircle dark orbs as round and glossy as puddles on a moonlit night. They dominate his brain. Behind those limpid lenses a continuous interrogation simmers and seethes.

He hasn't seen me because he is intent, staring down. Something below him in the grass close to the foot of the pole has tracked its image up through the sunlight into the glowing sponges of his retinas. He is drinking it in;

motionless – no, stiller than that, he is frozen. It's as though a sculpture in polished slate and copper has been placed on the top of the pole. So intense is his concentration that for the moment I am safe; I can shift my awkward position and lean back against the rain-laundered bark of a birch.

Anxious for her own future, a hen chaffinch decides to brave the vivid statue that has invaded their sunlight. She flutters out to mob the kestrel, uttering a broken little cry edged with hysteria and adopting a quite un-finch-like flight, hesitant and dithery in a way that impresses no one; certainly not the kestrel. He doesn't flinch. His gaze is as fixed as his stance. He ignores the chaffinch, not even bothering to acknowledge her presence. She dances twice around the pole, gives up and returns to the birches. The day is silent again.

Only later will I properly comprehend the emergent mini-drama that is being enacted here. For now all I see is a kestrel perched on a pole. My thoughts return to the sun. It has been at work for several hours, streaming photons my way. The ground is drying, the leaves unbuttoning their tulip wraps and motorways of chloroplasts are flooding in to work. I am forced to acknowledge (reluctantly) that only some of that solar radiation is for me. Happy though I am with my slice, I know that others are stirring too. The great tits and chaffinches have raised their song, breasts swelling, syrinxes oscillating, hurling it out, choiring the day with spontaneous, sun-charged exultation. Beside me the delicate petals of wood sorrel are lifting; their shamrock leaves are widening to soak in the soft confetti of sunlight that sprinkles the woodland floor.

There is a solemn explosion of life everywhere I look. Chemical reactions are raising their game. Protoplasm is busier than it's been for months. Decay is smouldering underground. Insect pupae are squirming inside their leathery wraps. Egg cases are splitting. Sap is ascending the birch stems to match the call for water and minerals from high above. Every opening leaf needs the hydraulic turbidity of filled cells to stiffen and grow. Columns of liquid power are answering a call to arms. Trance-like, the kestrel stares. With the patience of a gravestone he stares into the grass.

Somewhere underground, in some secret cranny of its own, a reptile blinks and stirs – stirred by some cryptic alchemy of electro-chemical sentience. Waking from long sleep it feels the surge of the warming earth around it. Its dreams had been of pure sun. There was nothing blind about this instinct. For all heliotropic reptiles that have to raise their body temperature to get going, the sun is an imperative, an irresistible call. They have no choice. To feed, to grow, to mate, they have to find the sun. Such is the lot of the slow worm.

Normally the slow worm (actually a legless lizard) doesn't bask in open sunlight as crocodiles and many lizards and snakes do; it prefers to absorb heat from stones. Beneath a sheet of old corrugated iron is a perfect place to heat up quickly and in safety – a quick warm for a slow worm. I have found dozens in such places – have even laid sheets down for that very purpose. Boy-naturalists indulge strange pursuits. You come back later and take a peek. You lift the sheet. Suddenly exposed to the light, slow worms look put out and urinate to make the point. And they are slow; they can't hurry off, are easy to catch. You learn quickly it's important to let them urinate *before* you put them in your pocket. Reptile urine has the rancid odour of over-stewed cabbages. As a boy I smelled permanently of school kitchens.

But this is May and the sun is high. There are no corrugated iron sheets available, nor, apparently, suitable stones. Slowly our worm-lizard ventures out into full sun. This ponderous legless lizard, who feeds mostly on small slugs, is stiff and slow. In the hand it has none of the taut, muscular flexibility of a grass snake or an adder or those almost prehensile, broad underbelly scales that zip snakes along so efficiently. Stiffly the slow worm levers his silvery inches between stems and stones using friction and the extended 'S' of his long body to slither forward. His black tongue flickers, testing the air. His blunt little head, the hazel-ringed eyes and pencil-dot nostrils prise through the grass like a bodkin. He is all metal, the thickness of a man's forefinger forged in shining blue steel. And he is utterly harmless – unless you happen to be a slug. But before he can do anything else he needs the sun.

I knew none of this. I saw only the statue staring into the grass. Then it fell. It was as though the sculpture had been tipped forward by an unseen hand. Still staring, on closed wings it fell through empty air to the earth. The earth rose to meet the copper falcon in a collision that would surely bring its death. In a single burnished dart it dived to the long grass, head first. I missed the yellow talons thrust forward.

I was too slow to see the black-banded tail feathers fan to brake the fall. It vanished. I was sure it must be dead. How could it plummet to earth without dashing out its brains? I stood up. There was no sign of the kestrel. The grass had swallowed it up.

The kestrel is a falcon, a member of that elite of raptorial, hooked beaks, all of which vie with the eagles for precedence. The vain and competitive aristocracy of the raptor world have never conceded a jot. Led from the front by the gyrfalcon and the peregrine, for dash and verve the falcons have it; for power and imperial splendour the golden eagle and its huge cousin the sea eagle cannot be matched. Hardened birders can never agree; the jury has long since given up and gone home. The kestrel and the merlin are the smallest falcons on the British list. Both can dazzle with aerobatic skill. Of the two the kestrel is the commoner, so familiar on our roadsides and motorway verges hovering for voles and mice, hawking the air for insects. The windhover is its old country name. It can face into a gale with wings half closed, holding its position with barely a quiver for minutes at a time. It stoops like a flash of bronze.

I peer through my binoculars. The grass reveals nothing. The whole thing was a sun-dream; I begin to think I imagined it all.

And then this little falcon, this flash of kettle, rises from the earth. It ascends on stiffly flickering wings. It rises and rises. Clenched in one black-taloned fist is a lanyard of legless lizard. Its yellow grab-foot had closed around a slow worm. The needle talons grip its tail. Sunlight glints from silver scales. It rises with the kestrel, twisting its head and thorax in an aimless confusion of defiance and despair. The kestrel circles the pole once and returns to its perch. Landing on one leg it shifts its grip, now pinning the squirming tail down with the other foot too. The slate-blue head bends to its prey and the grey bill opens; the hook curves downward like a claw. The slow worm inscribes one last, desperate loop. Levering against nothing but air it curls and flails and breaks. It breaks free. I see a flash of red and the broken body twists and falls, arcing through sunbeams to the ground.

The kestrel looked bemused. He stood with a squirming tail in his talons. Its bloody stump thrashed even more vigorously than before. The falcon looked first at the tail clenched in his feet, then down at the grass below. A sharp, yickering cry vented his frustration. He seemed to know that the prize was gone; gone the way of the survival game – some you win, some you lose.

The slow worm had played its last card. Its past and its future had collided in a moment of terrible truth. By sheer luck it had been caught by the tail. Evolution had handed it a trump to play when the chips are finally down: cast your tail.

Break free and go forth tailless into the future. Inside its tiny, metallic brain something akin to adrenaline was sending an SOS to its tail an inch behind its last vital organ. Tissues contracted and the pre-ordained hairline fracture built into its cartilaginous spine suddenly snapped. The blood supply crimped off, the muscles ruptured, the silver scales parted like slates on a shattered roof. It broke as though chopped. It shed the inches it needed least. The body cannot re-grow a tail, but the stump will quickly heal. Tailless, it can still feed and breed and function adequately for long enough to reproduce itself. That's all that natural selection cares about – one more chance to survive.

So my sun-loving slow worm had played its last hand and won the day. Hitting the grass, it lost no time in disappearing. The kestrel flew off with the tail; I climbed the fence and walked over to the pole. I scoured the long, dead grass, lifted stones and gazed up at the perch above. The slow worm had gone. Its dreams of the sun will never be the same again.

# 4

# King of the Castle

Crow, feeling his brain slip,
Finds his every feather the fossil of a murder.
Who murdered all these?
These living dead, that root in his nerves and his blood
Till he is visibly black?

                 – Ted Hughes, 'Crow's Nerve Fails'

*May 12th*   Regulation has polluted my whisky. The water
we drink comes from the loch. The Victorians built a dam
to increase its size and piped it to the house and the farm.
Before that it came in buckets. Bronze Age children
scooped it up in their hands. People have lived here and been
drinking the water from this loch for the best part of five
thousand years.

The water analysis man who arrives every year with his
little sampling bottles tells me comfortingly we have some
of the purest water in Europe. But now, suddenly, after all
those millennia of drinking and living, it is apparently no
good any more. The chemicals are fine: lovely iron and
magnesium and other trace minerals shoring us all up; the
electrical conductivity is spot on; the mild acidity renders it
soft and quick to lather; the bacterial count is nil – not a

coliform or an *E. coli* in sight; no unwanted salts or chlorine, not even a nasty nitrate, but the *colour* is wrong.

Somebody somewhere else, someone who has never been to the loch, nor perhaps even to the Highlands, has decided that our water *looks* wrong. Its *hazens* (whatever they may be – the *Shorter Oxford English Dictionary* fails to acknowledge them at all) are too high. The Chardonnay-tinted staining that comes with the clouds and the snow and the life-giving rain that gently bleed tiny, suspended particles of peat into the loch from the high moors, and which have graced my bath and my evening whisky for the thirty years I have lived here, is no longer acceptable to someone who doesn't have to drink it or even see it. 'You will be required to undertake remedial works,' insists the letter I have just thrown down in despair. I have another remedy in mind.

It's the second week of May and I'm escaping again. Some things are better ignored, treated with the contempt they deserve – survival is tough enough without creating problems that don't exist. The kestrel still burns in my memory's eye so I'm heading out to see what nature's wild wheel can uncover today.

It is early. The sun is awake, but still cool, the west wind light. I don't plan to linger. Sail-white clouds jostle in the marbled sunlight of the morning like club racers. There has been rain in the night and the infusion of leaf mould lifts headily from the scuffles of my boots. I breathe deeply. Last year's horse chestnut leaves still clutter the path in russet rugs, swirled into low dunes by winter gales. Picking one up, I see that the flesh of the leaf has all but gone, leaving only a filigree of veins and stalk with shards of translucent tissue trapped in the corners like broken glass in a ruined church window.

May's great trick is movement. It never stays still. No two days are the same, always pressing forward so that yesterday's images are diffused, atomised in the breathless rush for food, space and light. The new leaf is bolder now; after months of open tracery, shade is arriving to sharpen edges and deepen creases in the land's complexion. The great tits in the Avenue are silent. I pause to see what's up.

The hen bird, less custard and more mustard than her mate, comes in with a looping caterpillar in her bill. So that's it. Her white, speckled eggs – could be five, could be twice that or more in exceptional years – have hatched. I could easily take a look; the nest box has a hinged lid secured with a twist of wire, but it seems an unmerited intrusion at this delicate moment in their new lives, so I abandon the thought. She is in and out in a flash, a tiny buff and black torpedo exploding out of the hole with those white cheeks gleaming like a nun's alb. She alights for a second on a twig, just long enough to pull focus. She's as tight as a nut, sleek and pressed together like modelling clay. Did this really evolve from the amoeba by the gradual process of random change? Did Stanley Miller's experiment running wild for a few million years cause methane, ammonia, hydrogen and water vapour to fuse and spark into this bright, hot, fizzing fistful of protein; this seeing, singing, dutiful, nest-proud mother of five to eleven would-be replicas, blind and naked and unspeakably ugly, trapped in the moss and down cup she has so lovingly woven?

It's far too comfortable to live with assumptions. Although adult great tits eat a wide variety of insects, seeds and fruit, they feed their chicks almost exclusively on caterpillars. It is safe to say that without a steady supply of caterpillars they couldn't raise their young. So all they have to do is lay their eggs fourteen incubation days before the caterpillar glut emerges and that's them sorted – isn't it? But how do they know when the caterpillar glut will be? It peaks at widely differing times, sometimes by up to three weeks from year to year, dependent upon the weather, but particularly the temperature in late April.

If it's very frosty caterpillar eggs won't hatch because buds won't open, the leaves will be retarded and there won't be anything for the caterpillars to eat. These hatchling tits have to be fed immediately. They will quickly weaken, chill and die if each chick doesn't get a good feed in the first few hours. I do the crude sums in my head: let's say nine chicks, each needing at least fifteen of these squiggly loopers a day, plus a couple of good fat ones of other species if possible – that's a hundred and fifty-three caterpillars to be garnered in across the fourteen hours of daylight available to them, as well as food for the parents themselves to keep up their strength – call it one hundred and eighty. That's ninety per adult bird: six and a half per hour if they don't rest – a beakful back at the nest every thirteen minutes, including travelling and searching time. No wonder they're not singing. And they have to keep it up for the full twenty days before the chicks fledge and another week after that before they can feed themselves. So how *do* they know just when to start laying eggs?

Is there some grand programme out here? Are we back at school, obediently plugged in to a timetable? Is there a Fat Controller in charge, keeping everyone up to speed, frantically barking out rules and regulations like the Water Authority? Or is it just chance; are we all a mess of pottage and protoplasm, tossed in together like the kestrel and the slow worm – some you win, some you lose – and you just keep praying that your number comes up? Hmmm. Maybe I should have stuck with the hazens. I walk on, wishing the sun would get to work.

'Give me health and a day, and I will make the pomp of emperors ridiculous,' wrote Ralph Waldo Emerson in 1836 in his essay 'Nature'.

> . . . The simple perception of natural forms is a delight . . . To the body and mind . . . cramped by noxious work or company, nature is medicinal and restores their tone. The tradesman . . . comes out of the din and craft of the street, and sees the sky and the woods and is a man again. In their eternal calm he finds himself.

Somewhere in the Massachusetts woods, the cradle of American literature, the transcendentalist writings of Emerson, Walt Whitman and Henry David Thoreau were to change the English-speaking world's perception of nature.

They established a distinctive rhythm for this literature of meditative excursions. They mark a purposeful shift from the imperative Abrahamic diktat requiring the conquest of nature in Genesis – '. . . and have dominion over the fish of the sea, and over the fowl of the air, and over every living thing that moveth upon the earth' – later to be justified and permanently imbued in the founding principles of Christian society by the seminal thirteenth-century teachings of St Thomas Aquinas.

At a time when many of the great wildernesses of the New World were being opened up for the first time, Emerson and his colleagues leapt from the notion of taming the wild to harmonising with it in spirit and deed. The concept and philosophy of nature conservation as we know it owes much to these exuberant and assertive scripts. But they also perpetually question what it is all about. 'To what end is nature?' asks Emerson early in his famous essay, a question that presents itself to every naturalist over and over again. As science systematically strips back the scales from our eyes the questions loom larger, not smaller. 'God knows why I'm here at all,' a man I met working in the woods said enigmatically to me recently. A few days later I saw a teenager walking down the Inverness street with 'Perhaps the Hokey-Cokey *is* what it's all about' boldly printed across the back of his sweatshirt.

Out there, just over the fence and up the steep field, on a high spot where, like clenched knuckles, grey boulders nudge through the grass, sits a solitary hooded crow, a blackguard of the crow clan known round here as a 'hoodie' – a term as far away from endearment as you can get, but one often spoken with the sort of respect afforded to Attila the Hun, or, in Highland Scottish parlance, the Wolf of Badenoch, the fourteenth-century warrior chief (Alexander Stewart, 1st Earl of Buchan) who sacked Elgin Cathedral and many other sites. The hoodie has a reputation. It also knows exactly why it's here.

It is a handsome bird, strong and well balanced, with a black hood – as someone once said to me, 'as black as Calvin's bible' – and a grey mantle as pale and soft as a cloud that threatens a shower. Everything else is black, crow-black: the sharp, powerful bill, the gimlet eye, the tough, springy legs and scaly feet, the long wings and tail – the satanic reputation. It is, of course, a race of the carrion crow, *Corvus corone*, one of the arch-rogues of the bird world, but the hoodie is awarded its own ensign – *cornix*, 'of crows'. So he becomes the ultimate crow of all crows, the highly intelligent arch-knave of the corvid tribe, craftier than a raven and quicker to seize upon an opportunity; more cunning than his cousins the artful jackdaws, magpies and jays. Unlike the rowdy, gregarious rook, he is a loner, usually working alone or as one of a pair, furtive, sly and often seen to be malevolent with it. You can't impugn a hoodie; he's been there before you.

It is hoodies that will spot a sore on a sheep's back and harry it, landing over and over again, savagely pecking so that the wound stays open, letting in flies to lay their eggs. Before anyone notices it the sheep is down, 'struck with the fly', as they say round here. Hill sheep often lie undiscovered for days. Maggots will do the rest. A suppurating carcase is a hoodie's idea of nirvana.

It is the hoodie that will swoop down and chisel its stabbing bill into a clutch of four newly hatched curlew chicks, one by one, as they struggle to find cover among the heather, leaving them maimed and strewn across the moor like victims of a sniper, cheeping out the pathos of their own imminent destruction, moving on to the next one, and returning later to finish them off, while the yikkering cries of the frantic mother rend the air overhead.

This one bird on the rock looks innocent enough, sunning itself, occasionally preening. But it is neither innocent nor alone. Its partner is perched atop the lightning-scorched mast of a Scots pine, only just in my view some three hundred yards away to the left. Between them they can scan a whole hillside containing the spread hirsel of my neighbour Geordie McLean's sheep. They are waiting. Opportunistic patience is the name of this game. They are waiting and watching the lambing field: waiting for events to unfold, for an after-birth or a stillborn lamb, watching for the slightest chance to raid and plunder.

It is May and the wide pasture is dotted with ewes like a repeating emblem on a counterpane. Many are yet to produce. Little gangs of strong lambs cluster like school-children in a playground. They rush off in a game of Tag, tearing along the fence, halting suddenly and rushing back again. Then they scamper off to a low mound – it's Follow My Leader. The strongest lamb – at least a week old – gets there first and bags the high point; the others are jostling, pushing, competing. He holds his ground, bleating assertively

– King of the Castle. The air vibrates with their high-pitched, stuttering din. The expectant ewes graze quietly, apparently unaware of four black, scanning, scouring eyes.

Competition: that's what it's all about. We're all competing, all the time, although like Emerson we merrily choose to wrap it in fluff, sentimentalise it, rose-colour it, to conceal it in any way we can. We're not good at facing up to unpalatable truths. But we are all competing for space, light, food, mates and power, each and every last one of us: archbishops, civil servants, vagabonds and vicars, knaves, princes and prostitutes, welders and trapeze artists, bus drivers and bakers – even naturalists. Any excuse will do. Even the colour of our drinking water would become a competition for authority if I rose to the challenge.

The great tits are frantically competing for caterpillars; competing against other bird species and other great tits. The caterpillars are competing with each other for the starch-filled cellulose they need to grow; they're munching for all they're worth, gripped by the fear that somebody else's mandibles will get there first. The leaves are competing for light; far below, the roots are jostling with the root hairs of other plants for water and minerals, grabbing, grasping, gripping and hanging in there for all they are worth. The whole thing is one ghastly, urgently swirling, deadly serious game of King of the Castle.

Years ago I read in Sir Dudley Stamp's thoughtful analysis of nature conservation in Britain that our post-industrial societal values were no longer determined by those of primary food producers – farmers and fishermen – and that since most of us no longer had to worry about where our food was coming from our attitude to nature was one step removed from reality. Back in 1969 Stamp was right, as was Emerson in 1836. Relieved of the worries of primary food producers who, throughout the Third World, still struggle for soils and against agricultural pests every day of their lives, we can waft through the woods musing loftily, 'To what end is nature?'

A vehicle crunches slowly up the track and parks at the field gate. It is Geordie, now in his sixties, whose crofting family have kept sheep and cattle on this land for centuries. Tam, his black and white border collie, leaps from the back of the pick-up and clears the fence in a high, excited bound. Tam is a young dog and still has to be worked through. Enthusiasm for the task in hand is fine, but over-exuberance is counter-productive. Geordie calls him in with a wave of his long crummack and they move up the slope together with the dog at heel.

Those who give their lives to working with animals also gift themselves to the land. They know it and love it, and, over time, it adopts them and shapes them to its will so that they become a part of the landscape, blending with it in economy of movement and sureness of foot, hand and eye. The gentle philosophy of the hills and glens shapes their weather-sculpted faces, delivers broad smiles and a knowing nod in place of unnecessary words.

I watch man and dog walking quietly among the ewes. Tam drops to command, lying obediently while Geordie eases in and catches up a lamb with the looped handle of his crummack. He checks it out; the ewe grates loudly, a stammering 'He-e-e-e-y!' of disapproval. She stands her ground and faces him; crossly she stamps her neat little front hooves, first one and then the other. He gives her lamb back, placing it gently on the cropped turf. It runs to its mother and immediately suckles, tail a-shimmer like a ribbon in the breeze. Geordie is a primary food producer, although I don't think he sees himself or his hill sheep as competing with anything much, except perhaps the weather.

Most of the competition was over long ago. With fire and axe men cleared this land from climax forest, using the timber and burning the brush, exposing the fertility of the forest soils to the sun and the rain. Grasses rushed in. With competition eliminated, those colonising plants had the light and the nutrients to themselves. Pasture flourished and those long-forgotten men and women thought it was good. They planted their meagre crops and tended their animals here for thousands of years, keeping the forest at bay and slowly but systematically removing the unwelcome competition from wildlife such as deer, wolves, wild boar and bears. They went to bed with their bellies full and slept soundly at night. There is no doubt who was winning their game of King of the Castle.

But competition never sleeps; it is built into the very spiral of the DNA double helix. Like love and hate it is built in, a part of us all. Just as tribal societies all over the world persistently fought among themselves for the land and its resources and the security and the options for living that came with it, so did the Highland clans. That pressure never lifts. Even now our new Scottish parliament is fingering the legal rights of those who own the land. At least in this glen we no longer kill each other.

Unconcerned about land rights or food production, and also with his belly full, Ralph Waldo Emerson could afford to wax lyrical about the woods:

> I have enjoyed a perfect exhilaration. I am glad to the brink of fear. In the woods too, a man casts off his years, as the snake his slough, and at what period soever of life, is always a child. In the woods, is perpetual youth.

In his darkest dreams it can never have occurred to Emerson that, by exactly the same process as Geordie's patch of Highland hillside was shorn of its forest, his own Massachusetts woods would soon be almost entirely cleared. Nor that within the span of just two human lives – little more than one hundred and seventy years – the human population of the USA would be approaching 300 million and the world 6.45 billion, with such patches of wilderness (mostly deserts) that are left teetering on the very margins of ecological viability. Suddenly his question seems acutely relevant. To what end is nature now? And what if the Hokey-Kokey *is* what it's all about?

Geordie returns to his Toyota pick-up. I watch it bump away down the track; Tam stands in the back, head out at the side, tongue lolling and ears flapping in the wind. He has done his rounds; for now the competition seems to have lapsed, the lambing is going well, the sheep are okay. I walk on.

If I'm honest, I don't really like sheep. The Highland hills have suffered badly from overgrazing since the old cattle economy ended in the early nineteenth century and the Highlands' agriculturalists rushed into sheep. Wool profits and hill sheep fortunes have waxed and waned like a tide for two hundred years, but they have never gone away. Throughout the twentieth century the crofting world of small-scale agriculture seems to have pivoted around the sheep as its principal source of revenue and employment. It has spawned a sheep culture of its own, which is immediately evident to any traveller through the crofting counties: bare hills and close-cropped sward, lambing pens, dry-stone fanks, wind-tanned faces, quad bikes, collies and wool sacks hanging from their summer gallows. Yet I have come to respect those who have given their lives to caring for their livestock; those who never complain about the long, unsociable hours, the foot-slogging toil, the driving rain and sleet or the summer midges; all those who fiercely defend crofting as a way of life, regardless of whether it makes economic sense or not. I feel an empathy for Geordie and his black-faced ewes – 'blackies' – and their leaping, gambolling, bleating progeny, scattered across the hill like currants in a bun.

The trail takes me up the burn and through the spruce plantation to within a few yards of the old pine where the hoodie is perched. He is alert and wise to human movements. He has watched Geordie come and go – they both have. Hoodies know the range of a shotgun, the shape of a rifle. They know they are hated and that they are also dependent upon man's activities to raise their young. They could choose to live safely high in the mountains where contact with man would be minimal, but life up there would be tougher. Without the constant food supply provided by farming and crofting they would have to work harder, compete more, defend a larger range, and, like the great tits and the caterpillars, they would be far more vulnerable to the vagaries of climate and season. Their presence here is a calculated decision; a risk assessment perpetually grinds inside their black, angular skulls.

For a while this pastoral scene is idyllic. The birds sing; a buzzard wheels overhead, lazily spiralling higher and higher with the barometer. The sky is ribbed with the mackerel cirro-stratus of incipient high pressure. I see the hoodie's head tilt sideways as it eyes the buzzard, assesses the threat and weighs up the competition. It cries out: three rasping calls as rough as scraping your exhaust pipe on a stone, as if to alert its partner still back there on the boulders overlooking the slope. All hawks are a threat, even to these finely tuned predatory villains.

I'm close to the loch now. The drinking water nonsense is still fizzing in my head. I wander closer, almost as if I have to check out the colour for myself. If I'm not careful that letter could spoil my day. I must think like Emerson, be aware of 'the perpetual presence of the sublime'. It works. These eight acres of cloud-reflecting sky are as close to sublime as I'm likely to get today; I never tire of the surprise that greets me as I top the rise and see over the dam for the first time.

From the east the loch is sheltered by the woods. In these

conditions the surface immaculately mirrors the world in which we live. It has sun and clouds and woods brimming to its shores. Birds trace through and the ospreys and herons draw wide arcs around its rim. Over the other side, near the marsh and where the water lilies are surging upwards from their long winter sleep, my friend and neighbour, Pat MacLellan, is fly fishing, although, like me, he comes for the escape not the catch. ('Don't know what it is, John, but those damn trout just seem to laugh at me.') I see his rod and cast whip elegantly back and forward in double show. The green hull of his rowing boat is precisely replicated beneath him, and through my binoculars I can see his khaki baseball cap shimmering gently, a perfect upside-down image in the glowing water. We wave to each other and I turn away smiling. Pat always makes me smile.

As I walk away from the dam I see that the hoodie on the pine has gone. Something chills deep down inside my guts. I know it wasn't me that put him off. We had eyed each other up, that hoodie and I, and passed on. I didn't rattle him, nor, then, for all his reputation, did I have good cause to suspect him of any imminent foul intent. I leave Pat to the laughing fish he almost certainly won't catch (although, astonishingly, he holds the loch record!), and head back down the trail to the field edge. Up with the binoculars to check out the other bird in the boulders: not there. Now I know they're up to no good.

To gain a vantage point I have to head uphill again to a spur that overlooks the loch and the pasture. It is steep and I have to push hard against gravity for fully ten minutes. At the top I'm out of breath and can't hold the binoculars still enough to scan the broad grass slopes in front of me. I rest. The land is quiet. Nothing seems to have changed. The hoodies have gone, just vanished. I'm suspicious, but, fears temporarily allayed, I perch on an old log while the pounding in my breast subsides.

On the very edge of hearing, a cry as thin as tissue peels away from the bright grass slope like a sliver of paint from a barn door. I am not even sure I heard it. In a broom bush beside me a willow warbler takes over, claiming the morning in a long cascade of descending notes. I love him but I wish he would shut up. I clap my hands and he's off in a flicker of lemon tea. I hold my breath. The cry comes again, weaker, if that is possible, but higher pitched and so edged with pathos that I know my instincts were right.

I vault the fence and run out into the short grass. Two ewes start away from me, tails bouncing. Their strong lambs dash in behind them, heading away down the hill. In front of me, still a hundred yards out, is a small glacial terrace that runs across my vision in a low ridge concealing some dead ground. It seems to take an age to get there. As I top the rise I feel that low-slung clawing again in my abdomen. There is dirty work afoot and I am sure of it. But there is nothing: no lambs, no ewes, no hoodies, nothing – just a cropped green emptiness nestling in a Highland hollow on a May morning. I feel a little foolish.

As I turn to walk back down the slope the cry comes again. It is close, so close that I have failed to see its source almost beneath my feet. There, just a yard away, its outline blurred by a pale clump of last year's grass, is a lamb. It is tiny, lying with its back to me, so weak that it can barely lift its head. I realise straight away that it is the twin of one of the stronger lambs that ran off with its mother as I vaulted the fence. Ewes with twins are often bad mothers, abandoning a weakling lamb if it can't keep up, favouring the strong with milk so that the weakling gets steadily weaker. If the shepherd isn't quick to catch up all three and pen them so that the weaker twin can get its required quota of colostrum and first milk, it is certain to fail. On his rounds this morning Geordie saw the strong lamb and missed this little fellow, already failing, and the hoodies knew it. That is why they were so patient, so fixed in their stances and their watch. As usual, they were ahead of the game.

I scoop up the frail body in one hand. It is as light as a rabbit, and flabby with hollowness. Its legs dangle uselessly. It makes no attempt to resist. Then I see its bloodied face. On one side there is a bare bony cup where an eye should have been, and on the other the shrivelled remains of an eye lurks in its crater like a burst balloon. Blinded and abandoned it was bleating out the last faint strains of its imminent doom.

Like I said, you can't impugn a hoodie crow. Whatever foul trick you think it might be capable of, you are too late. It thought of it first and acted swiftly upon its surest, most devastatingly effective instincts. The birds had gone. They had done their fell work and cleared off to wait out the inevitable consequences. What they want is a carcase; their task was to immobilise it in such a way that food for their own young was guaranteed. There is nothing I can do but end the wretched animal's misery.

'. . . The simple perception of natural forms is a delight . . . in their eternal calm a man finds himself,' wrote Emerson.

# 5

# Dawn

. . . and then, in that utter clearness of the imminent dawn, while Nature, flushed with fullness of incredible colour, seemed to hold her breath for the event, he looked in the very eyes of the Friend and Helper.

> – Kenneth Grahame, *The Wind in the Willows*

June was once described to me as 'a few sleepless weeks charged with all the desperate, procreative amperage of spring'. It is certainly true that at these northern latitudes the long hours of spring daylight banish night to a brief, twilit apology. The sun's last stain trails below the horizon and emerges again an hour later with another name – dawn.

Dawn is the moment that sets it all a-spinning, sounds bugles, lights fuses, shifts moods and tugs insistently at the leashes of biorhythms. Dawn fires energy into red corpuscles and chloroplasts, explodes buds, fluffs out breasts, swells syrinxes with song, stretches out the incubating osprey's wings, whispers the shadowy red deer hinds back to the moor, charges the flick in the squirrel's tail, wafts the tawny owl back to his roost and, throwing a last glance over his shoulder, the reluctant fox vanishes into the damp darkness of his fetid lair. Dawn is a new look, another chance to tilt at the windmills of fate; it is its own alpha and omega, the exuberant manifest of hopes unknown. Dawn is the poetry of the incipient day.

By the middle of our June nocturnality really no longer exists. Bats are forced to hawk their insects in sunlight, foxes stroll and badgers scratch in the strong evening sun; both forage in broad daylight for much of what in that other long, introspective season from August right through to May is commonly called the night. Confused, our tawny owls hoot at noon.

And the desperate, procreative amperage? Yes, it is the season of heady affliction, of a certain brand of solar madness both comic and tragic at the same time. Perhaps it was what touched Shakespeare when he conceived the tangled plot of *A Midsummer Night's Dream*, bright dawns dragging him from his bed to take up quill and invent characters like Bottom, the clumsy victim of Puck the prankster, and the sun coming up to end the comic fantasy of the night in the forest. John Masefield had evidently been there too when, eulogising 'Beauty', the first lines to flood in were, 'I have seen dawn and sunset on moors and windy hills coming in solemn beauty like slow old tunes of Spain.' A Highland spring dawn is also charged with urgency and an impending sense of ephemerality – if you don't pay attention you'll miss it. Those of us caught up in this headlong rush at spring know all too well that it is finger-snap brief and that the perverse laws of delight dictate that it has to be repaid ten times over later on. Our ebullient vernal daylight may surge to twenty-three hours in fresh and exciting. At 3.30 a.m. the June air has a tang to it, like cologne; whether the sun is out or not, it is charged.

I have often asked myself 'Why?' Why for so many years have I indulged this anti-social preoccupation with the dawn? Answers are hard to locate. There is, of course, a fair assumption that I might see more; that at 3.30 a.m. mammals and birds will be caught off guard and the secret world of wildlife will reveal itself to me in a deeper, more intimate way. This is plausible, but it's only partly true. It doesn't *have* to be dawn, the moment of first light, *prima luce*, certainly not the absurd dawns of our Highland June when the afterglow skims below the northern horizon leaving barely an hour of twilight – literally, *twi-light*, the two-lights, the light of the day passing and the day emerging. They are the same animals out there, doing their animal thing at 2.30, 3.30, 4.30, even 5.30 a.m. – at any time within the parameters of 'normal' night when they are conditioned not to expect to meet humans at large. At 6.00 a.m. I can still catch the roe deer out in the middle of the field, or the red deer picking their way back from the river flats, and I can see the barn owls float off to hunt the marshes and the badgers to forage for earthworms far more conveniently at 9.00 p.m., still in broad daylight. Yes, the secret way into natural history by getting up early does exist (and I commend it to any budding naturalist who wants to get to know his subject well), but it is quite distinct from and should not be confused with the dawn disease. George Meredith had it right: 'Prose can paint evening and moonlight, but poets are needed to sing the dawn.'

I have come to believe that the dawn habit is more to do with the watcher than the watched. I think it is a deeply personal and distinctly self-indulgent desire to have the world to myself; to want to be alone with nature rather than having to share it with the sights and sounds of other human activities. To me each new dawn symbolises a fresh start, a glimpse of the world before modernity came barracking in. I see it as hope streaking rose-tinted across the horizon while the stains of human excess remain shrouded in shadow. I have become addicted, often just sitting up in bed to watch while the steely light knife-blades in among the trees and then sinking back to listen drowsily to the ecstatic, blithe, radiant, all-forgiving optimism of the birds. The spell of creation enthrals me, has become my all, my lodestar, my very reason for being. If the day is fair and the mood resilient, I cannot lie for long. I am up and away. Asked why I have done it all these years, the best I can come up with is, 'I love it.' For me the closing words of Thoreau's *Walden* hold a special truth: 'Only that day dawns to which we are awake. There is more day to dawn. The sun is but a morning star.'

*June 17th*   2.15 a.m. The air is cold, the grass metalled with grey dew. The forest edge of the eastern horizon, barely discernible, is serrated like a silhouetted hornbeam leaf. A pale smear of bright backing loiters behind the hills to the south-east, hanging fire, reluctant to get going. Above my head the morning sky is bandaged in layers; in an hour I know that the sun will lever into its lint fuzziness and the first hard shadows of the day to zebra-stripe the path will fade and vanish like mirages. By then the woods will be ringing with birdsongs, an orchestration sometimes so deceptively assonant that at first it seems near impossible to sort them all out. Rooks, jackdaws, blackbirds, song thrushes, robins, wrens, chaffinches, greenfinches, willow warblers, blackcaps, dunnocks, three species of tit and woodpigeons will soon be hard at it, melodious, percussive, piano, fortissimo, crescendo. The staccato drumming of a great spotted woodpecker – outbursts of mechanical speed and power – will ricochet through the trees like gunfire. In the distance throat-pouting cuckoos will float pairs of muted minims into the air like audible smoke rings, notes that seem to hang there, directionless and slightly sinister as if, along with the hawks, cuckoos have been forbidden to sing. The birchwood at the loch will be a riotous chorale of raw and fearless ambition. I must get there quickly.

I slipped out in the ebb of night, in that lingering remnant that belongs neither to dark nor light and seems unable to make up its mind, 'while Nature . . . seemed to hold her breath for the event', as Kenneth Grahame graphically has it. In hill country like this the dawn does not come suddenly. It gathers beyond the horizon like Viking invaders on a surprise raid, mustering the warriors, planning the assault, creeping into place, lifting, lifting . . . before silently spilling in across the fields and moors in a rush of steel, piercing, probing, rampaging.

In the Avenue I watched pools of shadow begin to shrink and the first hint of colour infiltrate the lichen-whiskered bark of the great lime and horse chestnut trunks as subtly as blushes on pale cheeks. I was ahead of the dawn, forging on up the trail as fast as I could push my legs without running. It was urgent; I wanted to get to the loch first, before it was taken by storm.

As I top the rise at the dam the world has turned daguerreotype, metallic and only touched with pigment in occasional blots of gold and yellow-green high in the trees. Everything else is a dazzle of silver and grey, clear as a post-horn. A cock chaffinch is undeterred; he perches high in a rowan sapling a few yards to my left and bellows with all the gusto and presence of a town crier. He is unaware that his brightly coloured uniform is, for the moment, a patchwork of gentlemen's dull suitings. (The cock chaffinch is actually one of our most colourful common birds, a mixed palette of pink, blue-grey, rufous, green, black and white, much overlooked because we are so familiar with it.) I am here and the loch is as still and pale as ice. Mist hangs in the birch fronds that trail the shore. It is time to sit.

Sitting is a ploy. I learned long ago that wildlife comes out to meet me more readily than I can call on it. Anyone who uses a wildlife hide knows that very well – the combination of concealment with the removal of scent and sound is a powerful tool to the naturalist. But you can't always take a hide with you. Silence and stillness may not conceal shape, nor remove scent, but they can be highly effective by breaking the mould – man doesn't normally sit still and is rarely quiet; sitting still denies the weft with which wild animals' warp of fear is woven. John Muir knew very precisely what I mean: 'Presently you lose consciousness of your own separate existence: you blend with the landscape, and become part and parcel of nature.'

It is also an excuse to watch the pageant of light and

shade. The busy walker creates his own waves and is too preoccupied with walking; unconsciously he spreads his scent in long contours of alarm. Two walkers more than double the impact of human presence; they become walkers and talkers. The wake of their verbal preoccupation fails to notice the enchantment of a breeze teasing with the water or the leaves, or the free kaleidoscope of delight acted out by clouds and the sun – what Walt Whitman called 'the exquisite apparition of the sky'. That said, sitting and watching can be soporific and I confess that I frequently fall asleep.

Waking, I often find I am not alone. Deer have browsed close, or small birds so unaware that they have momentarily perched on my hat. Foraging badgers have blundered into my feet. Chased by a weasel, a field vole once tried to hide under my knees, the weasel scampering over my lap. And I laughed out loud when an unwary bullock grazed up to me until its nose touched my hand. It got such a fright it leapt in the air, farted explosively, slipped and fell flat on its side in its panic to escape.

The hundreds of hours I have idled away at the loch or in its gentle woods, just sitting and listening, silently scribbling notes, dozing occasionally and waiting for nothing (or anything) in particular, have never been wasted. Sometimes on those clear summer dawns when the night seems to loiter, reluctant to concede its demise, it is possible to lie back, cerebral cortex pressed into the heather, and be lulled by the barely perceptible onset of day, and to watch the gradual disappearance of the last stars. The primal scents of leaf litter and sphagnum moss, the cool settling air, the pervading damp of the peat beneath and the far-off chatter of the burn all seem to come together in a cradle of primeval belonging not so far removed from the long-lost security of the womb.

And sometimes it all goes horribly wrong. One morning I had settled down against a tree in the pinewood, trying to solve the enigma of the red squirrels that come and go in our woods – are present and visible for weeks on end and then vanish for no apparent reason. It was just after dawn in summer, but warm – August, I think – probably around 5.00 a.m. In minutes I was fast asleep. Some time later a snapping stick awoke me – that unmistakable give-away that shouts of human presence. Wild animals don't snap sticks. I froze.

A man was coming towards me, along the path that meanders through the pines at the edge of the loch, carrying a bundle under his arm. Every once in a while poachers – usually local lads – visit the loch under cover of darkness to set night lines for our trout. I was sure he was returning with a bag to remove his catch before the world awoke, but to my surprise he turned away from the loch and headed uphill in my direction. Several times he stopped and looked back at the shining water. This was no lad; he was mature, greying, tidily dressed and bearded in a neat and managed way. He stood still and seemed to be doing nothing more than staring emptily across the water lilies, communing with the beauty of the morning. Then he looked around him as if searching for something. I was puzzled.

He was a stranger. I didn't recognise his careful, slightly stooped walk, nor his attire – a soft jacket and casual trousers – clothes one might attribute to a schoolmaster rather than someone deriving his living from the countryside. Yet he was purposeful. This was no early morning walker out for a stroll, and what he carried under his arm seemed shapeless, like a sack or a jacket rolled up or a bag without a handle or strap.

For several minutes this intriguing visitor stood looking back at the loch as though trying to locate something. At last he seemed satisfied and thoughtfully he placed the bundle on a patch of dry ground beside a pine trunk. Still convinced he was up to no good, I was on the point of getting up to confront him, when he suddenly knelt down on the bundle.

It was too late to move. These were not the actions of a marauder. He was doing nothing I could possibly object to, whoever he was, so I sat still. Slowly it dawned on me that he was praying. The bundle was a hassock – a prayer cushion.

After a few minutes' kneeling he arose and sat on the hassock, still facing the loch, straight-backed and cross-legged with his hands held out in front of him, forearms resting on his knees. His palms were turned upward and his forefingers and thumbs were touching in the characteristic pose of Eastern mystics in meditation. Zen had arrived at the loch.

Now I had a dilemma. I knew it would be impossible to leave without disturbing him; my only sensible exit route would take me closer to him, not further away. I didn't want to frighten him. There was nothing for it but to sit it out. Just how long do Buddhists meditate for while stimulated by beauty and simplicity? Perhaps it would be only a few minutes, but, then again, one glance at the shining loch gave me a sinking feeling that nirvana was at hand. I watched coal tits foraging in the pine canopy above me, I searched vainly for red squirrels and I closed my eyes to listen to the croaking call of a teal to her chicks somewhere out among the water lilies. After half an hour my backside was numb and I longed to stretch. He was still completely motionless. I wondered if he was in a trance. Were his eyes open or closed? I couldn't see.

I tried it myself. Fingertips touching, empty expression, staring straight ahead – but an itch on my nose refused to go away and I had to break concentration to scratch it. I tried again and felt my eyelids beginning to close. Meditation, it seemed, was not for me. After an hour I was miserably uncomfortable, becoming irritated and wished I had moved long before. I tried to doze. The man never stirred a muscle. I glanced at my watch: it was 6.45. He had been there for an hour and a half. Quite suddenly he placed his hands together in an Eastern greeting, bowed to the loch and stood up. He picked up his cushion and walked away.

There have been many other dawn encounters over the years: poachers dragging shot deer; down by the river a man once struggled past me carrying four snared salmon so heavy that he could barely lift them; and late on a warm summer's evening, as I sat quietly watching the loch, the desperate, procreative amperage of spring came rushing straight at me. A young couple half-walked, half-ran to within a few yards. Before I could reveal myself they spread a blanket on the pinewood floor and urgently tore off each other's clothes, hurling themselves stark-naked into a full, raw, clinching, coital embrace. That was too much. I leapt up and ran away, never glancing back.

*June 21st* 'Coming in solemn beauty like slow old tunes of Spain', this particular midsummer dawn is here. This is it.

A new day just hatched, just broken free – that's why it's called day*break* and the *crack* of dawn. It is pouring over the hill, rushing through the woods like a warm wind, flooding the fields, claiming ground every second, making the land new again, lightening and brightening everything quickened and silvered by its Promethean wand. I made it, breathless, but just in time to see it spill into the pinewood; a ghostly army filtering through the dark columns and out along the loch shore, shimmying the surface like a breeze, lifting it from pewter to the bright patina of old silver.

The robins knew it. Twenty minutes before daybreak we had the dawn to ourselves, just me and those pert, virtuoso cheerleaders; man and bird equally determined to be there first, claiming the day, as I pounded the path, pushing through their sternly defended territories. A robin seemed to be with me all the way, each one up and at it as I passed, prescient and powered, as confident and righteous as a high priest. And not in vain: with a message, with a challenge, with a tilt at the world, with passion, with pleadings, with longing, with a lullaby, with grace and hope, with the blood of thorns, with anguish, triumph and exultation, they tinkle and trill the irrepressible robin psalm to the first bright lances of day. Suddenly, as if at their command, the bird chorus has soared to an even higher, more urgent outpouring of joy. This is why I come.

I find it reassuring that my experiences of dawn have often been shared by others who felt compelled to write about it. Among the most celebrated of these must be Kenneth Grahame in his extraordinary digression from what is otherwise a jolly good, rollicking children's tale, 'The Piper at the Gates of Dawn', in *The Wind in the Willows*. It is almost as though Grahame felt obliged to salute the dawn with a chapter all of its own. Ratty and Mole could perfectly well have trotted off on their adventure to search for the otter cub, Little Portly, and have found him, without any need for Rat's disturbingly dream-like encounter with Pan. At once the music of the Pan-pipes (the dawn chorus) both enthrals them and brings the world into sharper focus: '. . . the rich meadow-grass seemed that morning of a freshness and a greenness unsurpassable. Never had they noticed the roses so vivid, the willow-herb so riotous, the meadow-sweet so odorous and pervading.' A page later the event turns into a full-blown religious experience for them both. Rat refers to it as the place of his 'song-dream', a 'holy place', while Mole '. . . felt a great Awe fall upon him . . . that turned his muscles to water, bowed his head, and rooted his feet to the ground . . . he felt wonderfully at peace and happy . . . an awe that smote and held him . . .' Then they see Pan, the Friend and Helper, holding the baby otter. 'When they were able to look once more, the Vision had vanished, and the air was full of the carol of birds that hailed the dawn.'

The pinewood is still. The dark trunks of the trees steeple upwards into vast cupolas of empty air. Nothing seems to move although high above me the canopy has already surrendered its darkness and a new world is bursting out. Birdsong issues from every direction, heady and intoxicating, but here on the needle-rugged floor nothing stirs. I settle down to listen and to wait for the sun. It is now 3.16 a.m. It won't be long. It's no longer dawn; that nascent spasm has passed through and vanished as silently as it came. What it has left behind is day, as full, fat and glowing as a ripe peach. Sunrise is now only minutes away and for the next two hours, as it lifts purposefully into high, near-motionless clouds, we shall be blessed with golden light and radiant warmth.

Now is not the time to sleep – anyway, this birdsong forbids it. But I close my eyes to concentrate. It's good to try to identify just who the flautists are in this primal nocturne and to listen out for a newcomer – a wood warbler or a blackcap, maybe even a pied flycatcher or a redstart, among several others that only occasionally pop up in our neck of the woods. When I opened them a moment ago I sensed I was not alone.

I have long struggled with this 'sense'. Truthfully, I am not at all sure it exists, and I suspect it may be a figment of conditioned imprinting and hindsight, but when it happens – or rather, I *think* it happens – it is almost always confirmed. If I try to remember now, aided only by my journal, *exactly* what happened that morning, I can't. All I can say for certain is that suddenly, for no immediately discernible reason, I was very wide awake. Bells were pealing in my head. My eyes were wide with expectation. My pulse quickened.

Did I see a movement? A flicker of shadow against the ginger biscuit of the needle-strewn floor? Did a fern frond stir? Did I just happen to be facing in that direction or did my subconscious antennae direct me there, tell me where to look? I shall never know. All I know is that I saw something which set my heart a-thumping. Instinctively I raised my binoculars in a slow, smooth ascent from rest to revelation.

The focus wheel rotated only a fraction. I was staring straight into the eyes of a cat.

> Tyger, Tyger, burning bright
> In the forests of the night,
> What immortal hand or eye
> Could frame thy fearful symmetry?

*Felis sylvestris grampia*. The Scottish wildcat. The black-striped, bushy-ring-tailed, amber-eyed, wide-eared, broad-footed, sabre-toothed, rare, exquisitely wild and reputedly untame-able wildcat of the Highland woods. The native tiger of the Great Wood of Caledon. The last of the European cats to stalk our glens – the lynx was exterminated in Scotland in medieval times. I was staring into the eyes of one of the great icons of Highland wildness, one of nature's last flings of defiance at the march of man's modern world, reputedly the shyest and the most ferocious mammal on the British list, and one of the hardest to see. Little wonder my pulse was racing.

This cat must not be confused with domestic pussies. As well as being bigger, stronger, heavier and fiercer, the wild-cat is as far from domesticity as you can get. Nor should farm cats gone feral be referred to as wildcats. They are not wild and never will be, however much they may hiss and scratch. The Scottish wildcat is a species, not a lifestyle accessory. Their ancestry is also very different. The closest domestic cat markings that resemble the wildcat are those of tabbies, but with black blotches and patches rather than the distinctive, charcoal tiger-stripes and golden-brown underfur of *F. sylvestris*. No one who has properly seen a true wildcat will ever confuse it with a feral tabby.

I saw my first wildcat at Loch Migdale in Sutherland in 1964. It was walking towards me down a forest path. A few yards apart we stopped and stared at each other for a snatched moment of sublime comprehension before it disappeared into deep bracken at the side of the track. I have never forgotten that brief encounter, or the way my heart seemed to stop, the image burning its way through my retinas like lasers drilling down hot corridors of optical electricity into the very matrix of my brain. In those few seconds I swear that the electro-chemical essence of that cat floated off and entered my skull. The print of its lightning-charged wildness seared home like a brand. Forty years later it is still there, as fresh and hot and spine-tinglingly vital as on that day.

Since then I have seen many wildcats, alive and dead; but none quite like that. And now I am here again – those same demonic, Oriental eyes, that inscrutable, flat-eared mask, the curl of that slowly flicking, clubbed tail. I freeze, binoculars still pinned to my face, elbows resting on my knees. The cat sits and stares. The tail's bushy, black tip is the only movement I can see.

In the nineteenth century the wildcat was almost exterminated by over-zealous gamekeepers. The celebrated naturalist-sportsman Charles St John writing in 1878 in his *Short Sketches of the Wild Sports and Natural History of the Highlands* opens his chapter dedicated to the wildcat:

The true wild cat is gradually becoming extirpated, owing to the increasing preservation of game; and though difficult to hold in a trap, in consequence of its great strength and agility, he is by no means difficult to deceive, taking any [poisoned] bait readily, and not seeming to be as cautious in avoiding danger as many other kinds of vermin.

Two years later E.R. Alston, in his *Fauna of Scotland*, agrees with St John, but adds, hopefully: 'It is still to be found, however, in the wilder districts of the most Northern Counties, especially in the deer forests where it is left comparatively undisturbed.'

In 1887 the much more thorough and systematic naturalist, J.A. Harvie-Brown, fills in some of the detail of persecution in his comprehensive book *A Vertebrate Fauna of Sutherland, Caithness and West Cromarty*:

Between March 1831 and March 1834, as recorded by Selby, 901 wildcats, martens and foumarts [polecats] were destroyed. One keeper in Assynt killed no less than 26 wild cats between 1869 and 1880, but of these only three during the last six years.

This appears to have been the low point. Evidence from taxidermists and fur traders suggests that the wildcat was in dire trouble by the last decade of the century, as, of course, were many other 'undesirable vermin' species seen to be a threat to the burgeoning game culture of the era in which the erne, or white-tailed sea eagle, and the red kite and the polecat were exterminated in Scotland and the osprey and the pine marten were forced perilously close.

The wildcat's reputation for ferocity and destructiveness of domestic poultry and lambs as well as game species made it a singular target, even though some of that reputation is myth. Wildcats are most unlikely to kill a lamb, although they will feed on a freshly dead one. But the wilder allegations of the wildcat attacking man, said to spring at your throat like a tiger, are unfounded, although when cornered and fighting for its life it is formidable. Charles St John describes how his terriers cornered one up a glen:

> I never saw an animal fight so desperately or one which was so difficult to kill. If a tame cat has nine lives, a wild cat must have a dozen.

In his charming anecdotal account of a naturalist's encounters in the Highlands, *Highland Gathering* (1960), Kenneth Richmond recounts a gamekeeper's tales of wildcats from Loch Ard Forest, just north-east of Loch Lomond.

> Pound for pound, the wild cat is probably the most efficient fighting machine in the world, and the most vicious. When faced with a dog it holds on with its teeth and tears away with the claws of all four feet. Dugald (the keeper) had once seen a sheep dog mauled in this way, an ugly sight and one he had never forgotten.

And later he tells of a Deeside keeper, Old Hamish, who 'had to have four stitches in his side where the beast had ripped him, slicing through a thick leather belt into the bargain'.

Yet after the turn of the twentieth century the pressure seems to ease. An interesting comment appears in Charles Henry Alston's *Wild Life in the West Highlands*, published in 1912:

> In proof that the wild cat is, up to the present day at least, by no means so near extinction as has sometimes been assumed, it may be noted that living specimens are offered to the Zoological Society every winter.

The advent of World War I, so catastrophic for the readily recruited young men of the Highlands and Islands, enabled the cat to stage a comeback, as Francis Thompson wryly observes in *A Scottish Bestiary* (1978): 'probably because keepers were forced to turn their attention to killing another enemy'. But two world wars notwithstanding, it is also certainly the case that the dramatic proliferation of coniferous forests after the Forestry Commission was established in 1919 will have greatly aided the return of wildcats as well as pine martens. Not only the additional cover in an open landscape of hills and moors, but the turnover of nutrients during ground preparation, often by deep ploughing, and the early thicket stages of the young conifers caused an exponential rise in vole and woodmouse populations, greatly to the advantage of the wildcat.

It is worth noting that the nomenclature has also evolved. All early records describe this mammal as the 'wild cat'. But as it becomes clear that there are also increasing numbers of feral domestic cats roaming the countryside, so the literature eases gently into the use of 'wildcat' for the real thing

– the noun permanently fused with its defining adjective to endorse the distinction of the real animal and its inseparability from primeval wildness. Almost all twentieth-century references are to *wildcats*.

But the species' biggest and most persistent problem is not persecution, habitat loss or diminishing food supply – there are plenty of glens and wild woods that could and until recently did hold wildcats.

In the twenty-first century it is in trouble again. A far more sinister threat has slowly been corrupting the species like rust erodes iron. Genetic pollution. Domestic cats were virtually unknown in the Highlands before the middle of the nineteenth century. With the advent of the railways and the great Balmorality sporting era the fashions of the Lowlands and England could and did migrate into even the remotest farms and crofts.

Wild toms cannot resist domestic moggies. Farm cats turned feral will interbreed freely with wildcats. Domestic cats are a blend of ancient Chinese and African cat stock and although they are physiologically quite distinct from the wildcat – there are differences in skull size and skeletal structure, dentition, gut length, tail shape, body weight and, of course, coloration – their provenance is close enough to produce a fertile hybrid. Once interbred, the genes will not go away. The more frequently it happens, the less and less pure the wild stock becomes – a paradox not lost on present-day researchers. The more wildcats there are, the more widespread the pollution seems to be. Some say there are no pure wildcats left in Scotland at all – a treasonable notion I sincerely hope is untrue.

What the hammer? what the chain?
In what furnace was thy brain?

My good friend Ro Scott is a professional naturalist with a
passion for wildcats. To the astonishment of other drivers
she is to be seen stopping her car and walking back to inspect
and collect dead cats on the roadside, looking for those tell-
tale signs of wildness, the rings and black tip to the tail –
and taking measurements for her ever-expanding database.
A study she did in the remote western Highlands in the
early 1990s suggested that there could still be as many as
3,500 unpolluted wildcats at large in the Highlands. But in
2004 the British Mammal Society published their estimate at
only four hundred – cause for concern and for conservation
action. Ro thinks their figures may be unduly pessimistic.
Her identification criteria (without DNA testing) are the
pelage and the other skeletal and dental measurements.
'Those wild genes are tough – really resilient,' she says. 'If the
measurements stack up and the pelage is right, that's good
enough for me – it's a wildcat. With the rapid expansion of
native woods we've seen in recent years there have to be
more than that.' She thinks that *Felis sylvestris grampia* is with
us for a good while yet.

I can see no feral genes today. Whatever impurities lurk
within its feline DNA, none are corrupting this pure moment
of dawn-struck *déjà vu*. It is Loch Migdale all over again.
The dark, parallel tiger-stripes line its flanks as a crazed

painter might have streaked shadows onto a Mediterranean landscape, and the diagnostic flattened, outward-pointing ears award breadth and power to the rounded skull. The club tail, as blunt as an aubergine, far thicker at the tip than a fox's brush, is black-ringed to a tip dipped in Indian ink. The paws are large and bulb-toed, concealing the scimitars within, and forelegs broad-set below a deep chest. The white whiskers flare. The mad, metamorphic eyes coldly fire. It hasn't seen me – the advantage of being here first and sitting still is paying out in pure gold. Wildcat eyesight is laser-acute, hearing fit for a gazelle. Its nose is less important, but since there is no wind I don't fear being scented. The cat is sitting.

Minutes slide past. It stands and turns side on, looking uphill through the pines towards the moor. Now I can count the tail rings – six clear black bars increasing in size to the heavy tip, which curls to horizontal and hovers apparently weightless and poised above the ground. Its flank-stripes lance to the forest floor. It looks around, alert and timelessly patient, but with the measured insouciance of a dictator, as though it has all the time in the world to check out the simmering amperage of this brightening day. I think this cat is on the hunt; it has that aura of feline menace, that lion-languid roll of shoulders fluid beneath the fur. Slowly it moves off uphill, diagonally away from me so that my last glimpse is that tail sliding into shadow as silently as the vanishing night.

I ease my binoculars to my lap and breathe again. A wildcat. A gloriously wild, supremely alert, sublimely adapted, bristling with health and power, utterly belonging wildcat. The image burns in my head like a Roman candle. This is as real and precious as a sighting can get, made vintage by the sharpening contrasts of the dawn. I sit still.

I sit still because I am reliving the image, because my strength has gone, because such things so rarely occur – the perfect dawn, the shining loch, the echoing birdsong and now this – that I need a moment to soothe my clanging neurons, to locate the 'save' button and commit it all to memory, let it all sink in. I'm not sure how long I sit – perhaps ten minutes, maybe not quite so long. This is a meditation beyond time, a private nirvana of my own. I'm calmer now, glowing gently until, higher up the slope, my eyes register another movement. Up with the glasses, gently pan left and focus in on a dark patch of shade. There it is again; it's coming back, soothing out of the bracken as softly as a curl of smoke.

It's coming back with something in its mouth, something is dangling from its jaws. Could this be a she-cat moving her kittens? My pulse is racing again. I have read about cats moving their young from den to den, as many mammals will if they are disturbed – something I have always wanted to witness. This is just the right time of year. I have witnessed pine martens and otters moving young, but not a wildcat. Reading about it merely whets the appetite and charges – sometimes over-charges – the imagination. She comes on. She is walking slowly and deliberately back down the slope towards me, holding her head high so that the kitten is well clear of the ground. For this I have waited years, decades. She comes on.

A low-angled sunbeam spotlights her; for a second her outline is top-lit, hard and clear. Her back burns as if on fire.

I stifle a laugh – I was getting carried away. It's not a kitten she is carrying, it's prey: a leveret, only a week or two old, limp and hanging by the scruff of the neck, just as a kitten might. I can see the long, slightly crumpled ears and the white star on its forehead. Brown hares are common in these woods. We forget that hares are woodland animals; it is us who have given them broad fields in which to lark their lunatic pantomimes.

I can picture the stalk, each paw raised and placed with neurosurgical care, then the crouched wait among the striped bracken shadows, invisible, as still as rock, those Athene-noctua eyes radiating dire intent – and the spring, a six-foot pounce with claws extended and the curved canine fangs puncturing leopard-like just once at the back of the head. And it's not a she-cat; this is a tom – a big-boned tomcat. He is sinew strong; chunky and thick set. This cat must be well over three feet long and sixteen or seventeen pounds of muscle, bone and aura. I am sure he is a tom.

I don't mind that it's not a kitten; I am just as pleased to see this big male carrying off his prey. Now he's only fifteen yards away, and he is going to pass by, along the trail I walk nearly every day, heading off to wherever it is he will choose to settle and feed. I cannot turn to watch him go. He's too close and will see my movement, so I grit my teeth and watch him slide through my ring of binocular vision without attempting to pan after him. It takes all my willpower, but I am desperate not to alarm him. I like to meet my wildlife in empathy, not to chase them away.

He passes through, gliding like a panther, shoulder blades ridging the fur of his back in a fluid roll that ripples down his taut, muscular body. And then the tail – Oh! That tail! That curling, definitive black club of authoritative affirmation, his badge of absolute wildness, the hallmark of his purest genes, disappearing from my view as though he had never been. I stare blankly at the empty forest floor. The sunlight is still levering in, prising the trees apart, tiger-striping the pine needles as though, if you had a really vivid imagination, you might think you had seen a wildcat lurking there.

> When the stars threw down their spears,
> And watered heaven with their tears,
> Did he smile his work to see?
> Did he who made the Lamb make thee?
>
> – William Blake

# 6

# Energy and the Big Deal

Underwater eyes, an eel's
Oil of water body, neither fish nor beast is the otter:
Four-legged yet water-gifted, to outfish fish;
With webbed feet and long ruddering tail
And a round head like an old tomcat.
                                    – Ted Hughes, 'An Otter'

Loitering suspiciously under a bush for minutes at a time, creeping stealthily forward, freezing as still as a rock – a stranger might wonder what on earth I was up to. They would be right to wonder – my entire demeanour changes as I approach the loch. Stealth has taken me over, pervaded my whole body language, made me inch by inch cautious and, above all, needle-focused, with every sense as keen as a blade. I come gently to the water's edge. It's something I learned the hard way.

Many years ago I popped up like a jack-in-a-box, only to find an otter on the dam, crunching his shark-sharp teeth into one of the fat rainbow trout we obligingly tip in each spring for his and our delight, but he had seen me first and vanished. All I really saw was a tail. I was left with gently expanding rings of light and a trail of bubbles; the remains of a fish dribbled from the coping stones. Those are the lessons a naturalist needs to learn only once. I remember softly cursing my oafishness as I stared emptily at the ripples.

In Britain the otter is iconic. Of all our wild mammals it seems to hold a special place in the human psyche. Immortalised in literature by Henry Williamson's Tarka and Gavin Maxwell's Mijbil, Edal and Teko, its grace and elusiveness seem to have posted it in lights – even fishermen are pleased when they see an otter. It is also a nature conservation success. Having watched it virtually disappear during my lifetime from most of the rivers of England, Wales and lowland Scotland as a direct result of river pollution and loss of wetland habitat, its robust return throughout the '80s and '90s adds a golden symbolism to its shy but captivating presence. After that day I approached the loch warily; it was a mistake I would never make again.

Our little fishing syndicate is composed of ten friends and neighbours who come after work and at weekends to flick their flies across the lilies and the shady pools in the hope of enticing a fish for their supper. They are a long-suffering lot. They accept that the otters and the ospreys have to feed too and they make an appropriate allocation in their stocking requirements. I like to think that they draw as much pleasure from seeing an osprey crash into the water or from a glimpse of an otter in the marsh as they do from their hours of elegantly casting solitude, and I hope that those exciting images of ol' nature spinning its predatory wheel bring them as much reward as taking a trout home for their own supper.

So I come gently to the brim. As the trail rises up the burn-side the first things I see are the birches and a gnarled old oak. These are the convenient green curtains I can hide behind. A few steps closer and a low bank of eared willows at the water's edge looms into view, soft and as grey-green as a lichen. I stop. From here I can scan the dam and the shoreline without being seen. To loiter, to stand still for a few minutes, is always wise and often productive. If a bird of prey is present, an osprey or a buzzard or perhaps the sparrowhawk that nests in the loch-side pinewood, its presence will be revealed soon enough by the other small birds. I listen for the ticking and fizzling alarm calls of tits and blackbirds or that eerie stillness which sings its own song, tells its own tale. I can't hope to remain undetected for long: birds of prey possess an acuity we can only guess at. But my wary approach gives me a chance to see them even if it is only briefly – something to log and file away in my journal, a bright moment to add to the unending cycles of wildness that whirl about my head.

If all seems clear I can ease gently forward until the glowing surface of the loch spreads before me like a silver sheet; stop again, up with the binoculars, hoping but not expecting. Blessed are those who expect nothing for they shall not be disappointed! That corrupted beatitude has always made me smile. And yet a careful search almost always rewards. The loch is full of surprises. Rarities drop in, such as the exquisite Slavonian grebe, black and cinnamon with outrageous marmalade eyebrows and a ruby eye, occasionally to be found diving among the bottle sedge stems at the marsh's edge. Or, in the autumn, with the first frosts, a family of whooper swans just in from the Arctic, cygnets in the ashen grey of first plumage and the dandelion bills of the adults shining in the sun. We get teal, tufted duck, flights of wigeon visiting from the river, and, just occasionally in the early spring when they are prospecting for nest sites, the haunting yodels of a pair of red-throated divers can be heard echoing back from the pinewood.

I have witnessed those flagships of conservation success, ospreys, fishing the loch more times than I can count. Pushed to the edge of extinction in Scotland in the nineteenth and early twentieth centuries by thousands of gamekeepers waging war on all hooked beaks (and just about everything else), they either just clung on – down to perhaps just one last pair nesting undiscovered in a remote wooded glen (which is the current wisdom being put about) – or perhaps re-colonised from Scandinavian birds blown off course. Whichever the case, from that first pair discovered nesting on the River Findhorn in 1955, there are now close to two hundred pairs expanding their range across the Highlands and beyond. No one thinks of shooting an osprey now.

A pair have built their huge, twiggy nest in an old pine less than a mile away from the loch and they return to it every year. In the spring one or other of the birds, occasionally both together, visits the loch on an almost daily basis. I have come to know them well. We are a perfect feeding loch, thanks in part to the sacrificial offerings of our friendly syndicate, although there is also a healthy stock of small wild brown trout of ideal osprey size, especially in the early morning hours of the long daylight months – May to July – when the female bird is on eggs and then later in the summer when they are frantically feeding three or four greedy young. I am sure the constant risings of the stocked rainbow trout help attract the ospreys, but in practice those fat, farmed fish are too heavy for the birds to take and they tend to concentrate on the little wild brownies which, possibly because of the acidity of the peaty water, rarely seem to grow to more than about three-quarters of a pound in weight – although there are a few exceptions. One June morning particularly sticks in my mind.

I was just in time. The male bird was perched on the very tip of a larch tree at the loch's south-eastern fringe. It was heraldic and imperial, crest raised, head thrust forward, ferocious eyes devouring the glinting surface spread below. As soon as I saw him and pulled focus he lifted and soared out over the water with wing-elbows flexed, power issuing from short, rowing beats of the long primaries. I saw the briefest hover, with wings high over his head in a V, and then they collapsed, the bird corkscrewing down almost vertically into a crash dive. At the last moment the blue legs thrust forward to their fullest extent and the black talons spread wide for the grasp. The surface of the loch erupted in a fount of creamy water and mocha bird. So steep was the dive he almost disappeared from view; only the open wings held him from total immersion.

There he sat, the crest still raised above murderous eyes and two spread wings resting on the water while the legs grappled invisibly below. It was immediately clear he had caught a fish. Had he not, he would have lifted off straight away. The short rest is a chance to recharge the wing muscles, for oxygenated blood to flood back in for the big heave to lift the wet bird and the fish up through the surface drag, up into clear air. Three times I watched him thrash for lift-off; three times his wings scooped high over his back, flailing magnificently; and three times he fell back. No matter how hard the wings thrashed, they failed to lift him free, so that he slumped back to the water. On that last heave I glimpsed the fish for the first time and knew instinctively that it was hopeless. It was far too big. It was a chunky, deep-bellied brown trout of at least four pounds, grasped firmly across the back by the piercing clinch of one scimitar-taloned foot. It squirmed and lashed, visibly twisting the osprey's leg with the power of its tail. It was too much.

For a few moments the osprey looked foolish. Indecision seemed to have quenched his fire. The crest fell. When the bird lifted again it did so easily; two scoops and it was free, then a shaken mist of fine droplets from bill to tail, and away he went, ringing the loch in a wide, panning arc of fishless fury. At last the cry broke from his gaping bill. Six sharp bleats of rage and frustration echoed round the birches as he lifted above the trees and disappeared back towards the river.

I don't know how often ospreys get it wrong; no predator enjoys one hundred per cent success. Maybe he was a young bird still chancing his arm, lacking the experience to know that wasted energy is dangerous. Maybe he just couldn't resist the olive-green back sliding slowly through the peaty water a foot down. In any event, I am sure he learned something from that mistake, as did I. My journal for that day records my excitement, asks questions, brings a smile to my face as I read it again all these years later. But that was not the end of the story.

Two days later I was back at the dam, peering through

the willows in the early morning. The sun was up and the whole loch burned so fiercely that I had to be careful not to look at the surface through binoculars. I skimmed the shore. No ospreys, a few mallard and a moorhen in the marsh and nothing much else – I thought. The birds were singing; all seemed calm. Then a flash of silver caught my eye.

On the northern shore, under the birches that lean out over the water creating shady pools of darkness, something glinted. My heart skipped to see an otter eating a trout on the bank. Sunlight mirrored from the fish's shiny flank had given him away. The otter was a long way off, a hundred yards or more, so I was able to watch it for several minutes. Then, never content, I thought I would test my skill at stalking closer.

I worked my way forward, but otters are not readily duped. Like all of the Mustelidae family their senses are finely tuned, harp sharp, never a missed note firing into a brain as bright and alert as a mongoose's. With hawkish eyesight and the nose and ears of a deer, sentries are posted in every direction. Man is always clumsy – I never stood much of a chance. I only got half way and I will never know what it was that betrayed me. The otter melted away into the loch, vanishing in the blink of an eye. In vain I scoured the surface for a trail of bubbles, sat still beneath a bush and watched for a while, but I knew it was hopeless.

The trout lay largely uneaten. The top of the head was missing, and a fleshy chunk had been torn from a shoulder above the pectoral fin, but the rest was intact. I turned it over with my foot and recognised it immediately. Its back was scarred with deep furrows and the muscle beds of each flank were deeply pierced with raw, gaping holes. It was the osprey's lost catch, the brown trout too heavy to haul away. But the wounds it had sustained in that mortal struggle had been too severe to allow it to swim as a trout should. Nature quickly prunes the lame and the halt. It had been easy pickings for the otter, which under normal circumstances would have been hard pressed to match the darting agility of a strong brown trout of this size. I left the fish for the otter to return to later and carried on round the trail, pondering these two incidents, the osprey and the otter, turning them over and over in my mind.

I had just witnessed two consecutive events of immense biological and ecological importance. One top predator, the osprey, at the apex of its own food chain had inadvertently fed another top predator, the otter. I had witnessed the accidental passage of energy from the peak of one food chain to another in a way I might not see again for years. It was a high-level transfer of energy sideways, a route not normally demonstrated in text-book ecology models and one which ably illustrated the point that natural selection is random.

Random. Random is wild, as wild and unreliable as the roulette wheel. Chance is the joker here, the high-stakes lottery that science can't predict or even measure adequately and none of us, even at our elevated level of consciousness, can plan for. Some you win, most you lose. Chance was the jackpot Darwin (and Wallace) won when the evolution penny finally dropped. What was then, and is still, so utterly phenomenal about their discovery – then, of course, only a *theory* of evolution – is that they had no notion of ultraviolet radiation from the sun delivering a constant barrage of mutations to all living organisms on Earth, and no concept of genes or chromosomes, the means by which those mutations could be passed on. It was like working out how glacial scenery was formed without ever having heard of an ice sheet or a glacier.

Our brown trout was itself a successful predator. To have achieved that size and age it was one in a thousand. There can be room for only a very few wild brownies of that size in our little loch. Its jaws were snag toothed and a continuous pillage glared from its cold, unblinking eye; it had achieved the status of super-trout. It dreamed only of smaller fish and invertebrates – a cannibal, as keenly devouring its own fry as anything else's. It lurked in the weedy deeps waiting and watching for any unwary movement. In a flash of olive-green and silver it powered out to snatch its prey. Had I opened its stomach I am sure I would have found the bony remains of many small trout as well as the chitinous shards of beetle and dragonfly larvae amongst a smorgasbord of other delicacies.

During its five or six years of life the four pounds of tasty, pink flesh that had torn free from the osprey's grasp that day had grown fat at the expense of hundreds of pounds of lesser fish and invertebrates. These thousands of small animals had in turn fed upon uncountable pounds of much smaller organisms collectively lumped together as freshwater plankton. These microscopic animals had themselves incessantly grazed upon millions of microscopic algae – green plant plankton. And it is the ability of these primitive plant forms to process sunlight and absorb mineral nutrients constantly washed into the loch by the rains that ultimately sustains the osprey and the otter.

Energy drives us all. Whether the petrol in our cars or the potatoes in our bellies, all our energy is derived directly or indirectly from the sun. The millions of thermal units of sunlight bombarding the surface of the loch, or the forest, or the mountains, or the sea or the entire planet are what drive photosynthesis, the powerhouse of carbohydrate production which feeds the world and which, long ago, laid down hydrocarbons in oil and coal reserves. With the rarefied exception of a few deep ocean organisms that synthesise inorganic chemicals issuing from volcanic vents (they have abandoned photosynthetic food sources and reverted to a much more primitive chemosynthesis), all the world as we know it is driven – and limited – by this free, ecstatic solar source.

Herein lies the rub. We know it; we have figured out the science of energy in atomic detail and yet most of us don't begin to understand its implications for our daily lives, nor do we acknowledge its fundamental importance to every one of us. Quite simply, we take it for granted.

Some months later I happened to find myself speaking to a class of sixth-form biology students from an Aberdeen school. They were bright and chirpy seventeen-year-olds. We were discussing food chains and the interdependence of all living things. I told them about the osprey, the trout and the otter. I presented the incident as an example of energy flow. On the blackboard I illustrated the whole cycle from sunlight to osprey and the random jump to the otter. Food chains were a part of their syllabus and I had thought my tale was a sufficiently interesting aberration to merit their academic attention.

Throughout the session an attractive blonde girl near the front looked bored. She chewed gum with an air of detached sufferance. She yawned provocatively. It was clear she had other things on her mind. A rampant sexual energy seemed to surround her in all directions, and she knew it. Her eyes were sultry with eyeliner and shadow, her blouse unbuttoned to expose a thrusting cleavage, and her skirt, in all conscience short enough when standing, as she slouched in her chair exposed acres of thigh. When it came to question time she glowered at me from beneath extravagant eyelashes. 'If this energy stuff happens on your loch, doesn't it also happen everywhere else all over the globe?' she asked dismissively, as though the whole subject was thoroughly tedious.

'Yes,' I said, as calmly as I could. 'It does. It's happening as we speak. That's the point; it's universal.'

'Well, if it's happening everywhere all the time, what's the big deal and why do we need to know about it?'

For a moment I was off guard. This level of almost palpably aggressive ennui was a surprise to me, a gauntlet thrown down, but one I was unprepared for and unready to accept. 'What is your name?' I asked, struggling for time to collect my wits.

'Sammy,' she answered without any expression at all, the eyes still simmering defiantly.

'Well, Sammy, we need to know about it because . . .'
I began. Then I checked myself, took a deep breath and
ducked out. 'Let me take another question and then I'll give
you a proper answer.' A boy at the back rescued me with a
question about ospreys.

I had felt my hackles begin to rise. Ire was clouding my
vision and I felt overcome by an irresistible desire to tell that
lovely young female, beaming all her youthful confidence
at me, what I really thought. But good sense held me back
and the moment passed.

What I had really wanted to say runs like this:

'The big deal, dear Sammy, is precisely your attitude. For
far too long we in the scientific West have been taking it all
for granted. Energy has sustained us to crazy levels of
profligacy and indolence and all we have done, generation
after generation, is take it for granted. These fossil fuels, the
sun's energy captured in ancient forests, jungles and swamps
over countless millions of years, have been stored and
matured like fine old clarets. They are the oil, coal and gas
reserves of the planet laid down almost as if the gods had
planned our meteoric rise from the primeval forest to become
the technological masters of the world, ours to draw on and
squander at our pleasure.

'The big deal, dear Sammy, is that we are drunk with
energy lust. It has gone, like good claret will go, to our heads.
It has allowed us to sit and indulge our every whim without
a care for the planet and its essential ecosystems we all depend
upon. It has encouraged us to fell the forests and drain
the swamps which were the very source of our good fortune
in the first place. It has handed us chemical-dependent

agricultural systems which expend ten calories of energy to grow and transport to the markets a single calorie of food. It has given us cheap intercontinental flights that are destroying the atmosphere. It has given us the technology to fish out whole oceans of fish stocks, pushing some of our very best food species to the verge of extinction. It has trained foresters to view trees only as crops of fibre, forgetting that a mature tree is giving back more to the soils and the environment around it than it takes. Their blinkered view of a forest as a harvestable commodity for quick profit overlooks the energy cycle we are talking about – the trees' ability to transfer the combined energy of sun and rain into global maintenance and long-term stability.

'The big deal, dear Sammy, is that for over two hundred years we have consumed our fossil energy bonanza without a thought for the side effects of air pollution, of carbon emissions, of heavy metals, of toxic chemicals, or the impact they may be having on the ecosystems of the globe and all the wildlife we profess to love.

'The big deal, dear Sammy, is that unless we wake up and pay some attention to what we are doing, your children and your grandchildren are certain to inherit an appalling mess.'

I had wanted to throw the book at her, to pour out all the accumulated frustrations of being a committed conservationist for thirty years. A part of me would have liked to have humiliated her in front of her audience of peers, over whom she knew she held authority and power – albeit in another field. I had wanted to tell her that hormones from contraceptive pills were now detectable in most of the fish and shellfish of the North Atlantic and were altering the breeding cycles of countless marine organisms. I had wanted to tell her that the essential support mechanisms of her own current, high-consumption lifestyle – the clothes, the make-up packaging, the iPods, the DVDs and the mobile phones, as well as all the glossy magazines that fuelled her life's materialist ambitions – were all contributing to the ever-growing mountain of waste, much of it imperishable and toxic, that would surround our successors for thousands of years.

But I didn't. I didn't tell her any of that at all.

Is it the loch and this circuitous perambulation of all seasons and all weathers over so many years that has drawn my fire? That has opened other doors, presented a bigger picture? Is it age? Just the passage of decades that has mellowed passion like the colour fading from an old photograph? What, I wonder, made me draw back from this surge of Luddite rage that yearned for a simpler, cleaner age? Or was it the stain of contagion, the certain knowledge that I am as guilty of a profligate Western lifestyle as anyone else – certainly far more so than this young woman struggling with her own biology to find a niche for herself in our complicated, messed-up world? I don't believe it is any one of these, but perhaps it is a bit of them all.

What I know for certain is that no one ecologically aware – as I profess to be at an amateur level – should be the least bit surprised at the way we use and abuse our energy. It is hard-wired in us all and has been from the beginning of time.

From the smallest and most primitive algae, through every level of every life form on Earth, the trout, the osprey, the otter, and right on up to man the arch-predator, the survivors are those which most efficiently engage with and consume the energy available to them. Successful species are the successful exploiters of energy.

The example of weeds on a patch of cleared ground demonstrates the point. When a forest is cleared and the latent energy in the forest soils is exposed to sun and rain, up springs a flush of weeds – plants often valueless to man, but ecologically they are winners. They colonise the nutrients and soils, harness the energy and multiply rapidly. They are the forest starting all over again, delivering nutrients back to the surface and dying back to decompose and replenish soils, while exchanging carbon dioxide for oxygen to support the many other forms of life around them. They are the building blocks of the new forest, eventually succeeding to shrubs and small trees, and ultimately back to a climax forest of great trees – one of the most stable and self-sustaining ecosystems known to science.

Man is the most successful species of mammal (I am tempted to say organism, but entomologists and microbiologists might disagree) the world has ever known, and it is our ability to harness and use energy that has lifted us to that dizzily exalted position. That we are also the most destructive of our own habitat and of the habitats of our food species is a by-product of our energy-centric lifestyles. Whether the primitive farmer felling forest to plant food crops, or nomadic grazers expanding their goat herds; whether the hunter-gatherers who burned scrub and forests to hunt their game, the trawler men who fish out whole age classes of the very fish their livelihoods depend upon, or the agri-businessmen who have so mechanised and industrialised food production that their once-fertile soils are now just a medium for chemically induced growth, mankind has always damaged his own interests.

Those human cultures in the world that have learned best how to exploit energy have systematically dominated those that have not. Some of us have grown fat and rich, many more remain uncertain about the next meal. This is not just human history, it is human ecology. For tens of thousands of years man's grand ambitions were held in check by the forces of nature. Famine, disease, parasites, warring tribes, droughts, plagues of locusts and extremes of climate held us back. The world was big enough to absorb the worst of our excesses because our population was small and vulnerable. But not for long.

The emergence of science in northern Europe in the post-Renaissance era was to change all that. The advance of medicine made survival easier and with every passing decade burgeoning technology made the harnessing of energy more and more efficient. Then came the fossil fuel bonanza – the coal-fired steam boiler, the internal combustion engine, oil- and gas-fired power stations leading to nuclear fission and the electronic age. The world was no longer small and we could replicate the success of exploitation at home anywhere we wished to, right across the globe. In less than two hundred years we have done what God had apparently instructed us to do in Genesis: have dominion over the birds of the air, the beasts of the field and every creeping thing that creepeth upon the earth. Now, it seems, we must reap the whirlwind.

The technophobic environmentalist mantra I would have

liked to dump upon the effulgent Sammy's head would quickly have turned into a rant. Rants are seldom productive; they're usually an active turn-off. Whatever frustrations may have churned in my gut that day, I knew that railing against her, or what my prejudices told me she and her generation stood for, would achieve nothing. I took a deep breath.

'The big deal, Sammy, is that it is up to you. We are facing a global energy crisis of our own making. The decision to plough on regardless or to use our heads and pull back from the brink is not mine, it is yours. It will be your generation who have to take the really tough decisions about energy and the way we use it. Will you be able to have one car or two? Are you to be allowed to go on driving as many miles as you like, or are you to be limited to a quota according to your profession? Is your total energy use to be monitored and your tax bill to rise with your consumption? Are you to go on enjoying cheap, unlimited long-haul flights to anywhere you like? Can we trust the free market forces of the capitalist West to deliver the decisions and economies we need to tackle global warming, pollution, over-fishing, deforestation? Can we get our heads around the concept of sustainable development and reverse the trends of ten thousand years of human history? Can we do it fast enough to rescue our lifestyles as we know and enjoy them from total collapse? For just how long are you and hundreds of millions of others like you going to be able to go on having your cake and eating it?

'The reason I want you to know and understand the energy cycle is that it will be your influence and your votes, and those of your friends and colleagues around you that elect

# 7

# Wild

It is in vain to dream of a wildness distant from ourselves.
There is none such. It is the bog in our brain and bowels, the
primitive vigor of Nature in us, that inspires that dream.

Henry David Thoreau, *Journals* (9:43)


'The best I can offer is wild,' warned the TV weatherman
this morning, just a touch too melodramatically. I got the
feeling he was covering his back. Perhaps his bosses are still
smarting from the stinging criticism to hit the Met Office
after failing to spot and forecast the last gasp of Hurricane
Floyd, which had spun across the Atlantic as a once-in-300-
years storm to arrive during the night of 15th/16th October
1987. Its rampant wildness was to devastate buildings across
much of southern England, topple 15 million trees, flatten
power lines for days on end and take the lives of eighteen
unlucky people. Later it was declared to have brought the
highest wind speeds to blast Britain since 8th December 1703.
Nature was wild that day and all that night. Sometimes we
need to know her wrath.

The much friendlier gales he forecast this morning were
at that moment salt-blasting the Hebrides, more than a

hundred miles due west of us here, on the far side of the Highlands' famous mountain spine which shelters and protects us from the saturated Atlantic winds. The mountains have the effect of drawing the teeth of these storms, so I knew that whatever finally arrived with us wasn't likely to be anything like so all-devouring. But it still drew me out.

*June 22nd* By lunchtime the tops of the Sitka spruces across the valley were swaying like yachts at anchor. Jackdaws and rooks lifted off into joyous packs, rolling and tumbling for sheer exuberance in the same way that sailing boats enthusiastically plunge through boisterous seas, all against a backdrop of high, surging cumuli as bright as sunlit snow. Wind like that demands attention; you ignore it at your peril. I hurried to the loch to see it chasing and rattling leaves at the water's edge and careening through the birches and willows with tantrums of swirling spleen; beside me it whirled across the surface like a child's frustrated scribblings on a page, while up on the moor long, melancholy exhalations uttered from the high mountain corries. The wind is as much a part of wild nature as any bird or bug. Wild was a good word for this wind.

This is an unusual early summer storm, a rambunctious westerly, piling in from the vast expanse of the North Atlantic. It is fresh; one of nature's vital rhythms sweeping through like a tidal wave, challenging, rattling, stirring, howling like a wolf, uplifting, purifying, humbling. But it has also been warmed by the mid-Atlantic Gulf Stream; *mild* is what we call it in our domesticated weather-speak, and that is misleading.

Mild in temperature it may be, but there's nothing mild about its petulant, goading mood. It brings to my face, eyes and ears a new awareness of the path, a turbo-charged arousal of thoughts, feelings, emotions – a sort of aeolian work-out. If this is wild, I thought, I like it. It got me pondering *wild*.

What is wild? And what do we really mean when we use that word in the context of nature and the outdoors? It is one of those conceptual abstracts that have no clearly definable origins; one of the several elemental conditions that have evolved with us over the hundred thousand years or so that *H. sapiens* has been steadily sloughing away from the rest of the natural world; words that stem from every aspect of life and the land itself, and have just always been there, a part of our daily lives.

Wild the notion, wild the unruly concept, has always been with us, dogging our heels ever since we were truly wild ourselves. Where the English word comes from is much easier to locate and tie down. *Wild* arrived in Britain with the language of invading Germanic warrior tribes in the fifth century: the Angles, Saxons and Jutes; and its recent derivative etymology is entirely clear: *wilde* in Old English and Germanic, *villr* in Old Norse, *wildi* in Old Saxon and Old High German, *wilþeis* in Gothic. It's a word that perpetually echoes our origins and has stuck with us all the way on our long journey from the primeval forest. But there is much more to it than that. Oh yes, much, much more. It is a word with a thousand faces: moods, feelings, emotions, impulses, dreams, hopes, lusts, longings and fears. It can be ferocious and utterly unforgiving, or tender and loving. It is birth and death; *wild* is the godless alpha and omega of the natural world. *Wild* shouts from the mountain tops, trailing great joy and great dread in its wake. *Wild* is the power *and* the glory.

My *Shorter Oxford English Dictionary* heads its long entry with: 'of an animal: living in . . . a natural state; not living with or under the control of humans, not tame or domesticated'. Wild is the original them and us. It's the adjective that has mapped our wrench away from nature's grip, and the word we fall back on when something or someone doesn't quite fit the manageable and domesticated, man-separated-from-nature mould. 'Wild man', 'wild-eyed', 'gone wild', 'run wild', 'wild and woolly', 'bewildered' and so on. When we use it to label ourselves we seem to be looking backwards to a lost age and condition we are now embarrassed about, almost as though we shouldn't fully own up to it any more. When we use it as a noun it leaves us firmly behind: *the* wild and *the* wilds – outlandish places where humans venture at their peril. Land going wild is land no longer useful to us; again, it seems to be going backwards, away from human values and influence. We couple it up with anything out there we can't control: wildlife, wildcat, wild boar, wild fire, wildness and the ultimate, exquisite refinement – wilderness.

Back in the Massachusetts woods of 1853, when we know from his journals (some two million words in thirty volumes) that he was penning his famous essay 'Walking', finally published in the *Atlantic Monthly* in 1862, Henry David

Thoreau famously claimed the derivation of 'wild' was the past participle of the verb 'to will':

> . . . 'will'd', meaning self-willed, free-acting and free-thinking . . . a 'wild' horse is a 'willed' or self-willed horse, one that has never been tamed or taught to submit its will to the will of another, and so with a man.

He took this directly from Richard C. Trench's *On the Study of Words*, published in 1852. To me this seems like etymological wishful thinking – a bit too free-willed – as though he was looking for a justification for his own mindset. Thoreau was a man obsessed with wildness: building his cabin in the forest beside Walden Pond and living as simply as possible, growing his few vegetables and harvesting wild fruits and game. 'Wild' was a condition he fervently sought of himself:

> Give me for my friends and neighbors wild men, not tame ones. The wildness of the savage is but a faint symbol of the awful ferity with which good men and lovers meet.

He admits Walden was an experiment; he was playing the native, the *primitif*, wishing himself to be self-willed and free-thinking, seeing if living wild – going back to nature – could work. 'I pray for such inward experience as will make nature significant.' And then again:

> I went to the woods because I wished to live deliberately, to front only the essential facts of life, and see if I could not learn

what it had to teach, and not, when I came to die, discover
that I had not lived . . . I wanted to live deep and suck out all
the marrow of life . . . and, if it proved to be mean, why then
to get the whole and genuine meanness of it and publish its
meanness to the world; or if it were sublime, to know it by
experience, and be able to give a true account of it in my next
excursion.

A hundred and fifty years later it is hard not to concede that
it was, in some considerable measure, a success, if not quite
in the way he envisaged. For Thoreau the whole experience
of nature was self-evidently sublime; even when, as his
unhappy expedition to Mount Katahdin revealed, nature's
meanness frightened him and ultimately got the better of
him, forcing him to turn back, he ascribes the blame to his
own frailty and psychological inadequacy, not to nature.
Thoreau's cogent, percipient, seminal writings, along with
those of a few others, are now celebrated as the founding
literature of the wilderness preservation movement in the
Western world. He would have been astonished to be told that
a century and a half later his work would still be in print in
twenty languages. Yet for all his heady philosophising about
wild nature, his experiment at Walden was but a brief twenty-
six-month interlude little more than a mile from a town. In
the end he had to give it up and return to manufacturing
pencils in Concord.

So where do we stand in the twenty-first century? What
have we done to *wild* the adjective and *wild* the concept?
What have we done with the noun that has so loyally dogged
our heels all the way from the woolly mammoth and the

cave bear; what have we done to *the wilds* themselves? Where have we parked the thing called wilderness in our complicated, cluttered brains? The answers are a sorry testament to the inspirational writings of Thoreau and Emerson, Walt Whitman, William Wordsworth, John Muir, Aldo Leopold, Gilbert White, Barry Lopez, Edward Abbey, Gary Snyder and now, most recently, Jay Griffiths, as well as the many other great philosophers, poets and lyricists of the wilderness movement. For the moment at least, we have lost the plot.

Wild is where we all came from and to where, ultimately, we will all return. Nature is far bigger than science and technology, than religious zeal, than economic forces and all the politicians ever spawned; it is infinitely bigger than democracy and people power and, despite our most arrogant anthropocentric protestations, it utterly dwarfs and swamps the creative genius of the human brain. (If a man or woman can create one work of genius in a lifetime, or think one truly original thought, they are remarkable indeed. Nature sparks originality and genius in every species, in every mutation, all the time, everywhere we look.) Just as, when we die, our nutrients return to the earth that spawned us, so we have not one twitch of control over the cosmos – the great natural workings of our planet and its solar system. One hefty meteorite colliding with the Earth or a major aberration on the surface of the sun or even an extreme volcanic event erupting from our own liquid core could wipe out every one of us, like the dinosaurs, in a matter of weeks.

However devastating the ecological crisis we may bring about by our own folly and greed, however many species we may drive into extinction in pursuit of our own amusement and comfort, we can never hope to control our climate or the many other natural forces that govern our lives. I am forever angered by politicians who repeatedly refer to '*addressing* the climate change *issue*', as though a tweak of the tax regime or a forthcoming White Paper will somehow make it all better. We are utterly powerless before the might of nature, so convincingly demonstrated by volcanoes, earthquakes and tsunami, hurricanes, typhoons, twisters, droughts and floods, encroaching deserts and rising sea levels. We all know we have the capacity to screw the natural environment up – dear God we know it – but I have yet to see a scrap of evidence that we can do anything better than backing off and letting nature heal itself. If we screw up altogether, we perish; but the planet goes on forever.

Thoreau is persistently misquoted. He did *not* say 'in wilderness is the future of the world'. What he did say was 'in *wildness* is the future of the world'. There is an important difference. Wilderness we understand, or at least we think we do – it is a place. Deserts are wilderness, as are great oceans, vast expanses of tundra or ice, mountain ranges, virgin forests and coral reefs – almost anywhere that human activities are marginalised by nature and it's tough for people to make a living. In Western culture over the past hundred and fifty years we have attempted to preserve some wilderness. The USA has designated wilderness areas by statute (they still have much more wilderness than the Old World) with the

Wilderness Act of 1964. The World Conservation Union has an official definition for 'protected areas designated as wilderness':

> A large area of unmodified or slightly modified land, and/or sea, retaining its natural character and influence, without permanent or significant habitation, which is protected and managed so as to preserve its natural condition.

(Note the contradiction: *'retaining its natural character and influence . . . which is . . . managed . . .'* My own definition of wilderness would specifically deny any hint of management at all.) And at the beginning of the twenty-first century almost all international conservation authorities recognise wilderness as an official term for just about anywhere that the forces of nature have primacy. But these are ring-fenced areas; they are quantities, and that's not what Thoreau meant at all.

Thoreau's famous *wildness* is a quality – the *Ur*-wildness in our heads. He was urging mankind to *think* wild, to remember our origins and to respect the forces of nature that spawned us, not reject them as something to be endlessly conquered and exploited: 'I wish to speak a word for nature, for absolute freedom and wildness.'

In the new and exciting American world of apparently unlimited horizons and of daily expanding industrial power and mobility, most people thought he was a head-case, and he didn't think much of them either: 'The mass of men lead quiet lives of desperation.' It wasn't until long after his death that the Western world on both sides of the Atlantic began to see some wisdom in his writings. It would have amused him to know that he had become a cult figure in America (he much admired the fame of Walt Whitman and Ralph Waldo Emerson); but had he known that his books would still be so widely read and quoted a hundred and fifty years after his death it would have done nothing to change his view of the human race. The fact is that Thoreau's famous wildness quote was a cry in the wilderness – and in the wilderness it has remained.

I came upon wildness as a seven-year-old child, suddenly and unexpectedly, at a fox earth so redolent with fresh scent that I started back, sure that a fierce animal, of whose identity I had no idea, was about to pounce and devour me. It was both thrilling and frightening; but its inherent dangers were insufficient to ward me off and its mysteries so alluring that I was certain to return. It was also private and personal, a secret all my own. I returned many times, only slowly learning who lived and moved within this murky pungence. It became a private escape then and it is yet.

Back then the countryside of my childhood was only marginally wilder than today, by which I mean that although agriculture had not become chemicalised and industrialised with all the purging changes that rapid expansionist era was to bring, it was still a man-shaped and manipulated land-scape of planted woods and fields growing crops and grazing livestock. It was a pastoral countryside of English villages still largely dependent upon its mosaic of small farms for the livelihoods of whole rural communities. Milk came from the next-door farm's dairy still warm and unpasteurised in enamel urns, and cabbages, potatoes and turnips were hand-lifted from the fields and sold door to door by a man whose whole career had been travelling round villages with his horse and cart. Quaint and wholesome though that now sounds, it did not mean that the countryside was necessarily any wilder than it is now. It was just being used in different, less intensive ways and consequently supported much more wildlife.

Young men went ferreting and long-netting for rabbits in the summer evenings; boys went bird's-nesting and proudly showed off their egg collections; when the local fox hunt came through, whole villages turned out for an important social event; otter hunting, badger digging and hare coursing were commonplace; grim-jawed gamekeepers in tweeds and gaiters ruled the woods and copses – everything that wasn't a game species was unprotected and liable to be shot as vermin. Every stream, pond, lake and river was fished by all boys and men of all ages. Country parks and nature reserves scarcely existed. The RSPB, now with well over a million members and by far the UK's most proactive and influential conservation body, was a tiny bird club, and the county Naturalists' Trusts were groups of genteel botanical ladies in tweed skirts meeting up with other mildly dotty enthusiasts bent solely upon recording local natural history. There was only one government conservation agency – the formative Nature Conservancy – and if there were any protected species (the 1949 National Parks and Access to the Countryside Act was the first attempt to legislate for the principle of nature conservation), no one in the country-side of my childhood had any idea what they were.

It was a different world; none of us could have foreseen how quickly it would all change. It felt benign and friendly and intimate in a villagey, *Cider with Rosie* sort of way, but it was not wild. There was no overt sense of the wild wood, nor of any landscape untrammelled by the hand of man. To find that elusive quality one would have had to go to the highest mountain tops or the remotest offshore island – and, with one or two notable exceptions, that has been more or less the case since the Romans abandoned Britain in AD 407. England's green and pleasant land had been substantially claimed, conquered, cleared, ploughed and tamed many centuries before my boyhood adventures took flight at the end of World War II.

Even the great forests of antiquity preserved by medieval kings and nobles as royal hunting parks – the New Forest, the Forest of Dean, Savernake, Wyre, Thetford Chase, Sherwood, Cannock Chase, Epping Forest and several others – were significantly shaped and used by the inexorable demands of men. They had all been harvested, re-planted, coppiced and grazed, and their undergrowth burned for hunting, managed for tanbark, cut over for charcoal and rootled over by domestic pigs for pannage for more than a dozen feudal centuries. Those forests – wonderful and remarkable though they are to this day – housed, sheltered and fed a thousand years of nobles, squires, sporting parsons, yeomen, farmers, game-keepers, carters, labourers, peasants, trappers, poachers, woodsmen, charcoal burners, huntsmen, cottars, tinkers, vagrants, outlaws, ne'er-do-wells, vagabonds and gypsies.

Even here in the far north of Scotland the once-widespread climax forest of the Highlands – the 'Great Wood of Caledon' as it has been evocatively dubbed – was being similarly exploited, but without the same measure of protection by nobility or the Crown. Slowly but surely it was cleared and fragmented, and, leaving only a few precious remnants, more than 99 per cent of its range was finally felled, grazed or burned out of existence to meet the ever-expanding needs of an exploding population of Highlanders. The immediate victims of this gradual but systematic deforestation were the wild ox, the reindeer, the wild boar, the lynx, the brown bear, the wolf, the beaver, the polecat, the capercaillie, the red kite, the sea eagle, the osprey and, to within a whisker of their twitching noses, the wildcat and the pine marten. The eventual victims, so often unlamented, were the wild flowers, the saprophytic decaying fungi, the specialised pine forest birds such as the Scottish crossbill and the crested tit, the unsung hordes of invertebrates, the vital and intricate mycorrhizal root associations, the humic microbes and, finally, the precious forest soils themselves. No, the wild woods of Britain were certainly not wilderness.

So what was this 'wild', this sidestep away from the bustling world of man I located and escaped to as a child? Where can you find this elusive, evocative, almost mystical, 'self-willed, free-acting, free-thinking', 'not tame or domesticated' quality that hit me full-face as I knelt to explore the dark entrance of that fox earth and which has haunted me all my life? It would take me more than thirty years finally to understand what it really was.

Annie Dillard describes it as 'a precise tilt of the will'.

There we go again – the will. However badly etymologically off course Thoreau's past participle may have been, he had a point. It *is* self-willed – all to do with the will. Wildness exists in us all, but we need the will to locate it and put it to work. The 'tilt' is that particular angling of reason and perception away from the accepted forces of materialism, domestication and tameness that have so divorced us from nature and our origins. In her striking existentialist essay 'Living like Weasels' (1982), Annie Dillard admits:

> I could very calmly go wild. I could live two days in the den, curled, leaning on mouse fur, sniffing bird bones, blinking, licking, breathing musk, my hair tangled in the roots of grasses. Down is a good place to go, where the mind is single. Down is out, out of your ever-loving mind and back to your careless senses.

I'm with Annie – I believe that you have to *want* to locate wildness, both within yourself and out there, in order to know it and to understand it. She continues: '. . . from a wild animal . . . I might learn something of mindlessness, something of the purity of living in the physical senses and the dignity of living without bias or motive.' And with John Muir, who insists: 'Only by going alone in silence, without baggage, can one truly get into the heart of the wilderness.'

By the age of eight I had perfected the art of escape. My mother was an invalid incapable of many of the usual functions of parenthood, so I was sent away to an astonishingly (by modern standards) unsupervised boarding school and, when at home in holiday time, often left entirely to my own devices. Where I went and how long I was gone for must have been a matter of real concern to her, but times (and hazards) were different then and the fact that somehow I always did seem to return for food and bed must have reassured her. Most importantly, I spent my whole childhood locked deep in English countryside (a relatively rare and privileged opportunity I was wholly unaware of at the time). To wander out was immediately to be in woods and fields, among rivers, marshes, streams and ditches – places, in those days, of endless wonder and discovery.

Of course, at eight years old I hadn't given wildness a thought, nor did I until well into adulthood. But my direct personal experiences – the discovering and the wondering – of those halcyon days were unquestionably wild. No one showed me badger setts for the first time; I found them myself and have never forgotten the thrill of working out on my own what they were.

I belonged to no clubs, read no guide books and possessed no field guides or maps. There were no way markers, signboards or interpretive leaflets to tell me where to go or what to expect to see, no television programmes and glossy magazines to whet my appetite. I had no specialist outdoor clothing. I caught butterflies in my bare hands just because of the allure of their dancing flight, eventually making myself a net out of a wire hoop, a bamboo cane and an old muslin curtain, long before my father bought me a proper one. I climbed to birds' nests high in trees – and I fell – on more than one occasion, walking several miles home with a broken arm or wrist or a badly sprained ankle. At my own hand I knew danger and excitement, real fear and searing pain.

I nearly drowned climbing out along a crack willow that a gale had tipped into a pond. The tree was alive and well, although almost horizontal, and its branches stretched well out into the stagnant water – perfect for a moorhen. My plan was to steal moorhens' eggs from the clumpy nest of weed skilfully woven into its outer branches. But the branches were too thin, even for a small boy. When I fell in I found myself stuck fast in oozing mud. Had it not been for the branches still within reach, and abandoning my gumboots (I never did admit what had happened to them), the story might have had a very different ending. But by then my enthusiasm for these self-willed, unsupervised excursions into what I perceived to be the true wild, and for my collections of eggs, butterflies, bones, fossils and many other memorabilia of the wild world, had become a passion. Despite getting into trouble for losing my gumboots, I returned a day or two later with a large spoon lashed to the end of a pole, clambered out along the same willow and secured my prize.

All those experiences and many other 'firsts' were wild. They were moments and places where human concerns, albeit childish ones, were largely absent. I had no watch in those days. My hours were natural and biological time, driven by light and dark, hunger, wet, cold, tiredness and pain. My emotions were honed and driven by my own direct actions and responses to what I was doing or what I found by my own intimate perceptions, bodily needs and feelings.

Without realising or analysing it I was responding to natural biological rhythms. I also now realise that without ever consciously identifying it as such, I had begun to see myself as a part of nature – I had run wild.

Much later, my first taste of real wilderness was in Africa, in the Kenya bush of the 1960s. On foot, unarmed, rounding a thorn thicket and coming face to face with a buffalo bull, a lion or an angry elephant focuses the attention like nothing else I have ever experienced. It is 'a careening splashdown into real life and the urgent current of instinct', a carnal, gut-clenching moment that tests your wits, your nerve and your body chemistry to the very brink. This is the ultimate definition of wild – knowing it, meeting it and tasting its ancestral fear. As Annie Dillard eloquently reveals, wild animals 'live in necessity and we live in choice, hating necessity and dying at the last ignobly in its talons'.

Britain offers few, if any, such animal-related experiences (unless you confront the criminal underworld, meet a violent lunatic or get charged by a bull), nor does much of the 'tamed' industrialised world, but when these things did happen to me in Africa I recognised the same emotional and bodily responses as those I had felt in boyhood. The sudden panicky sweat, the short staccato breaths, the thumping chest and trembling hands, and afterwards the sickening chill . . . had all happened before: when in my canoe I was charged down by a pair of mute swans; when I found a badger in a snare and in my naïve attempts to free it, it locked its teeth into my arm and wouldn't let go; when a branch high in an oak snapped under my weight and for a split second I thought I was plunging to my death; the gut-clenching shock when a tawny owl burst, talons first, out of a hole I was exploring halfway up an elm, mercifully latching on to my woolly hat and not removing my eyes. But ironically, it was not in Africa that I came closest to real disaster, but in the ancient woods of merry England.

In the late 1960s (in my early twenties) there was a resurgence of interest in deer in Britain. As a result of private deer parks' falling into disrepair during two world wars, introductions and escapes of exotics such as sika, muntjac and Chinese water deer, national reforestation policies and the reduction of gamekeepers and other rural workers after the war, deer of several species, native and feral, were spreading across Britain into areas that had not held wild deer for decades, and sometimes centuries. Hard on the heels of this phenomenon a scion of the British Mammal Society was to emerge as the British Deer Society, inaugurated at Woburn Abbey in February 1963. As a member of the former I found myself drawn into the latter. BDS founder members were a colourful mix of landowners, sportsmen, scientists, naturalists, zoo-keepers, wildlife artists and photographers, foresters, gamekeepers, stalkers and wild men of the woods. Many were great characters charged with a common enthusiasm for all things cervid.

They emerged from every background and from every remote and wooded cranny of Britain, stretching from the Highlands of Scotland, represented by red-bearded, bagpipe-playing foresters in kilts and tweedy, fore-and-aft bonneted stalkers for whom deer meant 'red', to the toe of Cornwall. There were khaki-and-combat-clad backwoodsmen with accents as thick as the soles of their leather boots; Teutonic, precisely mannered, loden-uniformed roe stalkers; bearded and bespectacled zoologists in duffel-coats and corduroys; landed lords in leather-elbowed tweed jackets; polo-necked, pencil-sucking artists with their sketch books; and florid-cheeked stag hunters in elegantly waisted hacking jackets and ancient bowler hats frayed at the brim. The Society's field meetings drew these colourful people together from all over the country, often fifty or sixty at a time, in a common and palpable bond of love and appreciation of deer of all species. They were also great fun; a sort of Robin Hood camaraderie of shared enthusiasm – not to say passion – for the woods and the deer produced some uproarious lectures and after-dinner speeches after unforgettable days out, always in some remote and exquisitely beautiful part of the British countryside.

At one of these meetings on Exmoor, the home of stag hunting in Britain for the past 200 years, I met a retired harbourer of the Devon and Somerset Staghounds called Hector Heywood. (A harbourer is the man who finds a suitable stag to be hunted and watches it for days before the hunt, knows its habits and where it goes to cover to lie up by day – a harbourer has to know his deer intimately.) I warmed to him immediately. He was a countryman to the core, born into a remote rural community dominated by stag hunting, in which, apart from brief military service, he had remained all his life. He was one of those 'uneducated', non-scientific naturalists who seemed to understand wildlife and the habitat that sustained it with an innate and awe-inspiring confidence. He loved deer and saw no contradiction in hunting them. Deer numbers had to be controlled and he believed that hunting was a rational replacement for natural predation by the wolf. I was to spend many hours in his company in the few months I knew him and I owe him a life-long debt of gratitude for what he taught me about Exmoor and its magnificent deer.

Exmoor red deer are the finest in Britain. The habitat is perfect: a mix of deep, wooded valleys known as 'combes', fast-flowing streams cascading down from high, granitic moors of heather and grass, and in between a mosaic of steep, stony-soiled, high-hedged stock farms, where the living was meagre and the hunting an integral component of the farming and land-owning community. The combination of good feeding on cropland, excellent winter shelter in the woods and careful selection by hunting had produced heavy-bodied stags with magnificent multi-pointed antlers far larger than anything I had ever seen in Scotland. Hector took me to see these superb animals at close quarters.

In the rutting season the wooded combes echoed with their roared challenges. Night after cool autumnal night we left the Land Rover at the edge of a wood and stalked a few yards into the darkness to hear the stags belling to each other. What goes on in those woods on dark October nights is as close to wildness as you can get in Britain. When two equally matched stags refuse to back down the combe reverberates with the juddering clash of their antlers. They lock together, surge and moan and churn the leaf litter to mud with their flaying hooves, break free for a few seconds, then crash together again in another long, heaving struggle. I was transfixed.

A few days later Hector was busy so I decided to go out on my own. At dusk I walked quietly into a remote wood through which the River Barle rattled enthusiastically over its stony bed. I used its happy burbling to conceal the sound of my approach. The air was rank with the musk-and-uric pungence of rutting deer. Up ahead I could hear a stag roaring and moaning his tetchy bravura. I crept closer, zigzagging steeply up the side of the valley through waist-high bracken. Finally I came to the edge of the wood. There he was, silhouetted in the fading light, surrounded by a group of hinds, standing proud, very much in charge of his patch. The deer were about two hundred yards away, but clearly visible in the twilight. My stag roared throatily at intervals of seven or eight minutes. I remember thinking I should have brought a torch to see my way home.

After watching him through my binoculars for a while I decided to try to stalk closer. It was exciting. I was practising field craft, emulating Hector's subtle, life-honed skills. I retreated into the bracken and crawled around the edge of the wood until I had a better view. The distance halved without my being detected and pleasure flooded through me. This was something I had always wanted to achieve: being a naturalist, out there, on my own, discovering, learning, emotionally locked into the subject of my vaulting enthusiasm – unconsciously but ineluctably going wild myself. I felt that warming glow of possessive fulfilment – this was *my* stag – in the same way that I had felt about finding my first badger sett as a boy.

Hector had told me a few days earlier that it was possible to 'call' a stag to you during the rut – that by cupping your hands to your mouth and imitating a roar, if the stag was really charged up with testosterone he would come out to the challenge, even if the roar was unconvincing. I couldn't resist having a go. Light was failing fast and, anyway, in a few minutes I would have to give up and find my way back in the dark. I roared my best, a long, drawn-out bellow finishing with a few grunts for added effect.

The response was electric. This huge stag turned to me, raised his head to display his impressive antlers at their fullest heraldic reach, and came high-stepping towards me. Twenty yards away he stopped and stared. He was glorious, imperial, haughty and huge; and he was mine. I don't know what possessed me to roar again, but I did. I think he must have seen the movement of my hands to my mouth, and even as the sound uttered from my throat I realised my mistake. He didn't wait again, he just came. He came charging across the grass so nimbly and fast that I panicked. I turned and ran.

That was the worst thing I could have done, a dire mistake. Had I stood my ground and shouted and waved he would have seen that I was human and pulled out. Man *is* the dread predator, our form and our scent defeating even the proudest cervine heart. But the night breeze was in my face. There *was* no human scent, and by running away I confounded whatever doubts may have flashed through his hormone-fizzing brain. I was an intruder to be seen off in no uncertain way.

I plunged downhill through the bracken as fast as I could run. Behind me I could hear his hooves thrashing through the undergrowth. He seemed to be very close. I blundered into trees, tripped and half-fell, gathered myself and ran on. Branches whip-lashed my face, briars snagged my hands. It was dark in the wood now and this was not the way I had come. The land fell away steeper and steeper so that I was hurtling blindly forward. Suddenly I was falling, falling . . .

My recollection is hazy now, but I do remember landing and a stinging feeling in my thigh and my binoculars hitting me in the mouth. Then I was falling again, tumbling and rolling, somersaulting steeply down a muddy, rocky slope. Finally, after what seemed an age, I thudded into a large boulder and a pain shot through my shoulder. Of the stag there was no sound, but I jumped up and ran on anyway; for a hundred yards, perhaps? I don't know; it was a blur then and it is a blur now. All I knew was that I had to keep running. Something visceral, something ancestral, plumbed into the deepest core of my being told me to keep running. I was running for my life.

I never saw my stag again. When eventually I did find my way out of that wood and flagged down a passing car I was horrified to discover what I looked like. By an almost spooky coincidence it was Hector heading out to Dulverton. 'What in God's name you bin doing, boy? You'm covered in blood!' He shone his torch up and down my body. I looked down at my left leg in amazement. My trousers were sodden with blood, my lips split and teeth chipped, blood streamed down my chin and on to my shirt, and my hands and face were torn with long briar scratches as though I had been savaged by a bear. My right arm hung uselessly at my side and my shattered collar bone protruded in an angrily swollen bulge. 'It's 'ospital for you, young fella.'

And 'ospital it was, in Taunton, an agonising hour of twisting lanes away. What was remarkable was that until Hector revealed to me the extent of my injuries I had felt almost no pain. I certainly had no idea I had broken my collar bone and, as it turned out, cracked my elbow. The two-inch gash in my thigh and my lower lip had to be stitched; the dental work would come later.

Would my stag have gored me to death if I hadn't run? Probably not, but to have connected with just one lunge of those long, sharp antler tines might well have punctured me deeply and dangerously, rendering it impossible for me to have made it to the road. As it was, I felt no pain and was steered by some deep, involuntary genetic compulsion. Adrenaline and stark survival took over; the all-defining difference between not even knowing I was injured and being injured on the rugger field, unable to play on because the pain floods in immediately – the difference between the real thing and a game – the yawning chasm between wild and tame.

What happened to me that day was wild. The stag was wild, the fear was wild, wild was the flight. When I returned a week later to survey the scene I was appalled to see how far I had fallen down that rocky slope and how far I had run and walked out to the road, surfing on a massive hormonal shot from my adrenal medulla, involuntarily increasing my heart and pulse rate, and the levels of sugars and lipids pumped into my bloodstream and fuelling my muscles.

Now, nearly four decades later, having survived many wild encounters in many of the world's great wildernesses and having (at last) developed a much keener sense of self-preservation, I have come to terms with wildness and grown comfortable with it, as I believe Thoreau would have done had he lived beyond the age of forty-five and been able to travel as widely as we now can. Yet those uncontainable matrices of nature's wildness – volcanoes and liquid lava flows, great wind and storm, gripping pack ice, raging wild fires, the solemnity of mountains and deserts, the tumult of oceans, vast swamps and marshes and the bewildering mazes of our last great forests – have never ceased to arouse me. They tug at whatever cerebral imprinting guides my deeper consciousness – the *Ursprache* wildness in my skull that governs my thinking, the same wildness that shaped Thoreau in the Massachusetts woods and that makes me *me*.

Standing at the water's edge on that June morning with power gusts of Atlantic westerly coursing across the moors, buffeting my face and whipping the waters of the loch into angry wavelets at my feet, I found myself in its grasp once more. As I pondered this uplifting fling of wildness a heron appeared above the birch trees a few yards to my right. It was struggling.

Herons are designed for stalking marshes and shallows, not for aeronautical displays. Its great looping wings cannot beat fast. They shoulder their way through the wind with tugs of power not unlike a rowing boat. This fellow had used the shelter of the trees to make his way up the hill following the course of the burn, a flight he will have made many times. Now, within sight of his marshy, trout-, frog- and newt-rich goal, he was forced to lift above the frantic swayings of the tree fringe and meet the gale head on.

When I first saw him he was losing ground. His wings rowed him forwards a few feet, only to be blasted backwards by the next gust. He came on again, seeming to try to out-power the wind, reached the same point and was hurled backwards a second time, disappearing from my view.

Then he came again, this time tacking towards me across the wind until he was almost overhead. He was lower now. I saw his yellow-ringed eye look down at me and a rasping cry of alarm or perhaps frustration broke from his dagger bill. But herons are not shot at or persecuted here and he seemed to know that; his need for breakfast was, for the moment, greater than his fear of man. I looked up and into the cavernous grey underwings. I could count the open fingers of his primary feathers and hear their humming vibrations as they levered downwards through the rushing air. Against his body I could see the soft, downy fringes of his breast, special absorbent feathers for cleaning fish slime and scale off his flight feathers, ruffling and streaming. His pinky-yellow bill pierced the wind and his snake-like neck was folded to a tight S and tucked down onto his breast. His long legs, the sandy colour of reeds, trailed to his tidily stretched and pointing toes.

Once over the birches he dropped suddenly and steeply almost to the surface of the loch, angling sideways away from me, cutting across the blasts, rising and falling with the fluctuations of the swirling eddies, hugging the bank and the shelter of the pinewood where he made good ground, rising at last, almost touching the uppermost branches, out into the gale again, on past the marsh before spinning back with the wind and gliding serenely down to the water's edge. It was a masterful performance; a combination of determination and an exact understanding of his powers of flight in very testing conditions. It seemed, suddenly and unexpectedly, to be a new definition of wildness.

The long trail of evolution has honed the heron for efficient fishing and wading, as with all living creatures, to catch the food that enables it to survive: the fishing-spear bill, the neck-spring for the lethal stab, the long, camouflaged wading legs. Add to the recipe a few colourful frills for display and breeding advantage: the flowing black crest feathers; the dual black neck stripe; the pink tinge to the underbill, colour that floods in during the breeding season; the sinuous neck for posing and posturing, the buttercup eye, and you have a basic heron. But it also needs to get to its fishing grounds, sometimes over long distances, expending as little energy as possible. These needs have provided it with broad, rounded wings which enable the bird to soar and glide, as well as power forward in a straight line. No fancy swallow tail or sharp falcon wings for the heron. This is a family saloon, not a Ferrari. So all the more surprising that it can cope with a gale.

Natural selection takes no prisoners. What use is a fiercely efficient fishing heron that starves in a protracted gale? Written in, there all the time but unseen, is the constantly refining ability to cope with the extremes of its habitat and the demands of the ecosystem to which it belongs, including gales and storms. Hebridean equinoctial gales can last a fortnight. Herons do well in the islands; every shoreline has its statuesque heron stalking the wrack and tangle. Perhaps not such a family saloon after all.

So where do we stand with this complicated concept of *wild*? I have said we have lost the plot, and I mean it. We have corrupted the concept and perverted the word. *Wild* now means something other, honed by danger, something to be wary of. I have to acknowledge that the great majority of people in Western society, even many of those scientifically and ecologically aware, have no real idea of wildness either in their own heads or out there, unless you happen to be talking about polar or grizzly bears or great white sharks, or some other potentially dangerous wildlife, most of which are fogged and distorted by myth and alarmist misinformation. To be meaningful all language has to possess a commonality of understanding. If my use of *wild* means something no one else understands, then I'm clearly not going to be able to make my point. The best analogy I can summon up is religion. Its real meaning lies in profound personal experience, without which it is rendered superficial, even, to some, contemptible. For most of us *wild* has passed out of personal experience into superficiality, something that used to be, something not really for us any more. Who needs wildness when television nature programmes can show you every intimate detail at safe close quarters without even having to stir from your chair?

If we want to experience wildness for ourselves the norm is now to do so in a 'safe' way, by going to a nature reserve where a ranger will lead you by the hand, or signboards and leaflets remove all the excitement and discovery before you have even set off on the trail. Overhanging branches are removed in case they scratch your face; stout bridges waft you over streams to keep your feet dry; steps and handrails are installed, lest you slip or fall. The emergency services are always on hand. To entice and please our urban and suburban majority we are sanitising, taming and domesticating for popular consumption the last of our most precious wild places throughout the globe and frequently trivialising the experience of the wildlife they sustain.

Richard Mabey, one of our most thought-provoking contemporary nature writers, with a deeply developed sense of wild, leaves us in no doubt about how he feels in his book *Nature Cure*:

> A few days later we went back to one of the wildest, wettest stretches of Broadland . . . We left behind all the paraphernalia of the countryside interpretation business, the hides with gates, the trails waymarked in five colours, the boards that tell you what to look for and what to feel about it, edifices that seem to have converged with the precautionary fences and smoothed-out paths of the new safety culture to convey an ominous common message: 'You are not encouraged to have First-Hand Experiences. They may hurt. Life is dangerous. Keep out.'

The current craze for ecotourism (which at best is an enlightening and personally fulfilling sustainable experience and at worst a euphemism for gawping at a wildlife spectacle regardless of the consequences for the wildlife) is spreading this lamentable malaise around the world – witness lion-gawping on the Masai Mara or grinding through the rubbish in an armoured tracked bus to see polar bears at the Churchill dump. Darwin would be shocked to return to the Galapagos and witness the 200,000 people a year who queue to be photographed with nesting frigate birds and giant tortoises. These usually profit-driven experiences mean little to their participants despite the occasional sweaty hands, thumping hearts and sudden surges of attention skilfully manipulated by a growing horde of semi-professional experts. For most people we have reduced nature and wildlife to a leisure-time entertainment spectacle and sanitised fun.

Is this too harsh? Am I arguing a lost cause which was only ever available to a handful of the privileged *cognoscenti* and career naturalists like me? Yes, I think I am. I have to recognise that few, if any, would seek to discover the wildness in their heads by almost being killed or badly injured by a wild animal. As far as I am aware, no extreme experiences were suffered by Emerson, Thoreau or Wordsworth (although Thoreau hated his expedition up Mount Katahdin), but John Muir actively sought out danger to explore the definition of wildness for himself by climbing a tree in a gale 'clinging on like a bobolink to a reed' for the sheer thrill of it; Aldo Leopold certainly knew danger at first hand and was to die tragically in a wild fire on a neighbour's farm.

The extremist route to discovering wildness is not disputed here; it is well documented by adventurers and widely debated by ideologues and deep ecologists, but they are always likely to remain a tiny minority in a world where majorities are everything. For the rest of humanity in the

ever-expanding world of Western influence there has to
be another route if we are ever to hope to bridge the perpetually widening gulf between wilderness conservation
and modernity. If pushed to choose, I'm firmly with the
weekend-fun wildlife enthusiast and the sanitised ecotourism
experience.

Whatever my personal wishes and feelings, I have to
recognise that for most people the way markers, signboards,
guide books and ranger services are not just helpful, they
are essential. We are so far removed from nature and wildness in our daily lives that they have become inaccessible
and incomprehensible without a helping hand. To feel safe
and to be able to enjoy the experience of wildlife, nature
reserves and wilderness areas at all, people have to be encouraged to go there and, initially at least, to be comforted and
guided – to know that others have been there first and that
help is not far away if something goes wrong. That is the
world of our own making and for now we must accept it,
warts and all.

The more people who are able to enjoy ecotourism and
the shrinking wildernesses of the world, the better we are
able to protect them from the insidious forces of exploitation and development, although that is not an argument for
encouraging mass tourism into fragile habitats. If ecotourism
provides jobs and economic improvement for locals and
encourages a sense of ownership and value of wild places
among communities who might otherwise have destroyed
them, then it can be justified. At least that way we get to
hang on to some of our wildlife and its precious habitats.
The trick for those whose responsibility it is to create and

maintain nature and wildness in our crowded world is to make it accessible without destroying its essential qualities at the same time. This is not easy and often means denying market forces and easy profit – forbidding the ice-cream kiosk at the cathedral door. There are many pitfalls on that route and so far the signs from around the world do not augur well.

But none of this political realism stops me wanting to tell those same enthusiasts – colleagues, professionals and consumers – that there *is* another dimension; there is a spiritual and life-changing engagement with the wild world available out there to everyone. Many mountaineers know it well. The trails, the guides, the handbooks, mobile phones, GPS systems, annotated route maps and the plethora of specialist climbing and safety equipment have done their worst to demystify even those towering bluffs and magical heights just as they have with nature reserves, but for many mountain men and women there remains real scope for wonder and awe and fear and for what Wordsworth so elegantly defined as 'a presence that disturbs me with the joy of elevated thoughts'. In these places there is a private, personal wildness we can still relocate in our heads and which can serve us well by bringing us closer to the dazzling creative genius of the very nature that made us what we are. For all his wandering in the wild Massachusetts woods, Thoreau knew it well:

> I shall never find in the wilds of Labrador any greater Wildness than in some recess of Concord; i.e. than I import into it. [*Journals* (9:43)]

I meet it every day. It is there in this gale fresh in from the Atlantic – the one the weatherman called wild. It stings my face, makes my eyes water and causes the birches and pines around the loch to heave and lurch like boats at anchor in a storm. He was right. Wild is a good word for this wind.

# 8

# The Claim

Who owns this landscape?
Has owning anything to do with love?
For it and I have a love affair, so nearly human
We even have quarrels . . .
        – Norman MacCaig, 'A Man in Assynt'

First stake your claim. This must be a law of nature, although I don't think biologists would sign up to it in quite those terms. There are words, such as *succession* and *colonisation*, which scientists use to describe the natural processes of species moving in and grabbing opportunities, but none of them seem to me to be all-embracing, nor do they express the rugger-scrum urgency of nature muscling in. None seem quite to grasp the surging reality of what is going on out there, every minute of every day in every season. The best I can manage is *the claim*. I like *the claim* because it also seems to chime with some inner connection, making it a private and personal coda for my own existence, for what I have done in my lifetime, claiming space and letting it possess me as I possess it to meet my own biological needs and those of my family. I witness manifestations of the claim everywhere I look. I find it in every visible living organism: plants, birds, reptiles, insects, bugs, mammals, fish, algae, fungi and bacteria. On my way to the loch I stumble across it every day.

*June 17th*   This morning I'm back in the pinewood. It would be good to see the red squirrels or the tiny crested tits – a species utterly dependent upon pine forest – that flit and trill through the high canopy; but today I have another purpose. I'm heading through to the regenerating birchwoods on the western slopes draining into the loch, to check out a warbler. A bird-watching friend has reported an attractive but, by warbler standards, unmelodious trill he thinks might belong to a wood warbler. I am sure it is – it wouldn't be the first time we have recorded this inconspicuous little migrant songster with a timorous tune in our woods – but I want to hear and ideally see it for myself before we record it formally among the year-on-year increasing list of small birds in our new, precious wild woods.

They are new because there were no birchwoods behind the loch when I came to live here thirty years ago; the land was desolate, sour moorland that had been grazed bare by centuries of livestock, principally sheep, right through the nineteenth century, and, throughout the twentieth, increasing pressure from rapidly increasing numbers of wild red deer. With the removal of the hill sheep and some effective deer control the birches have seeded themselves and waxed strong under the smiling sun, now proper woodland, maturing year on year, niches filling, new life streaming in and claiming the woodland soils, the minerals, the moisture, the leaves, the dead wood, the leaf mould, the shelter and the shade for themselves. That's what also makes them precious. They signal hope for our long future – man giving something back to nature after taking too much for so long. The spring bird list is just one way of measuring the success of the expanding woodland; the more productive the woodland, the longer the species list grows. These are some of the things naturalists get up to: watching, finding, recording and listing, although for many years I have been happy to leave the paperwork to others more scientifically orientated and methodically inclined.

Halfway through the pinewood a wet flush runs down from the moor towards the loch. The ground is permanently boggy here, almost running in winter, but dense with lush grasses all summer long. Where the red deer have picked their way through, their cloven slots have left deep pouches where water the colour of brandy stands and shines. Bending down to inspect one of these I see a tiny wriggling disturbance beneath the surface of the water. The same repeats from pouch to pouch, seems to be true for them all. Some sharp-eyed opportunist insect of the wet woods, most likely a species of gnat, has found these egg-cups of static water to be just right for their particular domestic purposes. They have nipped in and laid claim to these unlikely legacies of chance. Eggs have been laid and the aquatic larvae have hatched and grown fat, grazing on microscopic diatoms in the safety of the water. Hanging below the surface they have probed a tail-end snorkel upwards through the surface tension to breathe. They have claimed their private space and their world is air and food and the protection of the dark microponds in which the parent gnat so thoughtfully spawned them. I bend down to see more clearly. As the shadow I cast and the vibrations of my footfall alert them to danger, so they wriggle free from the surface and disappear to the murky bottom of their tiny, sherry-glass home. All unwitting, intent on another claim of their own, the deer have sauntered through leaving their trail of perfectly shaped pockets for something else to use. Nature never sleeps, opportunities are snatched, claims staked. That's the way it all works. Nature doesn't miss tricks.

Pondering the mysteries of chance and opportunity, the two immeasurable constants that shape our world, I begin to cross the broad, wet stripe in front of me. In the wettest runs, those that stay damp all the year round, bright red and lime-green sphagnum mosses in opulent, domed hassocks plump enough to grace the altar rail of any cathedral have forced out the grasses, taking over, claiming the moist, peaty sediment for themselves. I pick my way carefully through; I know the mud beneath is deep and to put a foot wrong will always bring the discomfort of a wet foot for the rest of my walk.

I found my warbler – that is to say, I caught its distinctive shivering trill and its thin, plaintive follow-on – stalked it in to only a few yards, and saw an almost liquid, citrine flash disappear through an eared willow thicket and up into a high birch. Song is often the best way to identify a bird. It was exactly where I was told it would be – where it had been before. I would have been surprised if it hadn't been there. It, too, had found its patch and staked its claim. Its tremulous and repetitive song, described by Gilbert White in Selborne as 'a sibilous shivering noise in the tops of the tall woods', was its best shot at informing the world and any other wood warblers that may be around.

Every time I make my circumambulation of the loch I pass several obvious boundaries. There is the wire stock fence containing Geordie McLean's sheep; a dry-stone dyke marks the boundary of crofting land from two centuries ago; I, in my time, have erected fences on my own ground; behind the loch a mesh deer fence at the rim of a Forestry Commission plantation unsuccessfully attempts to keep the red deer off the pasture land; and a line of long-defunct pig-iron posts with the wires almost completely corroded away reveals where in the mid-nineteenth and early twentieth centuries the crofters divided up their grazing rights on the high moorland. Fences and walls are the convention we humans have always used to mark out our claims to the land. Then we back it up with maps and deeds, just in case. But these visible artificial boundaries are as nothing compared to the other boundaries I cross in the course of my walk. I cannot guess at their number – I can only list a few of the most obvious to me.

We all make claims. Claims are an essential component of day-to-day life in the human as well as the natural world. Claims are how animal societies are ordered and maintained; they have to be staked out and boundaries have to be set and patrolled. Claims are made to the three physical dimensions of space and the further far less obvious three of scent, sound and time, some very brief, some becoming permanent, immutable features in the lives of the species concerned. Claims are staked to food supplies and the territory required to supply that food, and, almost the most vital of all, to mates. Food, a home and a mate, those three; life's triple imperatives we all need, and to which, sooner or later, we all lay claim, from the lowliest gnat larva in the footprint of a deer to those who run great government oligarchies like the Forestry Commission.

Three-dimensional claims are easy to see. Each fence post reveals a need on the part of the claimant: the forester, crofter or other stakeholder. The bigger the fence or the wall, the greater the need. Some animals have fence posts of their own. Beside the burn, a convenient linear physical feature, I find a line of badger latrines – shallow dung pits – which mark the edge of a badger territory. Badgers live in family groups, sometimes called clans, and are deeply territorial. They stake out their ground with scent from under-tail scent glands and with lines and groups of dung pits prominently placed. The intention is to keep at bay any other badgers from neighbouring clans straying into their feeding grounds. The burn is an obvious natural boundary and the badgers have used it to define their territory and reinforce their claim.

Resorting to modern technology to assist our knowledge of these crepuscular undertakings, one of my colleagues recently set a concealed automatic camera (Stealthcam) on a tree beside the badger latrines. He also sprinkled some peanuts around beneath the camera. In the morning the camera had fired three times, revealing a solitary badger devouring the peanuts as expected. It was reset and more nuts were put out, and he confidently expected the same result. But the next night produced a fine dog fox, precisely mirroring the actions of the badger, and, almost as a gesture of defiance, a sort of fox V-sign, defecating full and vividly right beside, but not in, the badger dung pits. The fox had claimed the peanuts – thank you very much – but seemed unable to resist scornfully defying the badger boundaries, leaving a handsome, black and twisted marker of his own.

Protective of their feeding and breeding grounds, the roe bucks constantly patrol their patches of woodland and take great trouble to skin the stems of prominent saplings with their antlers. They also have a scent gland, in their case positioned between the antlers, so that by rubbing up and down on a slender stem and peeling the bark bare they can create a highly visible marker post, greatly assisted by the obvious die-back of browning leaves when the sapling has been ring-barked, which remains a flag for other bucks to keep out, long after the scent has evaporated.

Otters spraint conspicuously in the same places over and over again. I know a stone at the water's edge just under the bridge over the burn where I will always find a fresh, black, slightly oily, fish-smelling deposit. At the head of the loch there is a large, mossy, bank-side cushion in the marsh where the bright green of the moss has been entirely burned back to a lifeless grey by the trampling and strongly nitrogenous sprainting of the otters over many seasons. They also raise their tails and spray their urine against way markers – a tree stump or a boulder – to leave a lutrine signal and a lingering scent that wafts off around the loch or is carried downstream by the movement of the water to greet any other otter passing through. Man's ability to detect scent is crude and vestigial. If we ever had it, we've lost it; evolved it out over millions of years of developing an intellect which rendered superfluous that particularly vibrant dimension of the natural world. It's our loss. We can only guess at what the full sentiment of the otter's message might be.

Scent is multi-dimensional. All I can see as I stroll my way through the many territories of the wildlife around my home are the visible signs – a pine marten scat parked prominently on a stone, the twisted cord of fox faeces very ostentatiously left on the path, roe deer and badger paths winding through the woods – but I am conscious that I am also perpetually trespassing. I wend my way through uncharted waves of scent too refined for my feeble and inchoate olfactory equipment. If only we could somehow colour each animal scent with wisps of smoke: red for roe deer, green for badgers, yellow for wildcats, blue for pine martens, brown for foxes, orange for stoats, purple for the red deer . . . the land would become a perpetual rainbow of magical, interwoven lattices, an intricate sunset of spectral beauty, twisting and turning with the contours like a mad Van Gogh painting.

Supreme in the claim-staking art is the red deer stag. He has it all; he wraps all six dimensions into his display with anarchic domination, to hell with anything or anyone else. In the rut his testosterone-driven bravura transcends all boundaries. He powers his authority throughout his domain. Like a body-builder, he has perfected his physical attire: the fine head of antlers, the shaggy, black mane, the rippling muscles, the haughty eye. Then he marks out his ground. He stamps and rips at the heather with his hooves and antlers, digging a wet, peaty pit in which he urinates and wallows. When he emerges, rank, black and dripping, to other stags and to his hinds looking on, his stature and his authority are hugely enhanced. His cervine pungence fills the air. Then he roars. He tips back his head and hurls his challenge to the winds, to the high hills, to the waiting, quaking world. It is one of nature's most refined utterances, once heard never forgotten; a roar that intensifies life and validates the wildness of the hills, the moors, the forests and the seasons. He repeats it over and over again, daring the world to venture onto his stance or to threaten his harem of hinds – roars that lay claim to his wives, his land and his future.

And then there is birdsong. Robins, unable physically to mark the land, choose prominent perches from which to sing vigorously, to keep neighbouring birds at bay during the mating and nesting season. My spring walks are uplifted by their rich, melodious and robust solos – a sheer joy to us, but a deadly serious signal to other robins. The heron hoarsely barks his grating claim to the marsh. The nesting ospreys and peregrines shriek theirs into thin air while mobilising their aerial brilliance to attack and see off any intruders. So do the ravens; their profundo 'Cronk! Cronk!' echoes from the sheer rock walls of the river gorge, audible up to half a mile away. When the security of their nest site is intentionally or unintentionally threatened, by either other passing ravens or perhaps a buzzard or a golden eagle just wheeling through, they too take to the air and use their size and very accomplished aerial skills, amplified by their low-frequency mountain calls, to harry away the intruder, often mobbing it relentlessly for a mile or more.

To a bird there is no poetry in birdsong. For all our fanciful notions, the plain truth is that birds sing to attract a mate and to form a pair bond – and to keep others out. Most birds, even those which happily flock together for a large part of the year, are deeply territorial when they need to be. Anyone who lives near a rookery knows that. As I walk up the Avenue every spring the pageant being enacted high above me in the twiggy tops of the limes and horse chestnuts is a constant racket of corvid clamour. The rooks are yelling at and to each other all the time. Rooks that feed side by side in the field, flocking in hundreds, suddenly become angrily defensive of their little perch of nest space. During the noisy building process one bird will sit and defend the nest against others building nearby, while its partner flies off to search for more twigs. All that wonderfully evocative countryside racket simply repeats over and over again: 'Keep off! This is *our* space.'

Our woods ring with chaffinch song throughout the spring, another species that flocks in large numbers in the winter. But with the breeding season the birds pair off and mate. While the hen perfects her nest and lays her eggs the cock birds perch prominently on the outermost branch of a tree or the tip of a bush and hurl out a constantly repeating refrain for all they are worth. Throats dilated and vibrating, their buoyant melodies weave elegance and grace into our spring, but to other chaffinches the claim message is clear: 'This site is ours!' Once the breeding game is done, the urge to sing evaporates and falls back to a pathetic, repetitive cheep. For the rest of the year they barely sing a note.

Every once in a while, the song doesn't seem to work. In my journal I hoard incidents like pocketed pretty shells from the beach. Much later they become touchstones, assuming a broader significance. One nesting season entry records a claim that seemed to have failed. Departing the dam an hour after dawn, I was walking quietly down the path when a ball of feathers tumbled through the pine branches above me and landed at my feet. I stopped in amazement. Three blue tits were locked together in what appeared to be mortal combat. With feet and beaks they gripped fiercely on to each other, and their tiny wings whipped angrily in an attempt to beat their opponents into submission. It was impossible to discern more than a ball of rolling, fizzing, flapping blue, green and yellow. It was impossible to tell who was fighting who; was it two against one, or were they all equally angry with each other? I had no idea whether they were all male, or whether an unfortunate female was caught up in a vicious mating triangle. That such tiny birds could display such anger was astonishing to behold. A high-pitched chatter of rage, as though emitted through clenched teeth, was all I could hear.

I was transfixed by this extraordinary behaviour. What fury burned in these pulsating, thumb-nail breasts to make them abandon the safety of the trees? What passion clouded their tiny avian brains? Did they know they had fallen to the ground; that all their defences were down; that they were doubly vulnerable to predation, rolling about on the ground broadcasting their presence with their angry chatter? Any pine marten, wildcat, stoat, weasel, buzzard, sparrowhawk, hoodie crow or fox in the vicinity could so easily have nipped in for a cheap meal.

After watching for several minutes, and seeing no victor or any hint of a breach in the impasse, I stepped forward and bent to pick them up. For a moment I was able to hold them in my hands, still fizzing like a bomb, tiny shoulders still ramming angrily home. Then the truth seemed to dawn; one bird let go with its bill, eyed me for a split second of awful recognition and tore itself free, quickly flying away leaving a dusting of sulphur-tinged feathers floating to the ground. The other two looked faintly silly and then broke as well. In a flash they were gone.

I have often seen blue tits as well as other tit species fighting. They can be fierce little tykes with a special street-urchin charm, aggressive and feisty by nature, denying their diminutive size, soft, pastel-hued plumage and endearing confidence on our bird tables, but I had never before witnessed such relentless spleen, none of them apparently prepared to yield a fraction of an inch. Whichever bird made the claim that day obviously didn't make it forcefully enough. Another bird, perhaps two, saw a chink in his armour and made a challenge.

Animals are by no means alone in staking claims. Every seed that falls and germinates is a claim in the making. From the first sprout veering skywards from the splitting seed case, and the first root hairs tentatively heading down, every plant, whether mighty tree or tiny flower, is grabbing space and opportunity to establish its claim on sunlight, soil and moisture. We see only the delicate nodding of the wood anemone; we overlook the innate aggression in its leaves and roots, fighting for the space to survive, mustering its inner forces, doing its last-ditch best to force any other competing plant out of its patch. Some species, such as rhododendrons, resort to dirty tricks to win their space. Their roots release toxic phenols into the soil so that nothing else can grow there. They poison their way to the sun. Others, such as beech trees, produce a heavy canopy of shade to stifle the photosynthetic chances of anything else germinating around them, removing competition for precious water and nutrients for their own roots at the same time as saturating the ground with capillary root hairs so that nothing else has a chance. There is a war going on out there, endlessly, inexorably, day and night, in every ecosystem and habitat throughout our wondrous world, and always utterly without quarter. There is no place for charity in the natural world.

In the wrong place some claimants are thoroughly unwelcome. The Victorians planted an American red oak in what is now my garden. In a hundred years it had grown well to become a fine, handsomely spreading tree until it was claimed as a desirable host by honey fungus (*Armillaria mellea*), a devastating parasite of trees and shrubs from which there is no escape. It infects roots and butts, eventually fatally invading the whole tree with a white, fibrous rot. With a heavy heart I felled the oak and removed the stump, burning it and all the brash wood in the vain hope that I could contain the spread of the fungus. I dug out the ground around the stump and replaced it with fresh soil from another part of the garden. But the fungal spores are airborne and will have proliferated far and wide long before I took action.

To me and in my garden context, the honey fungus ravaging so fine a tree was a plague I could well have done without. But from an ecological standpoint I should not be so quick to damn its name. In a natural climax forest, where honey fungus will certainly have evolved, there must always have been many more trees than it could infect, and its depredations will have done no more than create a constant supply of dead wood for many other species, especially invertebrates and other saprophytic fungi, to claim for their own particular needs. In the long term the tree would decay back to the soil to feed new growth. The spaces in the forest its demise created would also have freed up opportunities for other trees and plants to colonise. Nature's generous spirit always seems to have room for its own.

For those who have the time and the inclination to explore it, nature is a constant source of joy and delight to the human eye. But there is another view of this marvellous cosmos in which we gloriously spin. For the moment mankind has grabbed the initiative; the world has been our oyster since we discovered how to dominate it, there for the taking and the keeping in our time. We have staked our claim with a terrible and merciless vengeance. But we should not be so complacent.

The ascent of man has always been at the expense of the natural world; we have always destroyed our own habitat and the fellow creatures that would share it with us. But for most of human history the world was a big enough place to absorb our impact and to repair the damage as fast as we laid waste. When we felled forests they grew up again. When we broke camp and moved on to a new abode nature strode in behind with the beneficent process of re-colonisation and restoration. We left nothing behind us but ash, bone, redundant timber, dung and clearings, all of which nature can cope with in a flash. Then Civilisation strode into the arena. In awe of its compelling logic we stepped away from nature and abandoned the wild that had served us so well. We pillaged the forests to build great cities.

The advancement of knowledge and the birth of science and technology seemed to be everything we could have wished for, matched in scope only by the conceit and complacency that spawned it. What we had not bargained for were the numbers of human beings that would arise as an inevitable consequence of advances in medicine, energy production and global mobility. Nor had anyone given thought to the space we would need to feed those ever-expanding populations. We lived with the grand assumption that there would always be enough land-water-food-natural-resources for us all. For long enough there were. For several thousand years 'Moab was our washpot and out over Edom did we cast our shoes', and we got away with it; although perhaps we should have learned a few lessons from the felling of the great cedar forests of Mesopotamia which had built and ultimately brought about the downfall of the great Babylonian civilisation and the permanent aridity (much of southern Iraq) that followed our devastation of that great natural resource.

Three thousand years later we are still making the same mistakes for much the same reasons. Now, in such a short time, less than my own lifetime, powered by cheap fossil energy we have created mountain ranges of waste, and pollution has run rampant through just about everything we do. We have created chemical compounds far too complex for any known microbe to break down. Only God knows how long it will take evolution to come up with ways for nature to break down plastics, to say nothing of nuclear waste.

Very few who are ecologically aware believe that we can get away with such profligacy indefinitely. Only very recently have our leaders openly begun to discuss some of the very serious impacts we have imposed on our planet. In the last three hundred years we have pumped carbon faster into the atmosphere than it has ever known since life emerged, and the unimagined consequence of so doing has begun to release methane from the melting permafrost zones of the vast tundra wastes. Methane is a far more potent greenhouse gas than carbon dioxide. No one knows how or where the consequences of this new threat will come home to roost. Vast regions of the sub-tropics could be heading for desert, a potentially irreversible condition it would take hundreds of thousands of years of no greenhouse emissions at all to repair. Against this the felling of forests and over-fishing of seas look temporary and trifling. It seems very likely that one day we shall reap the whirlwind – forces of nature way beyond our control may claim back the global domination we have celebrated as so great a human achievement for so long. Perhaps it has already begun.

# 9

# Summer's Green Stain

O never harm the dreaming world
The world of green, the world of leaves,
But let its million palms unfold
The adoration of the trees.
                    – Kathleen Raine, 'Vegetation'

By mid-July the long hours of daylight have done their work.
The solar energy grabbed by hungry plants has exploded
into a jungle of luxuriant verdure. I call it the great green
stain.

   To begin with, when they first emerged only a few weeks
ago, those greens were vivacious and varied, too many to
count, hues as subtle as tweed, from the dark gloss fronds
of hard fern, through the lichen-grey-greens of eared willows
to the startling, lime-juice opulence of larch buds. But these
shades are as ephemeral as the buds themselves. Slowly, as
the lengthening days yawn by and the envious chlorophyll
continuously churns, the trees gradually merge to a universal
wash of summer lawn, almost as if they have consulted with
each other and agreed not to stand alone. They seem drunk
with green energy; that first desperate growth spurt eases
back. Leaves have stretched to their fullest reach and now

they bask. The fiercest competition is over; they have found their place and accepted their lot at last, resting like a drunk who has had his fill and finds he has a full glass in his hand.

This is the season of excess. The world is gorged and fat-full; cud-chewing cattle laze in August fields among grass too long to be kept in check by their rumbling guts and drooling muzzles. The first pyrotechnic burst of wild flowers has faded and gone, swamped by the mutinous shade of pressing foliage. Wood sorrel, dog violet and lesser celandine are nowhere to be seen and the northern marsh orchids have vanished from the moor. Their brief hour has passed, leaving only an invisible dusting of seed for another year, while locked in the mould of last year's leaves they shore up their secret arrangements. In their place blowsy foxgloves have erected spires of sensuous, lolling lips, where, high on nectar and furred with pollen, bumble bees drowse from bloom to bloom. Now the path is hemmed by the tall umbellifer stems of sweet cicely. Its tiny white flower clusters dust my jacket as I pass and the warm air is piqued with an aniseed tang. High above the loch the tiny green heather leaves give way to a summer resurgence of buds, the first hint of the famous moorland counterpane still to come.

The insect host is on us; flickering swallows and house martins hawk the vibrating air and the moth-filled nights echo with the sonic prattle of brown long-eared and soprano pipistrelle bats. Hatches of mayflies and lacewings have stippled the loch like rain and then gone, vanishing as fast as they emerged. Bronze-backed shield bugs and metallic heather beetles have drifted through, a wave of tiny winged gems sent, it seems, just to feed the darting second broods of hungry grey wagtails sprinting and flicking across the dam. Stiff-winged, the dragonflies and darters hover over the water lilies, and predatory tiger beetles – bright, long-legged emeralds – scurry across my dusty path.

These are the open-shirted, bare-arm'd weeks which embrace the middle of our year. They arch across the humid, cloud-filled blur between the bright summer solstice and the last call of the autumnal equinox. I catch myself muttering it softly as I stalk the familiar trail, now squeezed by hard-edged bracken fronds four feet tall: 'Summer'. I say it again, 'Summer'. The word seems to mimic the season and lean on the mms: 'S-u-mmmmm-e-r' – caterpillar-like, it has two entirely different ends, with a fat, luxuriant, foot-dragging middle. As the old jazz song croons, '. . . those lazy, hazy, crazy days of su-umm-er . . .' – that's where I'm heading today, away and into the mmms.

*August 2nd*   These are the days when it is often easier to slouch in the long grass and daydream than to seek out the natural history of my home. I wonder if the wildlife feels the same. I fancy some do. On the high moor, in little parties of five to eight, the red deer hinds have grazed up to a secure look-out and settled down like me to laze, collapsing in the soft, lilac haze of the budding heather, sleepily chewing the cud and watching their calves – now strong and part-weaned – skip and frolic until they, too, drop down to sleep through the afternoons at their mothers' sides. As I lie and scour the hillside through binoculars I have to pan back and forward many times to find them. Among the broad expanse of greens, browns and purples, so effective and surprising is the camouflage of their eponymous russet summer pelage that I have to wait for a movement – ears flicking at a troublesome fly or nibbling at a warble itch on their backs – to give them away.

If I stalk closer, crawling up through the rough heather stems on my belly, I can see them doze: eyes dulling, slowly shutting down, heads lowering until some, perhaps mostly young hinds, stretch right out, dead to the world, safe in the knowledge that older, wiser hinds have positioned them-selves higher up where they can watch over the moor, ever alert, ears and nostrils never at rest. These are the sentinels: the hind herd's sentries instinctively posted by evolution's long, relentless memory of wolves and bears and eagles, and, of course, man. It is a good day when I can stalk that close. Usually they detect me first and are up and away with one hoarse, throaty bark of alarm from the wariest beast. But when I do achieve it I am often amazed by the genius of their camouflage. The longer and harder I search, the more hinds I find; some tucked away behind heather and grassy tufts and others just so still that I have missed them altogether. Squinting slightly so that my vision blurs, I can make all the deer merge perfectly with their background, vanishing into the heather haze as if they were figments of my imagination.

In their authoritative way, zoologists have dubbed this *mono-procrypsis*. It is nature's carefully evolved mechanism for general protective camouflage. Broadly speaking it means that if you put all the varied background tones of a prey species' habitat – say, a deer – into a pot and stir it up, the blend you come up with is the hue most likely to fit in anywhere: rusty red for a deer, grey for a rabbit, brown for a hare, and so on. But it is even more subtle than that: the resultant hue is not necessarily the one most likely to work for us humans, but for the monochrome vision of their particular principal predators. They are difficult to spot in full colour, but filmed in black and white they vanish entirely. That is why almost all of these prey species freeze when they suspect danger is at hand. They are hard-wired to know that their best method of concealment is their coloration. Only when something tells them it isn't working, when their anxiety goes up a notch, do they turn and run for cover.

Summer is feeding time. The abundance of food and energy has to grow all the year's young – bugs, fish, birds, reptiles, amphibians and mammals, as well as plants – through the hazardous business of dependency into the much safer zone of near adulthood. Young trees are expanding root systems underground and casting their first deep shade to conquer competition from other plants around them and help the roots. The leaves must do their work, but it is the prowess of the roots that will dictate their future.

By now tadpoles are fat; they are absorbing tails and gills so that mini-froglets and toadlets can soon emerge into the swampy safety of loch-side vegetation. In August the wet ground around the loch path heaves with this anuran migration away from the open water where shadowy horrors such as the rapacious mandibles of the northern diving beetle and the snapping jaws of trout are a perpetual hazard. The toadlets and froglets, still only half an inch long, have moved on from feeding on water-borne diatoms and are now off in search of larger insect prey in the marshes. The frogs will stay in the wet rushes, but the toads will travel far into the woods, hills and moors. They will not return to the loch of their birth for three years. Some will travel up to three miles before plodding back to spawn as adults.

In the willow thickets young tits and willow warblers are shedding their first scruffy plumage for a finer adolescent livery. They call repeatedly, demanding to be fed by exhausted parents who must wish that they would make more effort to feed themselves. High overhead the eyas fledgling peregrines are screaming too. Few bird species hold such totemic appeal as the peregrine falcon and there are few more insistent cries than those of adolescent falcons, which, for now, seem incapable of catching anything for themselves. The long, drawn-out screams stop me in my tracks, hand to brow, scanning the sky for a glimpse of their crossbow silhouettes skimming the valley rim.

Even when to our crimped vision their powers of flight seem faultless, the juvenile birds stay dependent upon their parents bringing in prey. It seems that the leap from mastering flight to actually killing in a stoop is a huge one. I don't know if anyone has ever written about a wild peregrine's first kill, not even the mysterious J.A. Baker, whose poetic literary transmogrification from human into bird, *The Peregrine*, was such a galvanising influence upon naturalists of my generation. In *A Tiger in the Sand*, Mark Cocker records a most unusual sighting in Derbyshire where a compulsive (but unnamed) watcher of peregrines witnessed a hunting individual misjudge a stoop and hit the ground, knocking itself unconscious; but he doesn't say whether this was an adult bird or a juvenile. In any event it must be an extremely rare occurrence, as far as I can tell previously unrecorded.

On many occasions I have watched 'training' stoops by adolescent peregrines, pulling out at the last moment as if their nerve has failed, but I have never seen that first, life-fixing and life-denying follow-through. Like the ritual spearing of a lion by Masai youths in search of warrior status, in that brief, fiery moment the taken life awards the confident maturity the peregrine must perfect to ensure its own survival. If I have a wish-list of wild nature sightings, this is near the top. For now I shall have to rely upon the descriptions of falconers urging and coaxing their young birds in training to snatch at simulated kills on strings. No, it is summer, and for a while yet our young falcons are content to scream for their supper.

In the loch the young trout are quite the reverse. Independent from first hatching, this summer glut is what the fry were waiting for, and for them it must seem to be what life is all about. The surface is never still. An insect swarm parades above them all day and all night – a bonanza. The surface boils with their snatching somersaults as trout gobble anything so foolish, unwary or unlucky as to land on the water. For a few happy weeks our fishermen scarcely bother about matching their flies to what is buzzing around them. The fish are past caring, on a roll, bug mad, crazed by the crunch of chitin and the sweet tang of soft, juicy centres.

To the anglers' delight (and, occasionally, disbelief), they just snatch at any bug-like movement; so rich is the choice that almost any barbed treachery will score.

In the woods below the loch the badger sow has two rowdy cubs. She has been suckled to skin and bones, a shadow of the powerful, bear-like animal she was back in the spring. By August the cubs have been above ground for nearly three months and are now self-sufficient – I think they have given up trying to get milk from their poor, drained mother. So they frolic around her as she snuffles through the long grass and the dew to find the earthworms she needs to rebuild her strength before winter. But the season's pickings are good: there are nests of young voles and mice to dig out and fat ground beetles to crunch. Soon, as the fruiting season expands, she will gorge on starch-filled rhizomes and shoots of many plants, on windfall fruits and nuts, acorns and beech mast, blackberries and then on to the glossy bilberry harvest in the pinewood. Sometimes I find a crater in the ground where a badger has dug out a wasps' nest. The destruction is total; shrugging off stings which fail to penetrate their tough hide and coarse fur, the entire nest has been routed for the fat grubs in their paper cells. Shards of comb lie scattered far and wide.

Summer is kind to the badger unless it is too hot and too dry, driving the earthworms deep underground. When this happens the badger cubs can suffer badly. Earthworms can constitute as much as sixty per cent of their diet and are an essential source of protein. Digging in dry ground requires more energy and delivers a smaller reward, always a bad sign and, like spiralling into debt, it is a reversal of the fundamental equation for survival. Parched land spells death for undernourished young badgers, and the mature females, unable to regain the weight losses of lactation, may not come into oestrus for the autumn mating. In really dry years they may even be driven to kill poultry or to feed on carrion. Laying down the brown fat so essential to see all badgers through the winter becomes a battle against time, a battle lost before it is fought if the summer has been exception-ally hot. Deep underground on some icy February day when snow has kept them holed up for days on end, curled up in the grass and bracken nest of a dry chamber, permanent sleep will overcome any emaciated badgers lacking the strength to surface and forage.

August brings what are for me the two summer horrors: midges and humidity. My walks are now carefully timed to coincide with bright sun or a breeze, neither of which midges like. They favour the sticky, overcast days of oppressive warmth, days when the air can seem to be more midge than oxygen; days when effort exceeds desire. The deer have fled to the high ground, the horses stand miserably under trees, nose to tail, flicking helplessly as the puncturing horde feasts on any exposed flesh. Shaking manes, twitching flanks and stamping hooves reveal the morass of high-summer suffer-ance through which all horses must flounder. Less tolerant, our fishermen wear net veils or flick their flies through a haze of citronella; plumes of pipe smoke funnel from beneath fore-and-aft hats.

Yet there are those that welcome the midge, mosquito and gnat swarms. At dusk soprano pipistrelle bats emerge from crevices within the timber cladding of our fishing hut, the Illicit Still, hawking through the insect clouds over and over again as a dolphin invades a shoal of fish. In the weedy shallows of the loch, the wild brown trout, small, dark and now fat, about half a pound in weight, revel in the super-abundance of midges and gnats that waft across the surface like a chiffon shawl. Without comprehending why the fishing is so good, the ospreys cash in. Both adult birds work flat out carrying trout to the three fast-growing, almost-fledged chicks in the nest only half a mile away. Perhaps the midge swarm is a key factor in bringing the osprey three thousand miles from where it has wintered in West Africa to its breeding grounds in the Scottish Highlands. The perpetual presence of these fat, convenient, carrying-sized fish cruising beneath the surface has not gone unnoticed. Dawns and evenings at the loch are now guaranteed osprey watching, and the echoes of their shrill cries ring out from the shady caverns of the pinewood.

There is no harvest here in this Highland glen to define the waning summer. No drone of combines, or groan of tractors over-laden with straw bales. Those are the familiar signals of a softer landscape of prime soils tamed and managed by a harsher regime than anything in this glen. Our hazy upland of unploughed pasture and humped moors offers up no such comforting auguries by which to gauge the year's turning. The sheep have long since been shorn and the lambs are fat and rowdy. No, here it takes a kestrel's eye to spot the yellowing at the edges of the highest horse chestnut leaves, always the first to reveal their solar exhaustion. It will be another six weeks before the nights freshen and universal leaf colour creeps through the trees. That will be autumn proper, but for a little while yet, it is summer still.

# IO

# Pine Martens

I think I could turn and live with animals, they are so placid
and self-contain'd,
I stand and look at them long and long.

They do not sweat and whine about their condition,
They do not lie awake in the dark and weep for their sins,
They do not make me sick discussing their duty to God,
Not one is dissatisfied, not one is demented with the mania of
owning things,

. . . . . . . . . . . . . . . . . . . .

Not one is respectable or unhappy over the whole earth.
                    – Walt Whitman, from 'Song of Myself'


*August 17th*   Last Thursday it rained. For two August weeks,
by Highland standards, it's been hot; some days so sultry that
by the time I reached the loch I was desperate to swim. Slipping into its dark, moorland water brings an instant fix of
wellbeing, like finding a loved one well again after a long
illness, relief and pleasure trumping one another. But on
Thursday the heat cracked like a rifle shot. Towering
Himalayas of cumuli, crag-headed and boisterous, arched

heavily across a sky so charged that the distant, rolling thunder seemed to echo their discontent. Then it rained. On hot, static air rain fell vertically in fast, fat lines. It rained and rained. In seconds the path became sodden; the fine dust of drought that only minutes before would have taken flight on a puff of breeze was now swirling out from among the stones and flushing away in scummy rivulets and pools.

I took shelter under a birch tree, but knew it was useless; rain like that bends boughs and hammers leaves apart. I gave up and walked on; better to get wet properly than to be sodden in bits. At least I had the satisfaction of experiencing what everything else was being subjected to. I have often thought mankind scuttles for cover too quickly – another separation from the wild world. We habitually shun discomfort as though it is always bound to be bad for us, whereas if we stuck it out it might bring us closer to nature and provide some insight to the deeper truths of our place on Earth. Where do butterflies go in weather like this, I wonder? Birds and mammals are well proofed and can easily retreat to their own microclimates – the nooks and crannies, the burrows, cracks and crevices they know so well – as long as they're not flooded out. I know that the roe doe and her ten-week-old twin kids will be tucked away under the gorse and broom above the pinewood. They'll sit it out until the sun shoulders through again when, with a bone-rattling shake from ears to rump patch, they'll cast off the water in a cloud of mist and carry on browsing as though nothing had happened. The hoodies and the robins, the willow warblers and the great tits are well prepared for this. It is a daily life-chore to anoint, tend, repair and straighten the feather shield; for a bird to preen is to survive. Feathers well oiled shed water like slates on a roof. Only a sick bird lets water reach its skin.

But the red admiral so recently flaunting his emperor's robes among the buddleia blooms; and the scales of wing dust so fragile to touch; are those carnival colours waterproofed too? Where does he go? How does he hide his delicate finery? Does he crawl into the shrub's recesses and hunker down, wings closed and all six legs clinging on for dear life? And what about *Cordulegaster*, the golden-ringed dragonfly, who can't fold away his rattling, rigid wings and to whom water has always been everything? Is he out there somewhere among the lily pads, gripping tight, ducking the bucketfuls each raindrop must surely seem to be?

I walk on up the path. I'm on an early morning errand. I have to go and see if the fisherman's hut at the loch, the Illicit Still, needs firewood. That little hut is a Thoreauvian hideaway built right at the water's edge with a bed and a table, a paraffin lamp and a lumberjack's rusty oil-drum stove. Sometimes I work there, doors flung open to the loch, scribbling away like Henry David at Walden, escaping, musing, letting the closeness to nature its bank-side perch automatically affords sink in like an emollient balm. When outrageous fortune has slung too much at them, family and friends sometimes hole up there to lick their wounds. I like to keep it fuelled with firewood, ready for the next lucky incumbent.

The suddenness and ferocity of this cloudburst takes me by surprise. The rain-roar wraps me round, creating a silence of oppression like a great engine or a mighty waterfall, denying me any other sensation so that I move engulfed in a drum of wetness and incessant sound from which there's no relief, no escape. It is a rarefied experience; one I savour for its power and unrestrained wildness rather than for any sense of pleasure.

At the loch the surface is a fury of turmoil like water poured into a deep fat fryer. Rain-rods spear into it so thick and fast that visibility is crimped down to only a few yards. Its frantic chorus drowns out thought. The hills have vanished behind a curtain of oblivion. I sit down on the grass at the dam. I may as well swim – an appealing notion – nothing can make me wetter now. Although fresher, the air is still warm, the land still exhaling the long heat that has forced the clouds upwards to cool and burst, dumping in just a few minutes a cargo of Atlantic Ocean collected over many days. But even as I contemplate stripping off, I sense that I am not alone.

Lolloping up the path, the path I have just travelled, heading towards me at an easy, loose-limbed amble, is a pine marten. I know him immediately. He is a big dog marten who hangs about the house and stables and raids the bird tables for quick pickings after dark, always looking for an easy meal. His fur is plain chocolate with an orange bib punctuated by four or five dark spots between his forelegs. He knows us and we know him; acclimatised to human presence, knowing, like the hoodie crows, that while man and danger are synonymous (happily he doesn't know the full historical truth of that danger: his forebears persecuted to the very brink of extinction both for their very fine fur and because they preyed on game birds), man and food are also a virtual certainty – a risk worth taking. So our martens have chosen to live their wild and predatory lives in and around human abodes, rearing their young in the stables roof, snatching a bantam from the hen run when on light, summer evenings my wife is late to lock them away; raiding the rubbish bins after dark, ever watching, prying, calculating; forever pushing their luck with the insatiable, hard-wired curiosity of their race.

Normally we see this dog marten and his kind only fleetingly (there are at least four that habituate our corner of the glen). You see where they've been, not where they're going. Late one evening, knowing how much the blackbirds would love it in the morning, I put a large slice of stale plum cake on the bird table. When I next looked a few minutes later, it was gone. Not a crumb or a sultana was left. A marten had nipped in from the depths of a cotoneaster where it must have been watching, and snatched it up. All I saw was a shadowy form streaking away across the lawn and into the bushes.

The pine marten belongs to the Mustelidae, the weasel, stoat, mink, otter and badger family. Highlanders used to call them martin-cats; they are only a little smaller than a slender domestic puss but with a more fluid, ferret-like form and a long tail. They are common in our woods, and, like most of their musteline cousins, they are inquisitive and bold beyond redemption. They are breathtaking climbers, with long, hooked claws, as acrobatic as trapeze artists, which, combined with the innate opportunism of a back-street pick-pocket, is reflected in their nocturnal-diurnal ambivalence – whichever is most likely to deliver the pickings. They filch jam sandwiches from our bird tables – actually put out for them because we enjoy seeing them so much – and seem particularly partial to denning in roofs or the dark corners of any undisturbed building they can burgle their way into.

My good friend, the celebrated naturalist and photographer Michael Macgregor, told me that many years ago martens had chosen to breed in the roof of his house above his bedroom. So noisy were they, and so smelly (all mustelines have a musk gland under their tails) that he decided to remove them. He cut a hole in the ceiling plasterboard and carefully lifted out four small kits, placing them outside on a veranda, where the mother could take them off to a new den. He returned to the bedroom to repair the hole, but before he could do so the bitch marten had brought the first kit back. One by one she picked them up in her mouth, scrambled up the side of the house, squeezed in through a hole in the eaves and took them back into the roof. Some years later Michael built a marten den in his natural history visitors' centre at Acharacle. It had a glass panel so that people could see in. A pair of martens fell for it immediately, quite ignoring the voyeuristic public eyeing up their boudoir.

It is a delight to witness marten agility and to see their shining, dark fur with mango-sorbet bib, flowing tail, and their pert, intelligent little faces with eyes of bright jet. When you see them chasing red squirrels through the treetops it is a marvel to behold. But this sandwich and cake thief is primarily a carnivore. The marten diet is a broad church: eggs, small and sometimes not-so-small birds (I have watched martens climb from nest box to nest box, checking them out to see if a lid will lift or if inserting a paw through the hole will deliver a fledgling), voles, mice, rats, rabbits, squirrels, lizards and beetles, and then they turn to fruits in season – rowan berries, brambles, plums – and fungi and anything tasty, from plum cake to bacon rind, they can steal from man. If during the night a marten discovers a way into my wife's hen run the destruction is total – in the chill light of dawn a level of carnage akin to a medieval battlefield.

As a family group, martens are well distributed across Europe, Asia, Russia, Scandinavia and North America, varying bio-regionally through a number of different, but very closely related, tree-climbing species: the beech or stone marten, the American pine marten, the sable, the fisher or pecan, the yellow-throated marten, the Nilgiri in India and the Japanese marten. Ours, the European and North American species, *Martes martes*, is called pine marten because when it was first described its original dominant habitat was the old pinewoods of Scotland. But its association with pines is no more or less relevant than that. It might better be named the rock marten because in the absence of a convenient stables roof or hollow tree it happily dens among rocks. Nor is it strictly a woodland animal. Pine martens can be found just about anywhere.

Perhaps because of the rain, perhaps because I was sitting down and the visibility was so poor, this marten didn't see me. He stopped a few feet away, rose up otter-like on his hind legs and looked around, dropped down again and shook. With a flick of his supple neck his pointed little face inscribed a short, sharp circle which set off down his back in a tidal wave of muscular spasm engulfing him in a private geyser of water and mist. Despite the pressing rain the well-oiled fur stood proud again, and he set off once more, past me and on up the path towards the Illicit Still.

I am sure he was following my scent. He was checking me out – where there is man there is food. In seconds he was gone, and I was in no mood to follow. The rain had finally penetrated every last cranny of my clothing and, unable to shake like a marten, I suddenly wanted to run for cover. Home, a hot bath, some dry clothes . . . wild it had been, and I would not have missed it for the world, but the pull of breakfast, hot porridge and coffee, was simply too strong. I even forgot my firewood errand.

Two hours later the rain had passed over. The sun came barracking out in a frantic rush to reclaim the day and in minutes the land was steaming like a Turkish bath. I enlisted my old friend Duncan Macdonald as a helper and returned to the loch with a tractor and trailer to complete my chore.

We finished stacking the logs and dusted off our hands with that pleasing glow of a job well done. Well-dried firewood, stacked like sap-scented ingots, is as good as money in the bank, something you can depend upon – 'a bit put by', as my father used to say, 'to help you sleep easy'. The back door to the Illicit Still is only a few yards from the forest where, a few weeks before, we had logged a windblown pine. Scots pine burns almost too well, the sticky resin flaring uncontrollably, like a Roman candle, and can be a real hazard in an open fireplace. But the Still is equipped with an enclosed Canadian lumberjack's stove made from a steel, forty-gallon oil drum, with legs, door, sill and chimney collar bought independently in a kit so that when the camp moved, the old drum, was discarded and a new one quickly rigged up. Thoreau would have approved. We stacked a good pile at the Still's back door and went inside to deliver a basketful to the stove. As I passed the logs to Duncan I felt we were making a peace offering to Moloch before our friends arrived to take up residence.

When we emerged into the sunlight a few minutes later, someone yelled at us. It was a thin, angry, cat-like yell, misheard because we were talking. It cut us off. We stood in silence. It was close – somewhere just inside the pinewood, above us, only a few yards away. We gazed around. Then it came again, cross and fervid, and very close. This time there was no mistake; this was a shriek we both knew well.

The marten was not pleased to see us. It was clear that our emergence from the Still was an untimely intrusion he resented deeply. The shriek came again, and again. It left us in no doubt. 'Clear off!' it said – or words to that effect – 'Now!' We declined to oblige. Although I had seen him earlier, and we see pine martens all the time, it is always hard to pass them by. We have become accustomed to them, they to us. But familiarity has also fostered a level of contempt for humans, a contempt they are ill-disposed to conceal. This fellow had pressing business and he was not amused at being disturbed. We stayed, eyeballing his foul-mouthed spleen through our binoculars.

We could see him clearly, twenty feet up a pine, close to

the main trunk and within a foot or two of a woodpigeon's nest. The unhappy parent birds had made a sharp exit, but two fat, half-fledged squabs sat in the nest, dumb and defenceless – so much lunch. They were his, and we had arrived at the very moment of his claim. His indignation surged to outrage as we stood our ground. The invective came like the fizz from a well-shaken bottle of champagne, explosive and unstoppable, sprayed in all directions at once. It was a drawn-out eruption of curse and damnation – happily untranslatable.

Having made his feelings quite clear, he snatched the first squab and retreated to a crotch in the pine, where, still spluttering muted obscenities, he ate it all. We could hear the crunch of soft bone, see the wet mouthing of hot flesh. The squab's limp red feet fell, one by one, to the needly forest floor. Then he returned for the second. He grabbed it, glared at us for a stretched moment of pure insolence with the squab clenched firmly in his teeth and then slid, swift, elegant and shadow-like, up and away into the wood. Only his scratchy claws rattling on the pine bark gave him away; a smoke-curl of tail, a bark flake falling to the ground, an empty nest.

# II

# An Explosion of Flowers

Consider the lilies of the field, how they grow; they toil not,
neither do they spin.

Matthew, 6:28

*September 12th*  Emerging from the Avenue on a September
afternoon, leaving the darkling shade of the limes and
chestnuts and breaking out into warm sunshine and a soft
westerly breeze, within a few yards I am struck by two
commonplace events of the late summer, coming in quick,
unrelated succession, both of which stopped me in my
tracks and set me thinking about our long and complicated
relationship with flowers.

The first was on a patch of what to most people would
be wasteland – a corner of old pasture isolated by a bend
in the farm track and left uncultivated for many years. I saw
a cloud of winged seed lifting like smoke from the spiked
heads of a dense cluster of rosebay willowherb (*Epilobium
angustifolium*). It burst suddenly, as if a smouldering fire had
had new fuel tossed on. The seeds were set, poised, ready
and waiting to break free; that little breeze just happened
to gust through at the right moment. The tall flower heads,
so recently a welcome blush of magenta in a world of tired

green stain, rocked in the breeze, leaning with it, pointing their charged obelisks so that the wind raked through the laden spikes, releasing like ghosts thousands of downy seeds, each one a hope and a future, desperate for freedom, loaded with ambition. It was a moment to stand and watch.

Some seed caught on grass and nettle heads within a few feet, waiting for a bigger wind to take them on. Much more sailed off into the fields and trees, lifting and swirling, lifting again and disappearing from my view forever. Just like smoke, the seed plume vanished almost as quickly as I had noticed it. I walked on, pondering the mysterious and creative world of flowers and seeds.

A little while later my stroll was rudely and suddenly interrupted by explosions – sharp, snapping cracks like something brittle broken underfoot. They repeated over and over so insistently that they seemed to be trying to make a point. Again I felt obliged to stand and watch. But there was no mystery here; the source was plain to see right at my side.

In the process of making and maintaining a path, a track or a ride, whether by mechanical intent or simply by regular use, man creates a space. To the whole of nature, spaces are opportunities charged with potential. There are hundreds of plants and animals poised, waiting to exploit such chances. Natural clearings are rare, usually the consequence of some disturbance – a tree blowing over, a landslide, an animal such as a badger or a bear digging and rootling around for food, or thrashing about like a stag in the rut, and, of course, man's perpetual restlessness – exposing the soil to all comers. Spaces quickly fill. The natural world is well supplied with colonising plants that will motor in and take over. Unfairly and often in ignorance, we choose to label them weeds.

Here, commonly scattered across our hills and glens, we have wild broom (*Cytisus scoparius*), one of the several leguminous shrubs and flowers quick to take up residence in a vacant space. It is hardly surprising that my path is lined by dense thickets of broom shrubbery. Over many years the soils have been exposed by human activities and the broom continually piles in. Now, at the end of the summer, these crackling explosions are the seed pods bursting open in the heat of the day, showering their little, black, pea-like seeds far and wide. If we didn't keep beating them back the path would close over in no time. In less than two years it would be scarcely visible.

A weed it may be, but broom can be a valuable plant to man and wildlife. Its root nodules fix nitrogen in poor soils; its persistent leaf fall decays into new, more fertile soil and it provides shelter and a home for countless animal species, from tiny invertebrates up to the insectivorous birds – the tits, robins and wrens that colour and enhance my days – among many others that seek sanctuary and food in its shady caverns. Woodcock probe the soft new ground beneath its jungle of ridged stems where roe deer shelter and harbour up during the day. In winter voles and mice feast on the seeds and rabbits gnaw at its nutritious bark, and deer, cattle, sheep and goats will browse on its tart, leguminous shoots. But as well as all this, it is a flowering plant. In May and June the hillsides are lit by the strident yellow and coconut scent of broom and gorse flowers, some years so dense that the whole valley seems to reflect a headily perfumed daffodil glow.

It is harder to argue the benefits of rosebay willowherb, or fireweed, as it is often known. Of the two plants it is perhaps the more deserving of the pejorative 'weed', particularly among my generation, who remember the bomb sites of World War II thick with its mauve-pink flowers, for many a symbol of death and destruction and for many others an enduring symbol of renewal. However the human world may choose to view it, as a naturalist I have no doubt that many insects and other organisms enjoy its nectar and its pollen, and caterpillars munch on its succulent leaves and stems. But like broom, its ecological function – that of honest coloniser of spaces, and, by leaf fall and decay, worthy creator of soils – should be value enough for any man.

Willowherb and broom: both flowering plants, both angiosperms. It is sobering to think that our whole existence on Earth both was and still is a direct consequence of flowering plants. Fossil records have enabled us to plot the progression of life, plants and animals, from the earliest stirrings in lake and swamp. The appearance of flowering plants – the angiosperms – comes late on in the unfolding story of life and is the essential springboard for the warm-blooded bird and mammal era, a food source which, in an extraordinarily short space of geological time, was to change everything.

First you have to imagine a world without flowers, without flowering shrubs, without grasses and cereals, without nuts, fruits and berries, without birds and mammals, without humans. This long-vanished ancient world of more than a hundred million years ago was a dull green world of mosses, ferns and primitive trees, for the most part thronging around water, swamps, lakes and marshes because most of them needed ready access to water to reproduce, not by seeds, but by microscopic swimming sperm that could travel to the female cell only through water. Through these early bird-less forests and swamps plodded the great, magnificent, cold-blooded reptiles, the dinosaurs.

This was a crimped world of perpetual limitations. The plants were limited by their primitive physiology and the dinosaurs limited by small, reptilian brains kept firmly in check by cold blood, which, like the present-day adders, lizards and crocodiles, required the heat of the sun to operate their instinct-driven lives, and then promptly closed them down again to a motionless, unthinking torpor every time the temperature dropped. This defining limitation permitted only a far slower metabolism than that of any modern mammal or bird. On cold nights the dinosaur world must have been eerily quiet and uncannily still.

For all the remarkable diversity of the tropical Mesozoic age, with its leather-winged, bat-like pterodactyls soaring over-head on ten-foot wings, the colossal vegetarian brontosaurs browsing the swamps, the forty-foot, finned plesiosaurs chasing fish through warm seas, and with a host of ravening predators epitomised by the aptly named tyrannosaurs tyrannising just about everything, it was a ponderous, slow-moving world without song or much colour; a world so alien to the one we have inherited that I find it hard to visualise. Dull greens, browns and greys dominated most life forms and reptile sounds were a cacophony of grunts and growls, hisses and grating screams. The inspirational tonal variety of our own environment, the constant birdsong and diffuse colours we so often take for granted – the black-birds, robins, chaffinches and wrens and the many flowers of my daily trail – were still millions of years away.

To the present day our native pine, the Scots pine, *Pinus sylvestris*, is still tied to its wooden seed cone, just like the early pines that had freed themselves from water by the development of wind-borne pollen. The emergence of pollen-producing plants and the now mobile seeds from the primitive cone-flowers of their pine and spruce progenitors was to herald a whole new era of evolution for both plant and animal life. Plants were no longer dependent upon water, nor fixedly restricted to wetland habitat. Their increasingly mobile seeds allowed each plant to expand its range and, by natural selection, experiment with its own destiny, adapting as they went to new and challenging conditions. They could grow wings to be wafted by winds, or by burrs and hooks attach themselves to animals, to be carried over huge distances; they could be catapulted out by mechanical devices like the exploding broom pod, or, ultimately, make their soft casings so attractive to the new order of emerging birds and mammals that they could reliably be carted off in alimentary canals and deposited far and wide. Suddenly there were no boundaries.

This evolution, of course, took many millions of years to perfect, but it can rightly be seen as an explosion – a great bursting out to colonise, dominate and beautify a world waiting for them, a previously silent and unexploited land-scape of sands and gravels, bare rock and jumbled boulders. The flowering plants, these highly mobile angiosperms with their astonishing and rapidly expanding subtleties of colour and form – there are over six thousand species of grasses alone – brought with them an entirely new world, a world of wonder and boundless opportunities. Inadvertently they brought us with them too. It is perfectly possible that without flowering plants mankind might never have existed.

As this Cretaceous explosion, some 120 million years ago, was intensifying, so mammals and birds were gradually taking over from the reptiles. The one factor common to the success and progression of both was warm blood, supporting a high metabolic rate. Without constant heat the brain and the body metabolism is severely limited, as it is with insects, which have to scuttle for deep cover every autumn or perish, completely immobilised until the warmth of the sun enables their re-emergence many months later. The brains of both birds and mammals cannot operate without high levels of oxygen and food. The problem facing the emerging mammals and birds – at first only small tree shrews, and lizard-birds, the feathered reptiles of the Cretaceous – was just where this level of high-energy food was to come from.

Angiosperm means 'encased seed'. It is a concept quite different from the naked seed (the gymnosperm) of the ancient pines. It is a dazzling leap forward. The encased seed is a fully equipped mini-plant ready to go. It is protected, sheltered and fed by its soft, high-energy casing. You can drop it anywhere and it stands a far better chance of germinating than its naked counterpart, which can easily become water-logged or scorched by the sun. If the naked seed is eaten, the plant is dead. The encased seed lives on. The casing can adapt and evolve, become fatter and fleshier and brightly coloured to attract carriers and pass undigested through intestinal tracts. Thorns, hooks, sails, wings and hard shells can emerge to protect or assist dispersal over many miles; poisons can be built in; mechanical devices like my broom pod can burst out on sunny afternoons.

Throughout the process of dispersal by all these means and many more, a far higher proportion of the cherished seeds lurking within survived intact and poised to germinate. They penetrated every habitat from the sea shore to the mountain top and were successful, far more so than the old order of primitive reproductive mechanisms. The world was turning upside down. Flowering plants were taking over. Yet again the steady, incorruptible miracle of natural-selection-guided evolution had produced a winner; its rapidly exploding diversity forced into extinction many of the primitive and less adaptable plant species of the dull old world of spores and pines and reptiles.

Now broad grasslands could romp unhindered across the Earth's great plains and uplands, creating savannahs, prairies and montane grasslands; new tree species emerged in the form of great, broad-leaved forests with field layers of grasses and a myriad of bright flowers; between the trees shrubs and creepers rose up from the densely vegetated floor. Most importantly, all of them bore flowers, fruits and nuts supercharged with high concentrations of energy – energy initially designed to nurture the seed inside, but which quickly adapted to attract carriers.

The dinosaurs had gone; the Earth was cooling and mammals and birds were the future. At their feet lay the new, universal, life-expanding benison of carbohydrate-charged flowering plants, theirs for the taking. The fuel and the oxygen were there to support their mental capacity and their galloping metabolic rates.

As the explosion powered ever outward like the ripples from a stone hurled into a pond, a simultaneous new food source and valuable flowering plant tool was rising to the challenge. Nectars and pollens were re-inventing themselves to attract insect and bird pollinators so that the evolution of flowers and insects and dazzling creations such as the hummingbird now became inextricably linked. Insects would never look back, grabbing the new opportunities of this manna with a mind-boggling creativity to which we owe our jewelled butterflies, our honey and bumble bees, our wasps, sawflies and ants, our soldier beetles and cockchafers, our striped hover flies and our exquisite treasury of multi-formed and patterned moths.

In the heat of the tropics and southern hemisphere birds and flowers seem to have evolved together in astonishing leaps of mutual admiration. Honeycreepers, flowerpeckers, sunbirds, brush-tongued parakeets, white-eyes, sugarbirds and even crows hovered, crept, barged, plunged and stabbed their living from obliging flowers desperate to claim birds as their pollinators. Specialised bats, squirrels, rats and mice all attached themselves to the pollen and nectar bonanza. Flowers of every kind joined in with all the gay extravagance of a carnival. Suddenly we had orchids mimicking butterflies and spiders, sprung anthers flicking pollen onto unsuspecting foragers, alluring scents and aromatic oils coating petals to make them still more attractive and a pyrotechnic burst of theatrical colour and design as species after species produced bloom upon riotous bloom in rampant competition for this new and highly effective means of pollination – little wonder Ted Hughes dubbed them 'pits of allure'.

Now charged with this endless supply of high-energy food, mammal populations also expanded rapidly, producing the great age of the Pleistocene, about a million years ago, with its roaming herds of herbivores: mammoths and elephants, rhinoceroses, bison, buffalo, musk oxen and yaks, horses and asses, camels, llamas and giraffes, sheep and goats, many species of deer, antelope and rodent. Very literally, hard on their heels came the arch-predators: the great felines – sabre-toothed tigers, lions, leopards and pumas; and the dogged herd followers: wolves, foxes, jackals and hyenas; the omnivorous bears hedging their bets, and many more. In the burgeoning forests and jungles the tree-shrew had become a lemur-like creature enjoying the rich pickings of the fruit-laden trees. Monkeys and apes would soon follow in countless variations. Just one of these apes elected to stay on the ground and pick berries. Hominoid ape-men were born into a world rich with fruit, ringing with joyous birdsong and bright with the vibrant colours of flowers.

One of the big problems for the mammals and birds of the Pleistocene is that it coincided with a marked fall in temperature and the onset of glaciation and the Ice Ages. Now stuck with warm blood, it was to be increasingly difficult to maintain body heat and brain power through long winters of ice and no plant growth. Birds had an easier choice: migration. When winter threatened they could gorge with relative ease on the great abundance of summer plants, fruits or insects and then take off to constant food supplies in warmer latitudes. But many mammals could not move fast enough to achieve a great migration and had to find another mechanism for winter survival.

Hibernation meant achieving the necessary physiological adaptations – the ability rapidly to grow insulating coats and lay down fat reserves by dedicating themselves to a period of intense feeding every autumn; thence to bed in a snow den, a nest, a cave, a burrow, or, like the ingenious brown bear, beneath a wood ants' nest. But it wasn't to bed, to sleep in any human sense. That would have consumed far too much energy. It had to be a wholesale slow-down of all functions: digestion ceasing altogether; blood with-drawing from extremities to vital organs; heart beats dwindling to the minimum required to prevent the animal from freezing up; breathing barely detectable; dulled brains regulating only those essential involuntary functions. It had to be a specialised heterothermic torpor, but by definition one which rendered the beast utterly helpless, so conceal-ment also had to be highly effective. All this thanks to the high-energy foods constantly supplied by flowering plants. Whether wide-roaming herbivores, ursine omni-vores or awesome carnivores, whether grass-, seed-, flesh- or insect-eating birds, that energy – that flower power – was concentrated in the fats of the new-world animals now covering the globe.

Hunter-gatherer men, emerging as we believe in the seasonless tropics of Africa, did not have to worry about hibernation or migration. Theirs was a world of abundance, quite literally a land of milk and honey, to which the generous old gods added meat and fruit. Where better to fuel an expanding brain and the ability to stand upright among tall savannah grasses? How they might laugh with astonishment if they could see the way we use flowers now.

My journal fails to record much more for that day than the explosion of seeds. I walked on, but everywhere I looked I saw more and more seeds spreading or preparing to spread their chances to the winds and waters. The powder-puff heads of dandelions, hawkweeds and thistles strove to emulate the willowherb. Lesser burdock locked its ferocious, Velcro-hooked balls – maddeningly difficult to remove – onto my socks and trousers. The vermillion hips of straggling wild roses dotted the rough edges beside the burn. Ash and sycamore keys in gaolers' bunches rattled in the wind. On the surface of the loch the floating seeds of alders bobbed and jostled among those of rushes, *Juncus*, against the dam. In my pocket was a glossy conker – one of the first of the season – I had prised from its fleshy, spikily armoured casing under the horse chestnuts in the Avenue.

At the water's edge the rowan trees were laden with ripening berries, berries that would feed tens of thousands of migrating thrushes – fieldfares and redwings – on their chattering way south to Africa for the winter; berries which, as soon as they were fully ripe, would be gobbled by pine martens too. Soon the paths would be punctuated with vulgar ejaculations of semi-digested fruit in soggy little red piles, almost as though the martens were using the fruit as a purgative to effect a good clear-out. In both of these cases the seeds will be undamaged, their work still to be done, often to be carried off by mice and buried – a secondary dispersal, complete with being planted to boot. The field-fares and redwings will unwittingly scatter theirs far and wide, each seed ejected in a ready-formed bubble of excrement fertiliser high over the moors and mountains like scatter bombs ready to fire. Fuelled up on worms, cater-pillars, snails and bugs in Scandinavia, these thrushes have gathered in vast flocks to catch an easterly wind across the North Sea because that food supply is closing down for the winter. Here, most conveniently placed, the wild rowans, as well as the hollies and cotoneasters of our gardens, will fuel them up again for the great push south.

I drew a warming existential comfort from this thought. The scarlet flesh of our rowan berries at the loch linking up with Scandinavian snails to provide the energy surge for one of the great bird migrations of the northern hemi-sphere, spreading and creating a bright, new generation of rowan trees as they go – the inspirational, boundary-less interdependence of all living things.

But there is one more extraordinary twist to the man story of flowering plants. Our hunter-gatherer was successful – too successful. With spear, axe and fire he began to change and control his habitat. He learned to hunt in gangs, to set traps, to herd his lumbering prey species to their deaths. Probably by accident he learned to burn their flesh in the fire, making it easier for his fruit-designed stomach to digest. He prospered and his numbers grew. He cleared forest and drove those animals he needed for furs and meat to the brink of extinction; some never recovered. The cave bear, the giant red deer (*Megaceros*), the woolly rhinoceros and the mammoth were too slow to adapt, too big and cumbersome to hide, and, in the case of the cave bear, too vulnerable in hibernation. Caves were in short supply and always bound to be explored by early man. With the demise of the great herds, some of their primary predators also perished, the dire wolf and the sabre-toothed tiger fading away altogether, and the global range of the lion and the tiger, ever tied to their prey, began to shrink.

In those areas of the world where mankind was most populous he was now at risk of hunting himself out of meat. If prey species' populations crashed, he crashed with them. He needed another, more predictable source of energy. It was the flowering plant that got him out of the primeval forest and up onto two legs, and it was to be the flowering plant that was about to rescue him again.

Those same grasses that had sustained the great herds of prey were still there, still flowering and still producing a great profusion of annual seeds. It was to take only one imaginative human to realise that in his own time and his own place he could plant those seeds to suit his needs and the world would change again. From a handful of grains of rice or wheat, of barley or wild oats or maize, would spring all the wealth and cultural diversity of the modern age. Our surging populations, our great cities, our terrifying machines and weapons, our spiralling knowledge, our religions, our medicines, our dreams and our vaulting ambitions would all spring from and come to depend upon those few carefully nurtured seeds. The world we have created, our world, was gifted to us by an explosion of flowers.

# 12

# The Autumn Stalk

But to have been
This once, completely, even if only once:
To have been at one with the earth, seems beyond undoing.
                    – Rainer Maria Rilke, '9th Duino Elegy'
                    (translated by Stephen Mitchell)


Think mist hanging over the loch and the river, think migration, think plums and windfall apples, think fungi. And then think shadows; lengthening shadows and low-angled light. 'We are tilted. This was the first thing to understand,' wrote William Fiennes in *The Snow Geese*, his uplifting evocation of recovery from illness by following the seasonal migration of some six million lesser snow geese in North America. 'The axis of the Earth's rotation is not perpendicular to the plane of the Earth's orbit round the sun. It is tilted at about 23.5 degrees.'

It is the Earth's tilt that gives us our seasons, our ever-turning year. It is the tilt that takes us away from the sun, shortens our days, closes down our trees and flowers and insects, and causes so many of our birds to head south to warmer climes. It is the tilt that awards us our moody contrasts and gently stretching shadows. The further north we are, the greater the seasonality, the longer and darker the days of winter and the briefer and more heady the summer.

Here, locked into our northern bowl, hemmed in by the high hills and moors, we cannot hang onto the sun. In June it was our constant companion, days so long that night flickered like a distant memory; life was so bright and absorbing that we failed to notice the sun's high point, its greatest angular declination we call the Summer Solstice, slide by. Daylight had become a drug, hauling us out of bed and keeping us on our toes until late in the evenings. Even though subconsciously we knew it was slipping away from us there still seemed to be plenty of time. Who notices a few minutes a day when life is good? The Earth's tilt was kicking in by stealth. No one noticed the shadows creeping further and further across the lawn. It is a testament of our physical and psychological separation from nature that we largely disregard those signals, the solar totems of our year, which guide and direct our wildlife.

Because of the tilt, migration becomes a constant feature of our latitude. As the input of solar energy falls away many of our summer birds are forced to clear off to more reliable food supplies further south, while those that choose to breed in the Arctic return to us in the autumn. Long before frosts scamper through the glens and chlorophyll bleeds from the leaves, the summer migrants are the first to signal their anxiety. By the end of July, warblers, especially the willow warblers, whitethroats and blackcaps that laced their jubilant arpeggios through our gardens and woods all through the months of long daylight, have not only ceased their persistent chorus, they have gone. Unseen, they have slipped away like party-goers who have burnt out and want to go home early; one minute our warblers are there, lustily voicing their resolve, the next an empty silence seems to hollow out the cool morning air.

Unlike the geese and swans, which hang on in the Arctic until the last moment, the tiny songsters cannot make great migrations in one hop; they prefer to feed their way south over a period of weeks, maximising the benison of the abundant insect swarm as they go, conserving energy, resting and feeding up before the final push, in some cases as far as equatorial West Africa, or, in the case of swallows and house martins, all the way to the Cape.

*October 4th*     Today I saw a woodcock; nothing unusual about that. They are with us all the year round, most visible in spring, when the male bird can be heard 'roding' overhead in a broad circle around its breeding territory. Roding is one of those mysterious words of no clear origin, like a *skein* of geese, beech *mast* or a squirrel's *drey*, that appended themselves to certain species of wildlife so long ago that we've forgotten why and whether those terms ever belonged to anything else. Now it's too late. No one else goes roding on warm May evenings, just the woodcock. As display flights go, it is unimaginative. The woodcock inscribes a broad circle, sometimes taking several minutes to complete, flying low over the tops of the trees at an even altitude, emitting a low, burbling gurgle punctuated every few seconds with a sharp, sneezing squeak. This usually begins shortly after sunset and can continue until dark.

I am always excited to hear and see the roding flight, not because it is particularly notable in itself, but because it confirms the breeding presence of this spectacular, long-billed, barrelesque wader in our woods. It is also an important symbol. Its decision to inhabit the birchwoods is an ecological health award, a rosette of nature's approval that the woodland ecosystem is functioning properly, that the leaf litter beneath the trees is creating soil and that the worms and bugs and microbes that are ultimately responsible for the natural composting process – that are the future fertility of the woods – are all present and correct. That bill, straight, rigid and five inches long, is a soil testing kit, an assessor's probe, checking us out. I search for the socket-holes of his signature, the woodland graffito of a master craftsman, scattered among the leaf litter as I pick my way through the trees. To me these signs are a rite of spring I rely upon to shore myself up after the long, dark days, something I actively seek out to assuage an inner anxiety, knowing by some innate osmosis that if I don't see and hear the roding flight and find the signs, something will be terribly wrong. He raises my comfort rating, the woodcock; he awards me a badge I can wear with pride.

You never see a woodcock unless it moves. On the nest the bird is invisible. Even when I have seen a bird fly in, land and then weave its faltering, cautious route to its nest, as soon as it settles on its eggs it vanishes. I have stared for an hour through my binoculars, knowing full well the bird is there, seeing nothing. The exquisite subtlety of its camouflage is breathtaking. Thick, black bars carve up its domed and scalloped head, the cinnamon-pink and grey background plumage, and the dappling, barred and waved shadows of its rufous back, arrayed in that almost sensuous waving form of sand at low tide, banish all preconceived images of shape and form. The bird melts. Even the large, unblinking eye becomes a pool of deception.

Sadly, to inspect the plumage properly the bird usually has to be dead. They are very good to eat; the highly prized quarry of many shooting people because they do require skill to shoot and the culinary rewards bring a certain exclusivity, a cachet of good country living, to the dinner table. Therein lies one of the deep anomalies of country life. If I were to suggest to you that roasted chicken guts, the food-filled entrails of the free-range bird, should be spread on a piece of toast and served up for your supper, or perhaps a subtle consommé of worms, beetles, earwigs, maggots and millipedes, delicately laced with bird dung, most people's reaction, I think I can confidently predict, would be 'Uugggh!' and a grimace of disgust. I admit it doesn't sound very appetising. Yet traditionally, both woodcock and snipe are eaten whole without gutting – 'undrawn' is the technical term – leaving the bird intact, with its head and bill on, its insides full of heart and lungs, gizzard, liver, reproductive matrix and long, worm-and-bug-filled gut, including formative and fully formed faeces at the tail end. In most cases the shot birds will have guts full of food, actually not so dissimilar to the gut of a chicken, another woodland and jungle floor species relishing any bug or worm, any juicy invertebrate it can find. But in the case of the woodcock and the snipe, suddenly the contents of the gut are overlooked, even irrelevant, and the sticky, slightly slimy, dark brown juices emanating from it in the cooking – 'the trail', as it is known – are considered a great delicacy. There is, as the saying goes, no accounting for taste – or perhaps that should be 'there's no accounting for illogical discrimination'.

Except in very hard winters when woodcock sometimes struggle to survive, shooting them is not a conservation issue. It is a populous and successful species spread across a broad range right across northern Europe from the Alps to the Arctic, from Scandinavia to Siberia. It is also very hard to hit, so many get away unscathed. For my own part I am more than happy to eat woodcock, however it is served up, but, for my own complicated emotional reasons, I have long since declined to shoot them (or anything else, for that matter, except the occasional rat or marauding deer). It is a well-known phenomenon that naturalists who have been very predatory in their youth hang up their guns later in life without necessarily harbouring any distaste for field sports. The late Sir Peter Scott, once a fanatical wildfowler who was to become the father of modern bird conservation, is a well-known case in point, as were Gavin Maxwell, W.H. Hudson, Aldo Leopold, Richard K. Nelson and many others. Many big game hunters in Africa have become avid conservationists and safari guides preaching and teaching nature conservation – have indeed founded some important conservation organisations.

There is also a valid argument that the hunting life, that of genuinely pitting one's wits against wild quarry (quite distinct from 'social' hunting – the artificial rearing of exotic game birds and driving them over static guns, as is the practice of commercial pheasant shoots), brings the hunter into a deeper and more intimate, more objectively respectful relationship with the wild and with the quarry species than it might otherwise be possible to achieve from pure observation. This is not a point I would choose to press; for me to suggest that because I was an enthusiastic shot in my youth I am now somehow better equipped to appreciate wildlife than anyone else smacks of arrogance and conceit – a hubris begging nemesis aboard – but I do believe it is an argument that has some merit, if only that of the learning process. I fancy that in the youthful pursuit of game I honed my field-craft skills and absorbed some of the tough, natural realities of prey–predator relationships, such as failing to be good enough and coming home cold, wet, tired and empty-handed, that I would not have learned any other way.

Years ago I was out shooting woodpigeons on a friend's farm. At dusk we stood in the shadow of an old oak on the edge of a wood, waiting for the pigeons to come in to roost. A woodcock floated through and my friend upped his gun and shot it. His Labrador collected the bird and came back to him wagging its tail. He took the dead bird and passed it to his young wife standing beside us. For a few moments she held it, saying nothing, but I could see from her face that she was gripped by the stark beauty of the lifeless creature in her hands. After examining the plumage for a few seconds she placed it reverently on the ground at her feet. Then a surge of emotion overtook her; she turned, placed both hands on the trunk of the oak, and dropped her forehead on to them in a gesture of utter desolation. When she looked up tears were streaming down her face.

But it is not spring, and the bird I saw today was not roding. Only three feet away it lifted suddenly and silently from the ferny edge to the path as I approached the loch. It looped away through the trees, in a slow, hesitating flight with distinctive downward flicks of the curved wings, weaving and jinking to avoid the trunks and dropping down again into the ocean of bracken beneath the birches after only fifty yards. It was a glimpse, yet an instantly recognisable one because of that unmistakable looping flight. It stopped me in my tracks and with a smile on my face I watched the birchwood swallow it up. I love this bird.

It is October and this may not be one of our resident woodcock. It could be a winter migrant, just arrived from Scandinavia. Right across northern Scandinavia and Russia, when the first autumn frosts stiffen the soils so essential for its probing bill, the bird ups and leaves for frost-free feeding grounds further south. This is not a flock migrant, like so many of its wader cousins. This bird delights in mystery. It migrates singly or in twos, arriving in the night and immediately blending into the undergrowth of its woodland habitat. Perhaps this bird had just arrived.

My journal has another woodcock entry, not from autumn, but from June a few years ago, and not in the woods. As it turned out, it was one of the most remarkable ornithological experiences I have ever witnessed.

My wife, Lucy, was heading home in her ageing and beloved Volvo estate. Our country back road is narrow; emulating the river it winds, slalom-like, through steep birchwoods with bracken slopes on either side. As she rounded a bend she saw a brown bird fly into the car ahead of her and fall to the verge. Thinking it was a tawny owl, and knowing my habitual interest in such things, she stopped. It was a woodcock. She picked it up. It appeared dead, hot and floppy in her hand, but bloodless and apparently undamaged, so she put it in the back of the car and forgot about it.

Our paths crossed a couple of hours later. 'Oh! There's a dead woodcock in the back of my car. I picked it up a mile down the road,' she said. So I went to look. Woodcock are outstandingly difficult to study in the wild so the opportunity to hold one in my hand and to examine its inspirational cryptic plumage was irresistible. When I lifted the tailgate I was dumbstruck.

In the middle of the Jack Russells' tartan travel rug stood a fine adult bird. It showed no sign of fear or alarm. Instead, something entirely unexpected occurred. Its feathers slowly began to rise, not fluffed out but gradually lifting and swelling across its whole body as though it were being invisibly inflated. It angled its bill downward to almost vertical so that the black stripes on the top of its finely sculpted head stood high and proud. Its dark eyes neither blinked nor wavered, but fixed me with a deep, saturnine glare. Its wings began to lift and loop menacingly downwards, reminiscent of a cowboy about to draw, further increasing its size into what I now realised to be a posture of threat – yes, of threat! This small woodland wader, no larger than my two hands placed together, had recovered consciousness and was bravely puffing itself up to threaten me – the arch-predator – to insist that I back off. But I had seen nothing yet.

Transfixed, I watched as the woodcock's tail began to tremble. The spiky feathers emerged and stiffly erected themselves into a broad, spreading fan that grew and grew until they were tilting forward over its arched back: a ginger, black and white-tipped array of quite startling *haute couture* that would have graced any catwalk. The tremble changed gear, into rapid vibrations. Slowly at first, with increasing vigour and a clearly audible snare-drum roll, the rigid feathers rattled with menace. The woodcock rose up on its legs and started to dance. It strutted and posed and flicked its postured bill as though shaking a stick. It chasséd and turned, never once attempting to leave the wide-open car; it tangoed and swayed to its own wondrous internal rhythm. Then it uttered a thin, sneezing call as though to spit its defiance finally home. This seemed to drive it to yet further heights of self-belief. It rose higher on its legs and pouted yet more petulantly, every few seconds snorting this bill-shaking yelp of exasperation. Its black eyes grew wide and burned with rancour. In defence of its own life this exquisite creature was performing an ancient fan dance choreographed in the damp woods of its long, mysterious origins.

In total awe I stood and watched for several minutes. Finally, fearing that it was about to explode in a cloud of feathers I picked it up in both hands and carried it gently out onto the lawn. It never faltered. Even in my hands it sought to buck and wing its bird bolero. I placed it on the grass and backed away. The vibrations suddenly stopped.

For a full minute the bird stood still; it looked faintly ridiculous with wings akimbo and spiky tail up-rearing. It seemed to sense its own absurdity – that its moment of ire had passed. The bill righted, the fan subsided and the wings returned to its sides. Appearing momentarily embarrassed, it took three short steps forward in a little run as if to check itself out – to be quite sure it was a woodcock again – then it lifted off and winged away into the rhododendron shrubbery with that familiar and unmistakable looping flight I love so well.

The Highland autumn has its own particular quality, a seasonality so pressing and insistent that it defines itself unforgettably. The hills are ringing with the roaring of red deer stags. In upland deer country the rutting season is the year's high point, the moment for which the deer have been slowly building their strength and energy. In the gentle Gaelic tongue the word for October and the red deer roaring are synonymous – *an dàmhair* – an inseparable association by a people who lived their entire lives in close proximity to nature in these wild glens. By the 15th of the month the roaring is at its peak, dominant stags hurling out their claim to their harems of hinds all day and all night. They are almost exhausted, having shed a third of their body weight over the preceding three weeks of not feeding and constantly corralling, herding and covering their females. Many will have been ousted by stronger stags coming in, spotting the weaknesses, seeing their chance and taking over after only a brief clash of antlers, the vanquished stag wandering off in despair. But occasionally there is a much closer contest and the challenger has to fight hard for his turn to pass on his genes. The sound of clashing antlers and the heaving and groaning of the combatants can be heard ringing through the woods around the loch, sapping my attention as I walk.

Then comes the colour, never all at once, but slowly seeping in from the dying days of September when the first horse chestnut leaves yellow at the edges, through to the last days of October when the birches around the loch are fired with bright copper and tangerine. Wild cherries, known here as geans, blaze in the startling scarlet of guardsmen's tunics among the birches and pines, out-dazzling the rowans that line the burn's edge. Aspens need a good frost to claim the eye, but when they turn, suddenly and unexpectedly, they do so with a panache unsurpassed by any other tree. A violent citrus yellow, the yellow of brightest sunlit lemon you ever saw, matched only by the gilded flash on siskins' wings, makes the aspens stand out in the woods like sentinels – even from afar, never any doubt what tree it is. And when the sun strikes them they seem to hurl it back with a burnished glare as bright as newly minted sovereigns, a gold grander by far than anything Tutankhamen wore.

*October 12th*    I am out to see a stag I have been listening to all night. He came close to the house, perhaps only two hundred and fifty yards away, in the steep field that backs onto the loch woods. His hinds and their calves have been down to the rich grazing under cover of darkness. Although he is not eating at all – and won't again until the rut is over – he will have followed them down through the woods, constantly roaring and circling, checking them out for the next hind to come into season. In the field he would have held them there on the rutting stand of his own choosing, guarding them against any other stag that might arrive to fancy his chances. I know that at dawn they will drift uphill again, leaving the field over the fence, often with the give-away ping of the top wire plucked like a guitar string by a lazy cloven hoof. Once back in the woods they will melt away like shadows, their departure revealed only by the gradual softening of their stag's bellowing.

I lie in bed until I know they are well inside the woods. Stalking them in the dark is well nigh impossible, our crimped vision only adding to the technical difficulties of stalking wild animals as keenly tuned as deer. Standing at the open window I take a bearing on direction, where I think they are. I wait for the roars, coming now at ten- or fifteen-minute intervals, until they seem to have stopped in one place. That's where I think they will settle for the day, lying up in the rust-tinged bracken, the stag only perfunctorily roaring unless he is challenged. The dawn is gathering. It is time to move.

It has rained in the night, but the sky is clear now and I can still see stars, although pockets of mist loiter in the field hollows so that I can barely see the forest edge. First I must check the wind. A faint breeze is drifting up the glen from the south-east. Stringy wisps of cloud pass across a silver segment of moon sinking towards the western rim of the hills above the loch. I watch to make sure breeze and clouds are passing in the same direction. An eddying wind can be treacherous. It's okay, both are flowing in unison, the clouds and the handful of grass seeds I throw up matching the chill on my cheek. I cross the fence into the field – must be careful not to ping the wires.

Powering up the open pasture is quick and easy. I stop to recover my breath, calm myself down before I enter the woods; the rank odour of deer is all round me. It is raw and elemental, not the heavily overburdened stench of a cowshed or a pigsty, but warmer, closer to that of a potting shed with a hint of dog kennel. It's musky and earthy together, and reminds me of a brown bear I once met in a Finnish forest.

By the time I reach the forest it is daylight – still dim and the mist has slid away down the slope to collect over the river far below like a new lake, but daylight all the same, sufficient to see the leaf litter under my feet and to avoid that other great giveaway: snapping sticks. Deer don't snap sticks. Wild animals place their feet with precision and care; only humans blunder along. I test the wind again. I'm still well placed; the breeze is crossing my face, barely detectable, taking the dreaded man smell away from the deer. Slowly and carefully I move off along the fence until I find the place where the deer have crossed. Here their slotted imprints are clearly visible, deep where they leapt over the fence, lighter where they delicately landed and moved off through the trees. I follow. My stag is plain to see. His size and weight are writ large on the forest floor, a trail so fresh that it seems to call out to me.

Woodland stalking is an exercise in wildness that stretches

and teases every sense; it stirs every slumbering primeval instinct and tests patience and physical control to screaming pitch. Sometimes it means freezing, standing as still as a tombstone in an uncomfortable position for many minutes at a time, sometimes dropping onto knees in wet grass or boggy patches, or, when the wind shifts or an unexpected and unwanted roe deer comes tripping through capable of spoiling everything, having to sit through a totally motionless half-hour unable to scratch your nose and forced to ignore the midges grazing the rims of your ears, while the water oozing from sphagnum moss wicks slowly up and into your clothes wherever they touch the ground.

This morning the gods are kind to me: no roe deer to give the game away, no woodcock bursting from beneath my feet, no eddying breezes, no discomfort at all. My stag is up there, only half a mile away now, still roaring sporadically, still in the same place, still undisturbed. I press slowly on, stealthily, thinking carefully about the placing of each foot: heel gently down; ease forward; take weight on that foot; scour ground; take weight on crummack in right hand; ease forward again; heel, sole, toe; test before taking whole weight in case something hidden beneath the leaf litter might snap or creak.

I have to wrest my mind back to the task in hand every time it wanders off, moving from tree to tree like a guerrilla resistance fighter, watching, listening, feeling my way through the forest as if my life depends on it. Deer footprints are all round me. They haven't travelled in single file – far from it – they have spread out across the slope, and every now and again the stag has broken into a run along the contours as if to herd his hinds back together again. After a few more minutes the first rays of the sun top the hill to the east and tiger-stripe the needly litter around me. Now I can identify the woodland plants under my feet: clumps of hard fern, bracken in frost-touched patches, a penny bun fungus, the *Boletus* cep that is so good to eat and nearly distracts me. I *must* concentrate. The birch leaves flare from amber to grapefruit gold.

Why am I doing this? Why, when I have seen red deer so many thousands of times, and when I can drive a few miles up the glen and see deer by the dozen through my telescope or binoculars in open hill country, do I want to stalk a stag on my own patch? What, I ask myself, is it all about, this obsession with wildness, this gut need to be a part of wild nature and to join it at its own level to no obvious end? I suspect that many naturalists ask themselves these same questions. I'm sure many will have answers far better thought through and more plausible than mine. Scientists enjoy honing their field skills so that they can make first-hand observations; many amateur naturalists may seek to study their interest as closely and unobtrusively as they can; film-makers and wildlife photographers like to pit their wits against their quarry and will demonstrate quite extraordinary patience and suffer agonising discomfort sometimes for weeks on end to get that special sequence of shots. But I can boast none of these material goals. My needs are much closer to the hunter ancient and modern, the deer stalker whose triumph is fresh meat to carry home rejoicing at the end of the day, although I carry no gun and no longer have any desire to kill. I suspect that in the name of sport or deer control, deep down the modern hunter is responding to the ancient imperatives of all predatory species: the need to kill for survival.

Until the advent of systematic farming in Europe some five thousand years ago, virtually all men, and perhaps some women in some cultures, had to learn to hunt. Hunting was a daily chore upon which they and their families were absolutely dependent. In North America, and across the Arctic, in Australia and Africa and throughout Asia, hunting by native peoples as a regular source of protein persisted well into the twentieth century and in some places still exists. Only in the so-called sophisticated Western world in recent times has the modernist notion of civilisation sought to shut out our past and elevate us above and beyond our need for wild nature as a source of food. With the singular exception of fishing the oceans, in our own society hunting for food has been supplanted by the beguiling word *sport*, more accurately defined as social hunting, where the hunters require minimal field skills and often the quarry, such as reared pheasants, ducks and partridges and farm-stocked fisheries, make virtually no real connection with either wildness or nature. Yet hunting remains a fundamental human instinct in all of us, only denied and rendered redundant in relatively recent times. In our post-industrial society that denial has metamorphosed into a suite of moral judgements enshrined in regulation and statute as if to prove that man is now above such abhorrent pursuits, even further distancing us from our origins. Anthropologists argue that the competition and the cut and thrust of business have filled the vacuum and assuaged those carnal predatory instincts – that the trader is the hunter trapped behind the counter.

Whatever primordial instincts I am subconsciously responding to, I feel a need to be out there. I want to know
what is going on – have come to pride myself in knowing,
as far as our limited comprehension will allow, what wild
nature is up to on my doorstep. It is what I do. I fancy that
a big part of me also wants to be inside nature and not shut
out by the lofty and often misleading veneer of civilisation
and modernity, and consciously, if only for myself, to do
something to close down the ever-widening gap between
man and the wild. I see that gaping chasm as an important
part of the problem we all face, the global problem of sustainability. Our separation from the soil has run us and all wild
nature throughout the globe into serious trouble at a level
unimaginable when I was a boy only fifty years ago. I, for
one, don't want to follow the herd into the abyss.

His night-long roaring has etched this stag into the soft
wax of my subconscious. By roaring in our woods for three
weeks now he has burned his way in and taken me over. He
has come closer and closer in the darkness so that the slotted
hoof prints and the bottle-green dung of his harem of hinds
are a prominent and unavoidable feature of the field that
lies between the house and the forest. With his antlers he
has thrashed an oasis of thistles to stringy pulp; just inside
the wood he has virtually destroyed a young rowan sapling,
beating it up with his testosterone-driven bravura to such
an extent that to survive at all it will have to sucker again
from the roots. My sleep has been bombarded by his echoing
challenges over and over again. Louder even than the young
tawny owls in the great ash tree beside the house, louder
than the persistent braying of Geordie's sheep, cutting deeper

and ravens do. Another roar breaks the silence of the empty woods, although a half-hearted one. I know that very soon he will cease altogether, closing down for the day while he rests up, so I must take another bearing on his position to be certain of my route. I reckon he is only five hundred yards away now, so I must take extra care, a wariness as close as I can match to that of his hinds. It is 7.43 a.m. The human world is awake. I can hear the occasional car hissing along the glen road far below me. Somewhere over the other side of the valley a tractor has fired up and a dog is barking excitedly. The clunk of heavy farm machinery booms across to me – perhaps a trailer being hitched. These are distractions. I must shut them out and think wild again. I was slipping.

For a few seconds I steady myself against the firm trunk of an old pine. The scaly bark is friendly to the touch and reassuring, as though I have just passed a test, signed in at a check-point, reaffirming my connection to nature, okay to carry on. Twenty feet above me a red squirrel flashes away through the canopy with the ease of a bird. I hear his scratchy claws and see the flicker of his rufous tail. I am pleased that I got so close to him and a warm flood of pleasure diffuses through me like a nip of whisky on a frosty day. I am alone now, as far as I can tell, with the inevitable exception of a following robin hoping that I will break the soil (as all men do sooner or later) and reveal some succulent morsel for him. He flits ahead of me, tinkling out his threnody to the passing year, and then he vanishes, only to pop up again a few yards behind me, exploring my footprints in the needly forest floor. I could really do without him, but I don't think he will give me away – I have never known deer take any notice of robins – and, besides, I love him for his pizzazz and overt opportunism.

Extra care needed now. I'm down to perhaps only three hundred yards, well within the detection range of all deer senses. I have arrived at the edge of a small clearing of wet ground about fifty yards across. Each footstep has to be placed only after thorough checking out for anything that might make a sound. One squelch of water or sucking mud would have every one of them on their feet and away in a flash. Gently I pull the seed head off a sow thistle conveniently growing among the rushes and wavy hair grass. The down floats away from my hand and disappears behind me – exactly what I want to see. I raise my binoculars and scour the clearing, taking my time, peering into the gaps between the birches on the far side, searching for any clue, any sign of an outlier hind posted to keep guard. Nothing. The woods seem empty except for a dragonfly quartering the wetter patches of the clearing on rattling wings and the water-filled trails of deer prints where they have passed through. I decide not to cross the open ground – too risky, perhaps too wet. A hover fly, pretending to be a wasp in yellow and black stripes, inspects me up close. His mimicry doesn't fool me a jot and he seems to know it, hovering off about his business. I retreat and circle the wet ground to windward. Then I see the wallow.

In a wet and rushy place my stag has wallowed. He has torn into the wet ground with his lashing cleaves and dug himself a slushy, peaty hollow where he has gone down onto his knees, raking at the rushes with his antlers, throwing the debris far and wide. Water has filled the hole and he has gone right down, rolling, rubbing his head, neck and flanks into the oozing wet ground. When he arose, dripping and caked, he must have looked like some unimaginable, mythical creature of the underworld, black and evil and fantastic. The wallow is a wide, black, oval scar some twelve feet long and seven feet wide, trodden all round like an African waterhole. Mud lies in it as though it has been filled with molten dark chocolate, tipped in. The air reeks of deer musk and urine – his own signature, the pungent stamp of his driven, masculine authority over this land and his females.

I keep well back on dry ground. He is not long gone from here. I long for another roar so that I can find him again, fix his position for sure, but nothing comes. I think I can risk another hundred cautious paces in what I pray is the right direction. I begin to count, agonisingly slowly, a game of grandfather's footsteps without knowing where the old man is hiding. Seventy-six, seventy-seven, seventy-eight . . . and I'm hit in the face by another wave of heavy deer scent. A wall of musky pungence has drifted my way and stopped me dead in my tracks; the woods around me reek like a brewery. I know I am close. This little wind is a real friend. If their scent is coming to me so forcibly there is no chance of mine reaching them. Yet good as this confirmation is, I must now be patient. I am far too close to make a mistake. Slowly and silently I sit down and lean against a birch trunk. This is a waiting game. They aren't in a hurry to go anywhere, I know that; they may, in fact, have decided to settle for the day. Sooner or later something will give them away. It's their call.

Did I doze? I'm not sure, but now I'm wide awake. It is 8.22. Something – a mosquito or a gnat – has bitten me on the side of my neck. I long to scratch it, but mustn't. The sun is still merrily levering the trees apart, forcing its autumnal rays through and down to the forest floor. High above me troops of common crossbills and siskins flood over the canopy, their chipping and tseeping calls audible long after they have gone. Up there the sunlight has brought the coal and blue tits to life; I am happy to listen to them without looking up. I must do nothing to reveal myself to the ever-watching eyes and ever-twitching ears ahead of me. Only my eyes move. Time and distance blur; I no longer have any real idea how close or far away the deer are. I wait. Five minutes, ten, perhaps fifteen slide by; I resist looking at my watch, all movement is a risk, time is insignificant now. Oh! How I long to scratch my neck. Now a woodlouse is crawling up my corduroy trouser leg towards my knee. I am fascinated by his zigzag approach, his antennae probing this way and that as though he knows he's made a wrong turn, but can't work out how to go back. He reaches my knee where my hand is resting. I lift a finger and he pauses as though he senses trouble. I lower my finger onto his segmented, armadillo carapace and instantly he rolls into a ball, as tight as a pea (an old country name for woodlice is pea-bugs), tumbling back to the forest floor. Just as I am pondering how long it will be before he dares to open up again, the call comes.

A hard sound, a forceful abrasion of hard materials floods down to me from above and slightly off to the left. I recognise it instantly – and it is just what I wanted to hear. My stag has stopped roaring, but he is still peaceless, still fired up with sexual machismo, still needing to assert his dominance over the land he considers to be his own. He has chosen to take it out on a bush. I can't see it and I can only guess that it's the leggy, leguminous broom, *Cytisus*, because it is so quick to invade any woodland space, growing to six or seven feet high in a season, but I can hear the unmistakable clash of antler against a woody stem and a swishing rattle of foliage. Now the game is on in earnest.

I ease forward from tree to tree, sometimes a birch, then a pine, stopping behind each one to check out the shadowy ground ahead with my binoculars. All clear, so I abandon them to rely upon my own senses; I can't afford the extra movement using binoculars requires; besides, this is a wit-pitting exercise, the hunter versus the hunted, and I don't want to be found cheating at the moment of truth. I know very well there will be deer just ahead, perhaps closer than I think, so every footstep has to be teased forward, placed precisely and permitted to take my weight slowly and gently to ensure silence and absolute stealth. A half-sneeze freezes me in mid-step. It is a tiny, throat-and-nose-clearing wet-snort, barely audible, but it sets my senses fizzing like a firework fuse. I stare at the source of the sound and then I see it, a shaking head and a flickering ear. It is a calf, lying down. I watch its head settle back into repose. I can't see her, but I suspect its mother is right there, beside it in the long shadows of a spreading pine. My heart is thumping. I must back off.

Off to one side, moving so slowly that I almost fool myself, I ease away to the north, taking care to keep the wind in my favour. The hinds don't interest me today; they are an obstacle to get past to achieve my goal. My stag is still there, no longer brashing, but I do now know where he is. I must circle round and come at him from above. It seems to take an age to cover the fifty or so uphill yards to where I need to be. There is another huge old tree – a granny pine – up ahead that will do nicely for a spying position. It's gnarled and bent and has been broken many times by wet snow and deer browsing so that its deformed and contorted lower branches offer excellent cover. Five, four, three yards on painfully slow – not tiptoe but flat-footed, firm toe – and I'm there. My hands flatten against its flaky, ginger bark as I regain my breath and consciously try to ease down my thudding, booming heart. The tang of resin fills my nose, warm and aromatic like the familiar perfume of an old friend.

The rubbing and thrashing has stopped, but I can now see the broom bush looking decidedly beaten up, white stems gleaming where the bark has been frayed away in hanging strips. I know he's not far off. I ease round the old trunk, using my hands to steady myself. A happy swoon of *déjà vu* floods over me from years ago boyhood hide and seek, peeking out from behind the tree to see if they're coming. And suddenly there he is. There is my stag, lying down with five or six hinds around him, slightly below me on a dry, rocky knoll of heather and bilberry green. He is magnificent, what is commonly known around here as a wood stag – a beast that has lived in woods and benefited from shelter and rich pasture feeding. He is strong and heavy-bodied, black-maned and disdainful of eye. Even lying down he displays all the rampant masculinity of domination. With eleven points on his antlers, six on the left and five on the side nearest me, he narrowly misses being a royal. He has his 'full rights', as they say in deer parlance, the symmetrical brow, bay and trey tines on either side. The tip of the brow tine on this side is broken, so he has clashed during this rut; he's come out fighting and has not been found wanting. He has done his work, staked his claim and assured his genetic future, the ultimate, self-fulfilling imperative of us all. He is less than fifty yards away.

I know this is as close as I can get. I could mock a roar – of course I could. It's an old trick often used by stalkers to bring a stag forward. But I don't want to push my luck – besides, I learned my lesson the hard way long ago on Exmoor. Fired-up stags can be dangerous. No, I have achieved my goal and I am content. The prize is mine. I watch and I watch. There is little more to witness although I discover more and more hinds as I look around – and I can see another young pine tree he has beaten up a few yards away to my left.

That's it – I'm watching a party of red deer lying up to chew the cud and rest after a long night out in the fields. There is nothing exceptional here, nothing people cannot witness out in the hills any day of an autumn week, although perhaps not so close. But to me this is special. I have met my stag on equal terms; his senses and mine have matched each other in the absolute wild, no tricks or lures, no hides, no bait, no smart technology. I have seen this big old stag for myself; I have slept with his roaring in my dreams and breathed his musky scent at the edge of the forest. I have read the wind, followed his cloven trail up through the woods and found his wallow. Wild was the game, and wild the rules. I have relived the predatory skills of my ancestral past and, for now, I have won. And here he is. Now I know him up close and personal. If I ever see him again I will recognise him instantly. He is *my* stag.

# 13

# Iceland and the Whoopers

A fertile field is his free-sown life,
He has reaped his reward in the riches of battle;
Sadly I shall have served him if the seed he has given me
Should be wasted, not winnowed,
And blow in the wind.

> – From Egil's poem for Arinbjörn, *Egil's Saga*,
> translated and edited by Magnus Magnusson KBE

*November 26th*   I am out because today is extravagant –
an unseasonable gesture from the great god Sol, thrown
out like a bonus to reward our homage. Late November
is supposed to be windy and wet, but there is still real
warmth in this sun's benignant, healing mood. Days like
this have to be grabbed. We're in a count-down to far
tougher and rougher times, so I have to make the most
of it. When I saw clear blue from my study window I
knew I had to escape. Pressing emails can wait for once;
most of them are froth anyway, stuff people wouldn't have
bothered to write if they'd had to buy a stamp. I was off
up the Avenue as soon as I could break free.

The bracken has turned, but the sun soldiers on, fighting
back to the brighter memory of summer. Today's hillside

has that special autumnal opulence, Umbrian terracotta with a Midas glow wherever the sunlight strikes. I'm here on the dam because last night the whooper swans arrived from the Arctic, from northern Scandinavia – Lapland perhaps – or much further east, in Russia. Or they could well have come from Iceland. I can't tell and, unless a ringed bird dies and we get to know where it fledged, it's unlikely that I'll ever know, so I'll happily settle for Iceland, not least because I've just been there and enjoyed a gripping experience with Icelandic whoopers.

Every autumn I long for the swans to arrive. Some years it's October, sometimes I have to be more patient. This year – such an extraordinarily dry and warm summer that even in late October it didn't seem to want to end – I knew they would be late. But it didn't stop me listening out for them. I met whoopers first when I came to live in the Highlands all those years ago. They were exciting then and they are exciting now. I fell in love with them without realising it was happening, and then when I first discovered their nests in Lapland the bond became immutable, locked in for life.

In my twenties, in an attempt to learn more about Scotland as it was twelve thousand years ago after glaciation, I took a small winter expedition to Swedish Lapland. Quite by chance I happened across a whooper swan breeding ground far north of the Arctic Circle. It was a frozen bog, as silent and rigid as a Christmas card, but extravagantly beautiful, with high, snow-covered nest mounds dotted about across acres of frozen lagoons of moss and sedges, systematically repeating like relief patterns on a vast counterpane of icy crêpe de Chine. I meandered from nest to nest in a trance.

In one I found an addled egg, marble cold and nearly as heavy. As it lay in my mittened hand I imagined the summer: hundreds of these exquisite, yellow-billed swans and their fluffy, dove-grey cygnets dabbling in the safety of the boggy shallows, necks stained iron-ochre by the mineral ooze from which they grubbed the rich animal and vegetable vichyssoise which fattens the cygnets quickly through the short summer. It was an image that ran deep and stayed. Whoopers have been important to me ever since.

For many years I shared this fascination for these truly wild swans with my old, and sadly now late Scottish/Icelandic friend Magnus Magnusson. I miss the fizz and sparkle of his companionship, his wit and incisive interrogation. Far too often my self-indulgent soliloquy with nature goes unchallenged. We had worked together for over twenty years, first during his presidency of RSPB and later when we both served the government agency Scottish Natural Heritage, often in the far-flung wilds of the Highlands and Islands, exploring nature reserves and marvelling in the everyday currency of a naturalist's work. It was never enough for Magnus to be a figurehead or just a well-known name. His passion for wildlife was real and he would demand to be taken to see whatever it was we were striving to protect.

So many bright moments from those action-packed years: I recall standing with him in the piercing sunlight between rain squalls on the island of Barra as a skein of barnacle geese came honking and barking overhead, circled round and landed on a sheep-cropped green almost at our feet. They were immaculate, impossibly perfect in glossy black waistcoat and exquisite silver-grey barring. Magnus had a special affinity for barnacles on their way back to Greenland, passing his beloved Iceland, to breed. I remember his delight as bottlenose dolphins leapt high into the air, dived and skimmed around the prow of our boat as we ran the tide past Fort George in the inner Moray Firth. He often said nature was a great leveller; he loved the self-effacing indignity of bird-watching in the rain. Like schoolboys we laughed together sitting wet-bottomed among the yellow flags of a Skye marsh while a corncrake craked its ridiculous washboard call hidden only a few feet away in a clump of rushes and flowers of delicate red campion.

I happened to be back in the Arctic – in northern Svalbard searching for polar bears with my twelve-year-old daughter Hermione, in a land of glaciers and snowfields – in the same year that Magnus Magnusson escorted his daughter Sally on a wonderfully nostalgic expedition to Iceland to locate and explore their ancestral roots at Laxamýri. Sally had complained of the knife-edged Icelandic wind in May even though with characteristic Viking belligerence Magnus refused to acknowledge it at all, but I think that at –38°C our cold was in a slightly different league because we were so much further north – out on the pack ice of the Barents Sea, to try to see bear cubs when they first emerged from their birth-dens on the far-flung uninhabited island of Barentsøya – and it was winter, late March.

Quite unknown to Hermione or me, Sally sat down and wrote her engaging and revealing book about her father–daughter travels, *Dreaming of Iceland: The Lure of a Family Legend*. Quite unknown to Magnus or Sally, I also sat down to write *Nature's Child: Encounters with Wonders of the Natural*

*World*, about our own father–daughter adventures and the expedition to Svalbard. Both books were published in 2004. I remember the look of astonished delight on Magnus's face when he presented me his signed copy and I responded by giving him mine. We laughed, and, as on so many occasions during our working friendship, the whisky flowed.

Sally and Magnus's book inspired me to take Hermione back to Iceland two years later, not to research any smouldering Viking heritage, but to find some smouldering volcanoes. Hermione, then fourteen, was 'doing' volcanism in a school geography project. She had just seen pictures of the massive eruption of Mount St. Helens and the devastation it spewed for miles in every direction. It was, she pronounced, 'Cool!' When she came home she asked me whether there happened to be anything about to blow around here. 'No,' I said, 'mercifully not, but if you're brave enough to swim in steaming volcano-heated sodium silicate, I know just the place.' So off we went to Reykjavik in the Easter hols.

'Iceland is green, Greenland is ice', sing the old travel guides. Well, not quite. In April Iceland is icy. It isn't often that my children have asked to do something so laudably academic with their precious holiday time, so I leapt at the chance – besides, there is an inherent sexiness in nature's extremes that goads me on. Ice and steam, glaciers and lava, snow and fumaroles all seem to be taunting each other like male dogs building up to a scrap. You sense that sooner or later there is going to be an almighty punch-up; a dynamic tension sucks you in.

First we had to go and swim in that extraordinary silica

lake, Bláa Lónið, at Grindavík. It is a public facility attached
to a geothermal power station that permanently belches
steam into the icy air. To reach it you cross a vast lava field
of aggressively lunar scenery. Catastrophic eruptions from
Mount Hekla in the fourteenth century spewed zillions of
tons of plastic pumice across the Reykjanes peninsula like
chocolate icing crudely roughed across a cake. It crystallised
into sharp, coke-like palagonite, tinged purple with dolerite,
a rock that glows bronze in the sunlight, full of bubbles like
a mousse. As rocks go it is light and irresistible – or so it
seemed. I had to lug what felt to me to be unnecessarily
large chunks of it home because it was, Hermione insisted,
essential proof of her academic endeavours.

The tourist guides also make a big thing of Iceland
generating all its energy from geothermal heat. Hot water
comes free, which is terrific – as long as you don't mind
stinking of sulphur. The whole place seems to pong of bad
eggs most of the time. At the Blue Lagoon the water is so
stiff with sodium silicate that it shines as blue-white as
Persil, reflecting the frosty sunshine while clouds of steam
perpetually drift into a gentian sky. You float weightlessly in
thick milk, in places almost too hot to bear ($45°C$). They
claim it fixes your eczema, psoriasis, scabies, impetigo,
dermatitis and a host of other scabby maladies. You certainly
emerge with silky skin and, according to Hermione, 'hair
like a badger's arse'. But they also saw us coming. As you
leave you are seduced into buying a dozen cleverly packaged
and apparently essential oils and unctions with which to
tame the badger effect.

Next we felt we had to go to Geysir, the eponymous steam

spout called Strokkur ('churn') that draws a quarter of a million tourists every year. As tourist attractions go it is remarkably obliging. It blows off entirely naturally about every ten minutes, shooting a vertical spout of steam 60–100 feet into the air. A flimsy rope keeps you what is thought by the Icelanders to be a safe distance away – about 10 yards – where you stand with camera poised as this open well of boiling water menacingly heaves and surges. It is many thousands of feet deep, running right down into the molten magma. All that heaving is thermal inversion as the whole cauldron seethes and churns. In a very short time the unquenchable heat at the bottom produces a monstrous sulphur-steam fart desperate to escape. To a gasp of delight from the parka-clad crowd it rockets to the surface and explodes into the cold air like – well, like only a geyser can. A foul, hot spray drenches us all. As we leave we see a sign that tells us seven tourists are scalded every week.

After that we gave up tourism and reverted to being naturalists and steam-keen, badger-arsed volcanologists. We took off into the wilds in our rented 4×4 with ludicrously fat (but very effective) tyres across the snowfields to find fumaroles and vents of our own. The weather was sharp – just below freezing – but blessed with sunshine sparkling on a snowscape of high, broad-valleyed mountains, lava flats and ash chutes sufficient to delight any budding geographer. Steam wafted into the blue in all directions. Streams of boiling mud bubbled and trickled porridge-like through the snow in long, slurping runs.

We off-roaded from one fumarole to the next. Hermione was in her element. Clutching camera and binoculars we slithered through sulphurous slime and vile eruptions of crystalline sludge that wafted me straight back to the chemistry lab at school. Puzzled ravens chided us with rasping abuse – clearly this was not how Icelanders or tourists normally behaved. Above us whooper swans in broad chevrons bugled through the sunlight, just arriving to breed in the swampy interior. Snow buntings crowded around in chirpily fidgeting flocks of thousands, constantly moving, apparently fearless as they picked over the snow at our feet.

And then . . . and then, oh joy of every naturalist's desiring! A crossbow shadow suddenly skimmed across us, slicing the snow like a knife. Instinctively I knew what it was even before I had fixed her in my binoculars. It was one of those priceless events one reads about and then waits decades to witness. We didn't see the kill – it happened over the ridge, just beyond our view – but we saw our Arctic gyrfalcon in full rocketing pursuit of a covey of ptarmigan. The white grouse seemed to float through crystal air. As though in slow motion the falcon came from behind, angling down on flicking scimitar wings, overtaking them and scattering them in a flurry of white panic. And we saw her well: the shining white mask, the silver nape, an image to hoard away for life, that unforgettable delta dart, crimped in the stoop, a sabre sweeping through a land of ice.

On we went, bouncing on our obese flotation tyres (which had now proved to be invaluable) across snow-covered lava fields on our way to Mount Hekla. We even climbed halfway up it in –8°C, stopping to warm ourselves at fumaroles and sulphur pools of rotten-egg-stinking mud, which belched and steamed ominously on both sides of the track. If, as Hermione fervently hoped, these had been the precursor to a full eruption, we'd have been in serious trouble.

We had to abandon Hekla's towering pyramid; it was simply too ambitious. Far too high for a short winter day, although we had huge fun trying, wading waist deep through snow drifts and glissading down virgin slides. So we slowly picked our way back across its vast, empty, snow-smoothed lava field until, near the base of the mountain, we spied two whooper swans standing at the edge of a gently steaming, marshy pool. We stopped. Using the car as a hide we watched the birds doing nothing much for several minutes: preening a bit, dabbling in the pool and fluting softly to each other. We chatted idly as we sipped the hot cod chowder the hotel had given us in a Thermos, speculating whether they were a committed pair that had just arrived a bit too early to think about nesting, or whether they had never migrated south at all and somehow managed to hang on through the Icelandic winter.

What happened next was remarkable in my experience and I hurried to write it all down. Just then two ravens flew in. They made a spectacular contrast: the stark swan-white and the corvid-black; the angelic and the satanic; the pure of heart and the malevolent chancers; the delicate vegetarians and the ruthless scavengers of carrion.

At first we couldn't imagine what the ravens wanted with two adult swans on the frozen wastes of Mount Hekla in the middle of Icelandic nowhere. There weren't likely to be any carnivorous pickings for them and they couldn't possibly tackle full-grown swans, however Machiavellian their reputation. Then, to our great surprise, one raven hopped in and stabbed a vicious peck at a swan's flank. The swan rose up in immediate indignation, hissing loudly and flapped its wings angrily at the raven, which promptly flew back a few feet until it was safely out of range. The swan settled down again.

A few seconds later the second raven hopped in and tried the same trick, this time to the other swan. The same reaction, the same hissing ire lashed out at the raven. There was a pause while the ravens seemed to confer; then the first raven repeated it – his go – quickly followed by the other leaping in again. This recurred many times, over and over again, the ravens getting bolder with each advance and sometimes even making contact with the swans, although never even coming close to doing them harm. All that happened was that the swans got cross and flustered – much wagging of tails and shuffling of wings – and began to move away, arched necks and heads twisting from side to side to keep the black devils in view. So the ravens followed and when the swans stopped they adjusted their approach tactics and had another go. We watched, fascinated. 'Do you know,' I whispered respectfully (the mysteries of animal behaviour always make me respectful), 'I do believe we are watching a game.'

'It's not much of a game for the swans,' said Hermione with a 'Hmmph.' She was right. It was no fun at all for the swans – they were being bullied. It was a swan wind-up, raven sport entirely at the swans' expense: bored hooligans picking on gentle, defenceless victims.

Ravens are highly intelligent, like most of the corvid family.

No doubt that's part of the reason Corvidae are so successful worldwide as a bird family of many different species. Raven cunning is also well documented in folklore, fable and literature. But it was a real first for me – although I have read of their antics and watched wild ravens at home for hundreds of hours, I had never before seen them maliciously 'at play' with another bird species quite like this. After half an hour they grew bored at the lack of response from the swans, both of which had given up hissing and flapping and were just shuffling off, looking rather grumpy. So the ravens flew away, no doubt to find some other poor victim to taunt. We scurried back to the geothermal warmth of our hotel.

About ten whoopers over-winter in this glen. Some years it's a few more, some less. They always come, arriving in the night, just in from the far north in small family groups, sometimes six or seven together, adults and grey-necked cygnets flying in a broad chevron to pitch on the river or our little hill loch up on the moor. They stay with us until the frost grips the loch, when they move back to the estuaries and the foreshore.

The first I know of it is their bugling calls echoing out of the darkness as they pass. I rush to the window to catch the flash of moonlight on broad, silver wings. Then they become part of our winter, with us every day so that we listen out for the summons of their wild, nasal whoopings. In spring we never see them go – one minute there they are, standing about on the river fields, gathering in large flocks whiter than surf; long, straight necks like yellow-handled walking sticks, all softly fluting to themselves. These are wild swans, quite different from the posed, voluptuous ogees of their mute swan cousins sandwich-fed in parks and reservoirs and adorning the May pages of calendars; these whoopers are wild – a distillation of that faraway, Arctic wildness where they were hatched – finer, purer and then suddenly gone, tugged away by the stars and the lengthening days. They have lifted off into the northern night in undulating skeins. During the long, green summer we forget them, put them out of mind to concentrate on some of the incomers: ospreys, wheatears and swallows.

But on their return to the valley – just now – bugling their blood-tingling music across the night sky, they herald one of the most stirring moments of the incipient Highland winter. They seem to be dragging winter with them from the far north. Because they are so late this year I feel that I've been listening out for them for weeks. When it happened last night I was in bed and asleep – well, half asleep – I've never managed completely to close down that bit of my brain's long memory, the bit I've never quite fathomed, the quiet pool of dissonance that still remembers the primeval forest and labelled me a naturalist. I always seem to have one ear cocked to the wide-open window beside me.

I was out of bed in a flash. They circled the house in a broad arc not far above the trees, although I could see nothing, just hear this primordial, *sotto voce* oboe-utterance of the night, which, for me, together with the howl of the wolf and the fluting of common cranes, seems to define boreal wildness – one of the most evocative sounds I know.

I knew from their altitude that they were heading for the loch, so in the morning as soon as I could get away, I came up here to check them out. There they are, Icelandic or not, two adults and four strong cygnets energetically sifting through the marsh. As I appeared on the dam their heads shot up like railway signals and they whooped their little nasal anxieties to each other, nervous and fidgety. I shall watch them quietly for a few minutes from the cover of the birches and then slip away, leaving them in peace. They deserve a rest and a good feed after their long journey.

'What did you see?' Lucy asked me when I arrived back at the house.

'It's winter,' I said. 'Winter's just arrived.'

# 14

# The Goshawk

But Hark! the cry is Astur,
And Lo! the ranks divide,
And the Great Lord of Luna
Comes with his stately stride.
> – Thomas Babington Macaulay,
> *Lays of Ancient Rome*, 'Horatius'

*November 12th*　Sometimes things just happen. They catch you off guard and knock you sideways. The totally unexpected barges in and knocks your complacency for six. It's one of the tricks nature just likes to play to keep you on your toes.

I went to my desk early on at 7.05 a.m.; I have always worked best in the mornings. As dawn broke across the valley all the signals were of a singularly unexceptional early winter day: a morning mild enough, but with flurries of spitty rain on a bracing breeze from the west, this from a uniform, burdensome sky offering nothing to raise the spirits at all. I worked with one eye on the window, waiting for the rain to stop. At 9.30 a.m. I stared across to the river, in two minds about heading out or not. The day looked dull; nothing unusual about the rooks and jackdaws flocking back and forth from the river fields in rowdy mobs. My only thought was that they were making more of their day than I was mine. A buzzard glided idly past on fixed wings, unhurried about his business. Then the rain cleared and the sky began to lift from weary old lead to a cheerier top-lit grey – the friendlier pinky-grey of a collared dove or a greylag goose in sunlight. That did it – all the excuse I needed. I was up and away in a flash.

I didn't have much time; a man was coming to see me about computers at eleven o'clock, so I thought I would hurry round the loch in under an hour, just sufficient for some fresh air and a leg stretch, and on the way I would check out the peanuts I had scattered for a young male badger who had taken up temporary residence among the roots of a huge clump of western red cedar at the end of the orchard. It was going to be one of those mornings: a quick walk, some scribbled notes – perhaps on the badger, or a squirrel, or the number of mallard I disturbed from the marsh – and then back to my study for what promised to be a yawningly tedious meeting.

In the boot-room I hauled on my old trudgers (beloved Vibram-soled lace-ups, heavy and strong, that I hope will never wear out), grabbed my long stick, slung my faithful Swarovski binoculars round my neck, heaved into my old coat with a hurrumph of the shoulders and broke out into air as cool and fresh as a Glacier Mint. My mood went on lightening with the clouds. It's energising to hit the fresh air after being cooped up inside since before dawn. I took off up the Avenue, kicking the copper drifts of horse chestnut and lime leaves for sheer pleasure. At the burn I crossed the old farm track at the little bridge and turned west up the hill. As I did so I heard a thud behind me.

I turned round to look and listen. Nothing. I was about to press on when I changed my mind and decided to investigate. It had been a serious thud, not just any old thud from, say, conkers or a dead stick falling from above. It was weightier and more forceful in a way that would have hurt if it had hit you. There was something purposeful – even powerful – about it. I couldn't place it and it nagged at me. I like to name the various authors of nature's noises and pride myself on knowing most of the sounds around my home without a second thought.

Back on the track I could see nothing out of place. I cast around, wondering. Then I saw it. Beside the fence, only fifteen yards away, partly obscured by some dead bracken fronds, a large hawk sat crouched over a woodpigeon. The thud had been the pigeon slamming into something. I froze. Through my binoculars I could see that something was terribly wrong. The hawk – a fine male goshawk – was swaying with his bill agape, dazed. I realised that in the final gut-wrenching dash of the stoop, locked together, they must have hit the fence post, not the ground, and the goshawk had all but knocked itself out. I approached carefully.

He sat over the pigeon and glowered drunkenly at the world. Then he saw me and a surge of anger flooded through him. He lashed out with his wings in an attempt to take off with the pigeon, but fell back, panting. This goshawk was going nowhere. The burst of useless energy seemed to have defeated him, and he relaxed his grip on the pigeon, stepping off and lurching – he would have fallen over if he hadn't propped himself up on half-spread wings. The extremely lucky pigeon saw his chance and flew away with a clatter of grateful wings. The goshawk seemed unable to move.

Carefully and slowly I picked him up, coming in from behind and pressing his wings firmly closed with both hands, catching his legs underneath with my fingers so that he couldn't snag me with his talons, but I needn't have bothered. He was out of it, severely concussed, barely able to hold his head up. Then I saw the eyes. As his awareness came and went, so the brilliant yellow iris flooded with fire and then faded again, seeming to shrink back into his head beneath the hooded ridges of his brows. Just once on the way home he seemed to come alive and turned to glare at me. The eyes impaled me fleetingly and burned with inextinguishable murder.

I was captivated and engrossed by this rare chance occurrence. I do see goshawks from time to time; a few years ago they even nested in the tight-bunched spruces in the plantation woods that frame the view from my study window, but I had never held one before. A normal sighting would be a bird soaring buzzard-like above the nest site in spring, or dashing through the trees in a streak of power and grace – in either case no chance to examine its tightly sculpted form, its broad wings of Ballachulish slate and long, charcoal-barred tail, its horizontally striped and chequered breast feathers in grey and fawn like the waved sands of a low tide, the short, ripping downward curve of the beak as fierce as a fish-hook, topped with bright dandelion nares that matched the bright ankles and the twiggy feet.

I took him outside for one last, long look. Then I eased my grip to see if he was ready to go. The mad, marigold eyes now burned with an unquenchable anger as though they would explode. The talons pulsed into my gloves – for a moment I thought they would go straight through and curve deep into my flesh and I would be pinned down to the ground awaiting execution like the unhappy pigeon. His neck stretched disbelievingly, his head swivelled, scowling round just once before lifting from my gloves in one quick, downward thrust of his long, broad wings. He flew straight and powerfully up and away, rising all the time, straight to a dead branch near the top of a red oak tree some seventy yards away. His talons gripped the perch and he trod it, as though he was testing himself, and shuffled his wings at the shoulders before crossing them behind his back like a lofty schoolmaster. Then he rose again. Springing into the living air he lifted on quick, down-flicking wings directly and purposefully out across the valley. Over the river, now well above the skyline, he soared in a tight circle once, twice, and then he rowed away over the horizon. My walk was over, time up. I had to return to my desk, but not for long.

Something was calling me outside again. I hadn't done with this awesome, unsettling bird. I longed to see him again. As soon as I could get away I rushed out with my binoculars to see if I could find him. I drove a frantic mile up the glen road, and then a mile down the river side, searching, searching. But he was gone. He had vanished into the great beyond of hills and moors and woods that frame my world and his. I felt empty. It was as though someone I had loved and lost had returned for the briefest moment and then gone again, leaving me bereft. In the physical world I had lost him, quite possibly forever, but in my brain he still burned and raged like a fever. I went back to my study and started to research this remarkable raptor.

I kill where I please because it is all mine.
There is no sophistry in my body:
My manners are tearing off heads –
The allotment of death.
                    – Ted Hughes, 'Hawk Roosting'

The goshawk seems to have been first described by Aldrovandus in the fifteenth century. Aldrovandus, I read, graduated from the universities of Padua and Bologna with degrees in law, philosophy and medicine. He was an early naturalist whose first name, appropriately, was Ulysses (Ulisse Aldrovandi), and during his studies in hydrology, botany, zoology and ornithology he developed a special affection for goshawks, formerly known as goose-hawks (which gives you some idea of the power of these round-winged raptors). He named the species 'pigeon-hawks' after their commonest prey: *Astur palumbarius* – Astur because the species appears to have been first formally recorded in the province of Asturias in north-west Spain. In his 16 folio volumes of *Historia Naturalium*, printed in 1605, Aldrovandus calls the goshawk the bird of Apollo because he is sacred to the sun. This can only refer to his flaming eye. Later he states: *Attilae Hunorum Regi hominum truculentissimo, qui flagellum Dei dictus fuit, ita*

*placuit Astur, ut in insigni, galea, et pileo eum coronatum gestaret.*
'To Attila King of the Huns, the most truculent of men,
who used to be called the Scourge of God, the goshawk was
such a charmer that he bore it crowned on his badge, his
helm and his helmet.'

I read and read. In 1758 the Swedish taxonomist Carl
Linnaeus, perhaps also gripped by the flaming eye, thought
it deserved to be with the aristocracy of the hooked beaks,
the falcons, naming it *Falco gentilis*, but it was inevitable
that sooner or later its rounded wings would haul it off.
Nowadays ornithological taxonomists have recognised its
close relationship to sparrowhawks and other broad, blunt-
winged hawks in the family Accipitridae (which also includes
kites, buzzards, eagles and vultures), and awarded it its own
true hawk genus, *Accipiter*, retaining Linnaeus's specific
nomination so that, with characteristic scientific under-
statement it has become *Accipiter gentilis*, 'the hawk of
hawks', almost as though the boffins were lost for words.
It's hard to know which way to read it. Is it intended to be
the definitive species of the family, or does a flavour of
Aldrovandus's clearly stated respect and awe follow through
to Linnaeus, who honours it by subtly toying with the
superlative: as the rose is the flower of flowers, so is the
goshawk the hawk of hawks? If Aldrovandus had been
around to have his say I am in no doubt. *Ut rosa flos florum,
hic Astur accipiter accipitorum est.*

The more I discovered about this bird, the more remarkable it seemed to be. Every reference in every bird book
I searched seemed to be in awe of it. I found myself automatically turning to G in the indexes of volume after

volume, grasping every nuance. The word 'respect' cropped up over and over again. In one, a modest field guide to the birds of Europe with only the most token descriptions, the authors had broken with their own protocol and allowed the space to state clearly: 'Causes great consternation among crows, which give shrill screams and mob it with great respect and always keeping a line of retreat open.' Not just among crows.

I learn that it is known to take full-grown brown hares, rabbits, squirrels and rats as well as many bird species: wild geese and ducks, all the crow family, herons, pheasants and grouse, and even capercaillie, the biggest grouse in the world. Its chosen hunting method is solitary ambush in the bosky dusk, the true cobwebby dusk of deep woods, combined with rare aerial agility, often lurking in cover and shooting out to take prey by surprise or rolling sideways or upside down and snatching with one foot a rising bird from beneath. When hawking pigeons it takes on peregrine tactics, stooping from a great height and striking the pigeon in mid-air with both feet – this must have been what my bird did, until it hit the fence post.

For four days I read nothing but goshawks. The bird had infiltrated my dreams. In half-sleep I followed him jinking through the trees, perching momentarily before furiously launching himself at unsuspecting pigeons and crows. I heard jackdaws and rooks crying out in alarm, scattering with a clatter of wings. I felt the rush of wind in vibrating pinions as he stooped on closed wings at a heron over the loch, its rough-edged, startled cry waking me so that I sat up in bed convinced it had been real. And I dreamed of soaring with him on those long, blunt wings, high above the pinewood, circling, eyeing and marking the panicky trail of mallard far below as they fled the marsh for the river. More than once I awoke sweating, certain that the hawk was perched on the foot of the bed, those manic eyes flaring in the darkness.

My researches led me to T.H. White's engaging classic *The Goshawk* (1951), in which he tries to train a goshawk for falconry. Tim White's prose, primed with superlatives, respect and awe for this species, honours his bird:

> The yellowish breast feathers – Naples yellow – were streaked downwards with long, arrow-shaped hackles of burnt umber: his talons, like scimitars, clutched the leather glove on which he stood with a convulsive grip: for an instant he stared at me with a mad dandelion eye, all his plumage flat to the body and his head crouched like a snake's in fear or hatred, then bated wildly from the fist.

And then, almost predictably, since training his beloved Gos had been such a trial, he loses him forever. In a retrospective passage at the end of the book he muses:

> I remember him mainly by his armour-plated shins, with the knotted toes ending in their gripping scimitars. I wear a beard, and he once struck me on the chin. I can remember standing, grinning like a wolf, as the blood plied and roped itself in the hairy tangle, while Gos went on feeding. I can remember the feathery 'plus fours' which covered his upper thighs, and the way in which the muscles there would clench convulsively when he was in his tyranny. He was a Hittite, a worshipper of

Moloch. He immolated victims, sacked cities, put virgins and children to the sword. He was never a shabby tiger. He was a Prussian officer in a pickelhaube, flashing a monocle, who sabred civilians when they crossed his path. He would have got on excellently with Attila, the most truculent of men. He was an Egyptian hieroglyph, a winged bull of Assyria. He was one of the lunatic dukes or 'cardinals in the Elizabethan plays of Webster.

I have handled aristocratic peregrines, heraldic ospreys and haughty eagles, tiny, darting merlins and many kestrels and owls in my time, always with great respect. Slightly in awe, I have loved them all; birds of prey are possessed of an hauteur which supersedes arrogance – a sort of languid superiority and indifference to the entire world. But I had never handled a goshawk before. This *Astur* made a deeper and, I suspect, a more lasting impression on me than any of the others. Even holding him for only a few minutes, I knew instinctively there was no flicker of clemency in his soul, nor any hint of submission, only a total and all-consuming terrorism. That unforgettable eye flared like the sun, and entered my skull. I tell you, he entered my skull and lives there yet.

# 15

# Pop Goes the Weasel

Weasel! I had never seen one wild before. He was ten inches long, thin as a curve, a muscled ribbon, brown as fruitwood, soft-furred, alert. His face was fierce, small and pointed as a lizard's; he would have made a good arrowhead.

– Annie Dillard, 'Living Like Weasels'

*November 27th*  Before leaving the house today I had phoned a smart department store to enquire about buying some special perfume my wife had said she would like for Christmas. Since I detest cities and almost never go into a shop (although I have always found proper, old-fashioned, small, country-town ironmongers irresistible), the prospect of doing it by mail order was appealing. The woman I spoke to was brisk and confident, but also very helpful. I told her the brand and I quickly learned that it was available in various forms. 'I want the best,' I pronounced resolutely, as if the very suggestion of anything less was an affront – besides, I didn't much like the sound of 'toilet water'. Quite unfazed she said 'Yes, sir, of course,' and then she revealed the price, adding 'plus postage and packing'. I gulped. 'Are you still there?' she asked after a few seconds of silence.

'This must be the most expensive liquid in the world,'

I said at last, struggling to muster a little equilibrium after such a vicious body blow. 'Do you realise that's *five times* as expensive as whisky!'

'Oh, I'm sure it is,' she announced in the same superior voice, but now with a clearly detectable tonal seasoning of 'Who-is-this-twit?'

'I'll let you know,' I answered feebly, and rang off.

It was all very shocking. It had never occurred to me that a tiny vial of perfume, which, in small doses is designed to evaporate off into thin air, could command such a flagrantly disproportionate price. I went off the idea and set out on my walk, pushing vigorously uphill, hoping that the bracing November air would clear my head and that perhaps some other inspiration would happen along.

The path was ribbed with dry leaves of birch, hornbeam and willow in multiple shades of cigar ginger through to the sunlit-daffodil dazzle of aspen, piled into ridges and banks by the winds. I zigzagged along, scuffing my feet through them just to relive that familiar wild-wood rustle so evocative of childhood walks in scarves and welly boots. This tonic quickly restored my humour so that I forgot about perfume; a faithful old ruse that has helped me shrug off my grumps more times than I can count.

After half a mile I emerged from the forest at a dry-stone dyke which now separated the moorland from the woods, but which over a century and a half ago, when it was first erected back in the age of subsistence crofting, had been lovingly and skilfully built at back-breaking human cost to separate the old 'in-bye' land where crops were grown, from the great unfenced expanse of upland grazing. With

Highlanders moved off the land in the early nineteenth century (the infamous Clearances), or simply deserting it for a better life elsewhere, there was no one to repair the old walls and they often fell into rubble.

This one had crumbled badly, totally collapsing in places where marauding red deer desperate for the better grazing down by the river had jumped up onto the top coping stones, immediately pushing off again in a forward leap, simultaneously kicking the stones backwards. Once there was a breach, deer lining up to use it night after night, often twenty animals at a time, quickly plucked out the stones until there was a wide gap. After years of prevarication we had finally got round to doing something about it.

As is common in all country districts, our walls are made from local stones gathered off the land and from the beds of streams; in our case they are the metamorphic schist and gneiss of the mountains, hard and heavy, rounded by ice and melt-water, the jettisoned cargo of retreating glaciers. To fit them together in a stable structure seems to the uninitiated to be an impossible task. To do it well, well enough to withstand snow, frost, wind, storm and lashing rain as well as the rubbing of cattle and horses, and the desperate acrobatics of deer, so well that it will last for centuries, requires a creative synergy between hand and eye, the legs, back and biceps of a shot-putter and a total dedication to the craft.

Tim Neilsen had (very sensibly) abandoned an accountancy career for the altogether more stimulating skills of a dry-stane dyker. When I asked him why, he said there really wasn't much contest. The freedom of self-employment, the creative dexterity, the fresh mountain air, the wildlife, all this compounded with the absence of bureaucracy and regulation, the satisfaction of the job well done and the not inconsiderable rates of pay he could charge for his highly skilled and sought-after handiwork had proved irresistible. Tim had arrived with a young helper to tackle the repair job – a process that often means unbuilding the dyke first and then building it up again. It's an art that I love to watch – that subtle convergence of eye and instinct when the stone he bends to pick up, turned thoughtfully by calloused, knowing fingers, slots precisely into the gap he had in mind. So I went and sat quietly by while Tim sorted stones into piles of different sizes and shapes as surely and meticulously as a cashier sorts coins.

I perched on a stump, a huge old Caledonian pine felled long ago by Canadian soldier-lumberjacks who had been sent north to pillage these and many other Highland woods for the insatiable and all-consuming demands of World War II. The stump was now almost completely rotted, a deep, moss-filled crater and an incomplete ring of wood just wide enough to support my backside. I peered into its dark, fungally interior – something wasn't right. It seemed that the moss had been recently disturbed. I pried further, carefully lifting a domed, green hassock of *Polytrichum*, marsh hair moss. Underneath was a bed of soft, dry, fibrous and needly litter with the sort of heady, mother-earth scent you'd expect from someone practising aromatherapy in a potting shed. This layer, too, seemed loose. I pushed my fingers into it and came to fresh, dry oak leaves. How could fresh leaves get underneath moss? Now I knew someone was at home. A finger teased gently into the leaves withdrew smartly – it was very prickly.

from another stump I laid carefully over the top as a token of my esteem. Foxes and badgers will unroll a hibernating hedgehog and rip out the soft tissues, leaving only the empty, spiny skin as a macabre flag to their efficiency. We have plenty of both predators foraging through our winter woods, and while I don't believe in interfering with nature – a complicated ethic I have often struggled with – I certainly didn't want to be the cause of her demise. I asked Tim to keep well clear of her stump and I finished off with a couple of dead spruce branches across the top for good measure.

Hedgehogs, dormice, horseshoe bats and adders (among many other species) all hibernate properly, secreted away the whole winter through. Their temperature drops and their heartbeat and metabolic rate close right down, a condition from which they are unable to recover until a sufficient period of warmth arouses them; whereas badgers, red squirrels, and some other bats just become a bit sluggish with the cold, hole up for a few days at a time during the worst weather, but often break out again with a thaw. But the clever little pipistrelle bat, our commonest, has evolved a heterothermic torpor which switches on and off with self-evident non-chalance. When the cold snap comes he winds right down to minimal heartbeat and much lower body temperature, which, since there aren't any flying insects about anyway in those conditions, is very sensible. He sleeps soundly until – Bingo! – as soon as the wind shifts to the Atlantic west and the temperature lifts to permit a few moths to venture forth, the pipistrelle fires himself up and pops out for a meal.

One frosty winter day many years ago we were demolishing an old barn when we came across a dozen pipistrelle bats huddled together deep inside the hefty gable, built in the manner of all old farm buildings in the Highlands, of large field stones and lime fill. Over the centuries the lime crumbles and falls or washes out and cavities and crevices appear – perfect refuges for bats. The huge stones were being hauled out in bucketfuls by a digger. The driver, a friend and neighbour who was sympathetic to my interest in wildlife, called me over. He had stopped just in time. The bats were unharmed but definitely semi-torpid. They were incapable of moving at all; just little furry bundles of slightly twitching, leathery ears and wings. We carefully collected them up in a cardboard box and took them into another old building, where they stayed until the temperature rose. One mild day still in mid-winter I went to look. They were gone. They had awoken, crawled out and taken flight to hunt. I don't know where they went for their next shut-down, but these old buildings and slate roofs are so well supplied with deep crannies that I am sure they quickly found a new roost.

It seems likely that some hibernating animals in the UK (and, of course, elsewhere) will suffer from rapid climate change. Such creatures need frosts to trigger their torpor and long periods of cold to keep them torpid. The worst thing that can happen to a hibernating hedgehog, for instance, is to wake up in mid-winter because the temperature is too warm, only to find there is nothing to eat, and then to be caught out and about if a cold snap comes along. There is already some evidence that hedgehogs are breeding later and later in the year and that the young don't have sufficient time to forage for the essential fat they need to lay down for hibernation. Those animals almost certainly perish, but colossal foundation boulders bedded deeply into the substrate for a firm footing, boulders that must have required several men with levers to prise into place. It was a bit of the wall you never normally see, and I was impressed. These huge boulders made the base of the wall, the basement course below ground level, fully five feet wide. I stood pondering the effort needed to create this linear edifice and the men who did it. Glimpses of their history and their motivation were silently revealing themselves to us. There was something heroic about this dyke.

The men who built it laboured mightily: hauling the boulders in from the fields and the burn beds on pony sledges and crude carts, many stones far bigger than a man can lift on his own; laying them out in long, heaped lines for the skilled dykers to pick from; smashing them with sledge-hammers (named because they were carried on the sledges for breaking boulders too big to lift) to provide the in-fill; running to help when the shout went up for levers and muscle – men returning to their cottages sore-backed and exhausted at the end of the day – and all this epic of physical achievement for minimal pay or perhaps none at all.

The Highlanders must have needed the dykes very badly, an essential prop to their primitive subsistence agriculture, a vital protection of the cropland upon which they all depended, the reward of permanence and security greater than the human cost of construction. They weren't just building for their own needs, although that was an important part of their self-evident motivation; they were building for their long future, for the unborn generations of crofters to come, who they undoubtedly imagined would need dykes just as much. When this one was erected there would have been little thought of emigration.

The exposed sections were also revealing. Each beautifully aligned outer course leaned in to a rock-filled centre as the wall rose, packed around with chock stones and hefty tie-stones, flat and long, that crossed right through the middle to lock it all together. Rebuilding it was a slow and achingly laborious process, yet deeply satisfying to see the final structure, so functional and pleasing to the eye. One thing is certain: if those men were paid at all, it wasn't by the hour.

But it was not the structure of the wall Tim had called me over to see. Deep inside the base of the wall he'd found someone else's winter quarters. At first I thought it was a woodmouse nest, but it was too bulky and intricately crafted of moss and grass with a few blackbird feathers worked into a sheep's wool lining. I knelt on the firm earth to see. I teased open its woven layers. I was unprepared for the flood of animal musk that assaulted me. A tidal wave of evocation pulsed through, swamping me with instant recognition and familiarity. 'Weasel,' I said.

As a schoolboy I had reared an orphaned weasel called Wilba. There never was a cleaner, more alert and intelligent, more mischievous, more spontaneously playful and utterly enchanting animal companion. He was blind and helpless, and I dripped milk and glucose into his tiny mouth. He lived. In a few days his eyes opened and his teeth broke through like needles. As the weeks passed he grew strong and inquisitive, living variously in the breast pocket of my tweed jacket or in a small cardboard box in my desk, enacting the proverbial recipe by popping in and out of the inkwell hole present in all school desks in those days. When a master came along I pushed a book over the hole to keep him in place; as soon as the coast was clear I let him out again, to the fascination and complete distraction of my fellow pupils, running riot over my work and my person.

Being a mustelid, one of the family that have a scent gland under their tails (polecats, otters, badgers, stoats, martens etc.), it made everything, including my entire wardrobe, reek of that wild, sensual, animal unguent that was for so long the foundation of most expensive perfumes. And here it was again, calling as loudly and resoundingly as a scent can call. I was sure that back in the summer this nest had housed young. A litter of mouse bones and mangled fur cluttered the passages leading to it. The nest itself was still clean and fresh, quite unfouled, as is typical of most members of the weasel family; I felt sure it was still being used as a winter bed, perhaps by several at once.

As I bade Tim farewell to continue my walk my head was full of weasels; I became engulfed in a nostalgic weasel haze. I had often seen them nipping in and out of dry-stone dykes, but never really given thought to the walls as a breeding site. Having now seen such a nest, so brilliantly sited, like the hedgehog's, deep and secure, and explored the inner structure of the dyke, I realised how ideal these ancient upland walls were in every respect. Weasels must imagine that dry-stone dykes are built entirely for them: dry, safe and sheltered – and long, linear hunting galleries to boot.

The crevices and interstices are so numerous that a weasel can pop in and out almost anywhere he chooses. He reigns over these stone walls; he is the undisputed gallery king. His cousin the stoat – whom he rightly fears – is too big. A stoat might find one or two gaps he can squeeze into, but once inside he will be severely limited. No, the weasel is the unchallenged lord of this labyrinthine metamorphic fief. He can climb to the heights at his pleasure, impaling the world on bright, intelligent eyes from among the coping stones, four and a half feet above the land. He can run the long boulder canyons deep inside, drop down on unsuspecting mice, raid their nests, nip out to the forest or the moor, and dart back in again for sanctuary when the watching buzzard stoops or the fox prowls. When brute north-easters rage and snow piles up in drifts forcing most animals underground he can curl himself up in a nest far away from the slicing cold. At breeding time he can impress his weasel wife with choices: an extravagant array of impenetrable, vaulted palaces as grand and secure as Camelot.

Weasels are tiny. The best demonstration of this I have seen is in an old nature pamphlet on weasels by the late Professor Ian Linn of Exeter University, in whose formalin-reeking Hatherley Laboratories I once gleaned some basic zoology. He tells of an old West Country saying that weasels are small enough to squeeze through a wedding ring. This is illustrated by a photograph of a weasel skull comfortably passing through a gold band. Using his head as a gauge Wilba could squeeze into tiny apertures; so supple and slender was his body that if his head could pass through, so could everything else.

Tiny they may be, but the measure of a weasel's heart is in terror, not size. Pound for pound they are among the most ferocious predators I know – some say the fiercest, vying even with the wildcat. A glance at the jaws tells a horror story in itself – full carnivorous dentition, a Himalaya of jagged teeth fronted with four curving fangs – the canines – long, sharp and very strong. Its jaws are also built for power and leverage; the skull has wide zygomatic arches – the cheek bones – to accommodate the braided thongs of muscles passing through them, and a pronounced ridge at the back of the cranial cavity where the neck and jaw muscles meet and anchor. If a weasel latches onto your finger you have the devil of a job to get it off. Just as well it's small – the notion of a weasel the size of a leopard is something at which even God's heart quailed.

Mice and voles make up their principal prey, both of which are also rather unadvisedly drawn to the cosy basements of dykes to build their nests, although weasels will not hesitate at killing prey many times their size and weight: rats, squirrels, rabbits and hares. So our wall weasels have the best of both worlds: a perfect hunting ground stretching for miles across the hills and an ideal home, all thoughtfully and painstakingly erected by the skilled hands of men like Tim Neilsen.

I walk on. My brain fizzes quietly; the dark ur-pungence of musk is surfing primeval tides inside my head. All those years ago that weasel entered my arteries and invaded my heart. Now, brought face to face with fresh scent, I can think of nothing but weasels. 'Just what is going on here?' I ask myself. Weasels in the wall galleries and caves, hunting mice, under the ground, under the snow – a whole other weasel world spinning and churning beneath my feet. I must have passed by a thousand times without properly thinking through what goes on within. This wall is a linear Serengeti of cyclical fecundity and predation locked away inside its own private citadel. Mankind has laboured and brought forth a weasel cathedral. I want to shrink myself down so that I can pass through a wedding ring; to follow the scent through those dim, vaulted galleries and caverns, feel the pulse quicken, see the sparkle in the hunting eye, the raised paw, sense the fear-bolt pierce the mouse's leaping heart. I want to be there for the pounce, hear the muffled scream, witness the tiger fangs crunching into the base of the skull, the bead of blood staining the golden fur.

> Wee, sleekit, cowrin', tim'rous beastie,
> O, what a panic's in thy breastie!

I know exactly why there's a panic in his breastie. He and his kind have evolved over hundreds of thousands of years of panic – pure weasel panic. The spectre of the tiny, murdering weasel lurks in every twitching synapse of his mousy being.

I had to teach Wilba to hunt. Like most predators, weasel instinct needs parental guidance to acquire skills. I weaned him on tiny slivers of mice caught live in Longworth traps; later I killed them and opened the skin just enough to reveal flesh and flowing blood, immediately before presenting them to him whole. Even as a tiny kit, Wilba would lunge at the wound and bury his tiny needle fangs into it.

After a few weeks I no longer had to kill them – I just released them into his box. Instantaneously his body became tense, sinews as taut as violin strings; the little, angled face thrust forward, jet eyes burning. The wretched mouse cowered in a corner, paralysed by the omnipresent musk of his darkest dread. Inseparably, the pounce and the kill flashed – a sudden dart of chestnut fur, a blurred lunge as the four daggers closed on the back of the mouse's skull and fixed there. In a second the mouse was a lifeless corpse being dragged by that same death clinch into the private confines of Wilba's lair. Later still I took him into the woods to hunt for himself, only resorting to trapped mice if he was unsuccessful.

For a few short weeks this daily ritual was to become deeply engraved upon my psyche. Not only was Wilba growing and learning, soon to vanish back into the wilds that spawned him, but I was learning too. I was fourteen and although a keen formative naturalist I had no deeper training than the freedom of a wild country boyhood. Then, as now, the brutal realities of carnal nature were not taught, nor were they widely understood by the generality of the public (although in an endearing code the remarkably unsentimental Beatrix Potter had less than gently alluded to them by telling her child readers that Peter Rabbit's father had been killed by Mr McGregor and eaten in a pie). In school such essential truths were barely mentioned; certainly no one had then or subsequently ever explained to me that death and killing lay at the throbbing heart of all nature – and this stark exposure with Wilba was surely both, as real as they get, hour after hour, day after day.

To be there, lying full length among the ground elder and the damp Devon grass; to be anchored by the life-trust this tiny, instinct-driven carnivore had unthinkingly placed in me;

to witness his expanding skills honing the ferocious killing machine he would need to be to survive; to have his prey proudly dragged back to me and paraded – shown off – inches in front of my nose without ever letting go; to watch the feed until his tiny belly bulged, and then to take him home curled up in my pocket, was a deeply private and personal catharsis I have never forgotten.

As I turned back to the house that bright November afternoon, my head was still brimming with weasels. It had been that scent: that quintessentially wild, indefinable, time-eliding pungence that had spun me back all those years; had gifted that happy remembrance to my walk. That did it. If scent could be that evocative, could reel me back forty-five years in a jiffy, bring the lump to my throat and the prickle of lost innocence to my eyes, I reckoned the perfume was probably worth the money after all.

# 16

# Winter

Yet I have glimpsed the bright mountain behind the mountain,
Knowledge under the leaves, tasted the bitter berries red,
Drunk water cold and clear from an inexhaustible hidden
fountain.

– Kathleen Raine, 'The Wilderness'

There is a winter in all of us. A settling back, a reflection,
a long exhalation, a sigh of both apprehension and accept-
ance. Yesterday I watched Geordie gathering his lambs and
bringing them in off the high pasture. The young collie, Tam,
barked and circled excitedly. Geordie raised his crummack
in admonition; I couldn't hear the scowl, but I know it was
there. Tam obeyed instantly, dogging in to heel. The ewes
clamoured and huddled, their fat lambs barely distinguishable now to the untrained eye, just a jostling shoal of fleece
mindlessly bleating away, out of my vision down the farm
track. Those sights and sounds won't return to the hills for
many months. The lambs have gone to market, the breeding
stock held on the low ground all winter. It's a closing down,
a withdrawal, a transhumance of spirit and soul; winter is
coming on. That's the way things are.

The sun struggles now. It has lost its nerve. Senility has

crept in so that it seems to be being bullied by the clouds, shunted and hustled around its low ellipse almost as if it is an unwanted stranger, now ostracised and subordinated as if it's in the way of the weather's pressing business. Day by day the sun that has given so much, that led from the front with such power and panache for so long, has deserted us. It crawls crab-like, ought-not-to-be-here-like along our lumpy horizon and ducks away again behind the mountains long before a sensible day's work is done, leaving us groping in the dusk. The Highland winter is a lonely affair.

It is winter. In the marsh and the trackside ditch, in the loch's peaty mires, in the pinewood, under bark scales, beneath stones, in burrows and setts deep underground, in lofts and old sheds, beneath the slates of roofs, in drifts of leaves and rotting stumps, in wood stacks and muck heaps, deep inside clumps of grass and dry-stone dykes, the pulses of life have slowed. Like the tourist hotels and guest houses the nature of the Highlands has shut up shop; the signs have all come down. It is winter. The bugs and weevils are hiding now, the worms, the millipedes, the caterpillars and leatherjackets, the wood ants, the damsel flies, the frog and the toad, the newt and the rainbow trout, the adder, the slow worm, the woodmouse and vole, the squirrel, the hedgehog and the fat, snoring badger are settled in for the long, dark cold.

Many of the flying insects are dead, like the corpses of dragonflies gripped to the stems of rushes in a last embrace, as rigid as wire. Their work is done; their future lies in the eggs, now secure among water-lily leaves frost-browned and rotting beneath the ice. The long-eared bats have vanished from the roof, migrated off south in pursuit of warmth and insects; dozens of twitching bundles of fur and membranous ears jammed into the apex under the slates, there one minute, gone the next. All but the toughest birds have headed south; the golden plovers are long gone from the hills, their plaintive, piping calls faded away in the night, down to the estuaries and the mud flats where they have gathered in flocks before pressing on further south. The high hills are empty but for the golden eagle and the snow-white ptarmigan; above the loch the buzzards scream back at the croaking jeers of ravens and hoodie crows, the only sounds, the only movement to be seen.

Always impulsive by nature, my walks now become opportunist as well. I duck the December sleet squalls and the stinging rain, picking my moment and dashing out when the day allows. It is no less interesting; natural history may slow with the season, but it never stops. There is always something to see and note down, always something unexpected and exciting. Two mornings ago I met a fox, as red as a rowan berry, luminous and fired, backlit by the low, lifting sun. With his nose to the ground he was trotting down the track towards me so lightly and soundlessly that his pads seemed barely to be touching the ground. I saw him first – always a score – and he kept coming. At fifteen yards he caught my scent and looked up, startled. I could see his sharply drawn breath and, in a fleeting instant of horror, the man-dread flashed in his wide, amber eyes. Men and foxes do not keep company in these glens of crofts and hill sheep farms. In the blink of an eye he was gone, vanished into the broom bushes beside the path.

Seconds later I saw him streaking away across Geordie's steep field heading up to the dark depths of the forestry. He knew I was watching him go and he was taking no chances. What intrigued me was his use of cover where there was none. The field undulates and ripples with secret hollows and defiles of dead ground. This fox knew all about men and guns. At full tilt he kept out of sight so effectively that all I saw was a rufous blur streaming from cover to cover until he topped the high ridge and disappeared for good. As J.A. Baker evinces so powerfully in his elegiac masterpiece *The Peregrine*, 'We are the killers. We stink of death. We carry it with us. It sticks to us like frost. We cannot tear it away.'

There is winter in me. As Shelley insists in his 'Ode to the West Wind', I know that winter means that spring cannot be far behind, that the skies will clear and leaf will burst again; birds will stream into the loch-side woods and fill them with jubilant song, swallows will hawk and swoop over the surface of the loch and chatter once more from the beams in the stables roof. Hovering house martins will gum their sticky mud cups beneath the eaves. The sow badger will bring her fluffy cubs above ground and the otter bitch will whistle to her kits in the marsh. If they survive the long, perilous migration from West Africa, the ospreys will drop yet more sticks onto their already weighty nest mound in the top of the pine tree beside the river. These things I know and they give me the hope and optimism I need to see me through the long, dark days ahead.

Winter turns me introspective. In the long evenings I stare into the flames of the log fire – I could not survive without a fire – and think about the land and its wildlife, about the people who have lived here down the centuries and what drives us to be what we are. Knowledge becomes a burden, all thought a penance.

Mankind has come so far. The achievements of Stanley Miller (who died in California aged seventy-seven as I was writing this book) and his experiments to create amino acids now seem archaic in the terms of present-day organic chemistry. We possess phenomenal knowledge about the hard physics and the biochemistry of our planet and its life-support systems. Our information technology can watch us from outer space, Google Earth can home in on the car parked outside our houses, we can send messages round the globe in an instant. And yet we face an apparently catastrophic global ecological crisis. Accelerating global warming and climate change will affect us all. Billions of people will become homeless as rising sea levels flood low-lying countries such as Bangladesh. Millions more will run out of drinking water. The world's fish stocks are plummeting as a result of over-fishing. We are no longer just the killers, we are now the destroyers, tipping the world into a new epoch of extinctions more devastating than anything previously imagined. Man-kind's progress has become manic, an insane rush downhill that was always going to end in a crash.

Our rush for what we call 'progress' is a particularly cutting-nose-to-spite-face brand of blindness. In the business and commercial world and in almost every walk of life I can think of, when the cause of a serious problem is known and understood and those in charge continue to ignore it, blindly pressing on towards damage and destruction, it is condemned as professional negligence and people act quickly to remove those responsible and put in place the necessary remedial policies. Yet in both local and global environmental politics we press on regardless.

In the West, democracy – the political system we pursue with almost religious zeal and which is supposed to deliver emancipation and uphold freedom – seems to be floundering, out of its depth; it has no mechanism for telling the great majorities who nurture it to stop. Perhaps one day the environment will prove to be its nemesis. Politicians claim to understand the issues but argue that the devil is always in the detail and that no one can make sweeping changes to human behaviour and survive politically. So we tinker at the edges or we don't make any at all. Since Kyoto in 1997 we have wasted ten whole years, ten years of not just agreeing to differ, but ten years of not even agreeing to discuss the issues.

Of course the devil *is* in the detail, but that is no excuse for crass short-termism and negligence. The facts are plain to see. In the final analysis, commercial profits and glossy lifestyles and consumption-driven economic growth are not the life-support mechanisms our leaders would have us believe; they are indices of our own greed and selfishness. What matters to us all far more than anything money can buy or any return on capital, and what in any logical fiscal system deserves to be treated at a higher level of importance than even health, defence and constitutional affairs, are the real life-support systems – clean air to breathe and water to drink, sustainable crops to feed us, a pleasing place to call home and a secure future. And the single biggest factor threatening all of these is human population growth. The planet cannot support the numbers of human beings it presently has without sustaining great damage and losses to the global life-support systems upon which we all depend.

Unchecked population growth is the gravest threat humanity has ever faced. There are already over 6,600 million of us (September 2007) in the world. That figure currently expands by an astonishing 75 million every year (2006 figures). That equates to more than a million people added to the surface of the Earth every five days. A million more mouths to feed, a million more calls on the Earth's already badly creaking natural resources *every five days*.

Numbers of this magnitude are often meaningless and unimaginable, like the number of miles to the sun. We should each of us have a map of the world on the wall in our homes, in a prominent position. Every five days we should take a red marker pin representing a million people and stick it in a habitable point on one of the five continents. After a year or two it would be hard to find places to go on putting pins. And yet, in the name of the popular vote and for fear of upsetting anyone, our leaders stubbornly refuse to address it – in fact, they continue to encourage growth by every means they can.

It has been a delight to lead my life in a wild and beautiful place without overcrowding or urban sprawl and all the pressures and complications that come with it. To be able to study wildlife as a profession has been an honour, a privilege I hope to pursue for many years yet. But it would be irresponsible of me, and a denial of everything I cherish, to write about the uplifting qualities of wildlife while failing to emphasise the over-arching threat human beings present to those very qualities.

The academic debate about the significance of nature, wildlife or wild land in our lives sits at one extreme end of the whole environmental movement. For most people such an abstract notion as nature is an appealing luxury, a bit like theatre or field sports, but for many it is irrelevant to mainstream life, while to others it is entirely fanciful, simply not on the same page as jobs, lifestyles and wealth creation. It is easy to see why politicians are reluctant to discuss the core issues of population and the incipient ecological crisis we are all contributing to. But the ecosystems that support our wildlife are precisely the same as those that support us. We are in there whether we like it or not.

All wildlife needs fresh air and water and a habitat it can call home. Wildlife – all living plants and animals, forests, oceans and the micro-organisms that create our soils – is a resource we all need, whether directly for food, timber, shelter, for medicines, education or research, or indirectly for our sanity and security and spiritual wellbeing. It is also the essential key to natural restoration: that process by which nature heals itself, by which forests grow back and fish stocks recover if they are given a chance, a process we cannot undertake on our own. Ultimately human survival on planet Earth will depend upon the stability of the great ecosystems that have served us so well for so long. Wild creatures are the canaries in the mine. We ignore them at our peril.

Throughout the eighteenth and nineteenth centuries the

Highland population grew too large for the poor-quality land that fed and supported it. Communities in these glens teetered on the brink of starvation – two successive failed harvests or an epidemic of potato blight would have been catastrophic – so they left. In droves they drained out of the glens, as people did throughout the length and breadth of Europe, some ten million of them, and emigrated to North America and other parts of the undeveloped world. That option is no longer available to us. There are no more great continents waiting to be exploited; every continent is now over-populated. It is time to face the problem.

*January 4th*   As Christmas and Hogmanay festivities – those two flagships of consumerism – drew to a close I needed to get out. I took to the loch and on up through the pinewood to the hill beyond. A mile from the house I was in wide, snow-covered, silent moorland. No sun, but a chill, grey burden of cloud, as Kathleen Raine wrote, 'unspeakably troubled', and wisps of mist clutching at the hills. Rime clung to the broom bushes and dead bracken in white-feathered shrouds. There is an Iron Age fort a thousand feet above my home, a strategic viewpoint over the glacial valley, built three thousand years ago for defence and early warning of raiding tribes. It is a diversion from my usual trail, but a place I often go to sort things out. Life seems more sensible up there somehow, easier to throw out the dross and home in on a few truths.

In the snow it is easy to spot the red deer out on the moor.

They stand out like flecks on ermine. I scour round with my binoculars. None today. Last night was cold, −12°C – so cold that the snow crust over the heather will carry my weight unless I stamp my feet, and then I crash through to my knees and have to wade out again. Cold like this drives the deer down into the shelter of the woods, where they have stayed. The moor and mountain are unforgiving in winter. Those without sufficient reserves of fat, or carrying heavy parasite burdens, or the old or lame will not make it through hard weather like this.

My eye is drawn to a patch of darkness on a distant slope. I pull focus. It is a deer, but a dead one, one of the hundreds that will succumb to the constant winter struggle to sustain heat and energy. Then – a movement. Steadying my glasses I can make out the unmistakable hunched silhouette of a golden eagle perched on its flank. It raises its head and glares in my direction, its wing-shoulders flexed like an imperial statue, haughty, almost as though it knows I am watching it. I'm sure it is a big female, a bird I know. Two minutes later I see the reason for her wariness. A second, smaller eagle – her mate – appears above the skyline idly circling on broad glider wings. These are our 'home' pair, occupying a range of some thirty square kilometres, of which we sit at the south-eastern edge. They come and go across our glen all the time, nesting in one of several time-honoured eyries within a few miles of where I live. I am pleased that they have a meal.

Scotland has the highest density of golden eagles in Europe, especially in the mountainous western Highlands and Islands. But that information is misleading. It seems to suggest a healthy ecosystem in which the top predator is doing very well. Not necessarily so. The land conceals many lies. My good friend Dr Jeff Watson, one of the world's leading authorities on golden eagles and author of the definitive work *The Golden Eagle*, tells me that the most reliable measure of success of a species like the eagle is chick production. Throughout continental Europe, where golden eagles are widely distributed, the annual rate of reproduction is 1 to 1.5 fledged chicks per adult breeding pair. That is a healthy level of production and tells us that there is a reliable supply of prey species – notably rabbits and hares and members of the grouse family – throughout their range and that the adults are more than adequately replacing themselves. In other words, although the graph is never a straight line, over ten years it demonstrates a sustainable and gradually expanding population. In the west of Scotland the picture is very different. Chick production is a miserable 0.3 per year, and in the dryer east, which is better for rabbits, hares and grouse, it is still only 0.8–1 chick, well below what it should be.

The reason for this anomalous situation is that historically mankind's intensive use of Scotland's hills has not allowed for the sluggish natural restoration process imposed by our acid rocks, our wet oceanic climate and the seven long months of winter north of the 57th parallel, all of which are inimical to the creation of humus in the soil, the basis for all fertility. Other comparable areas of golden eagle habitat in Europe have more fertile soils, a much dryer continental climate and a shorter winter. Long ago we deforested the Highlands and we have systematically burned and overgrazed the hills for centuries, eliminating natural scrub vegetation (including heather) and unintentionally replacing it with coarse, un-nutritious grasses – a process which destroyed habitat for grouse, hares and other small mammals and moorland birds and the invertebrates they all depend upon. The eagles ought to have failed with them and disappeared long ago, but they were able to hang on because of man's high levels of carrion from sheep farming and the artificially maintained wild deer population on sporting estates. That remains the case today. Without the presence of large numbers of deer and sheep, golden eagle chick production would plunge to an unsustainable level and the population would tip into decline. Jeff also tells me that hill sheep die 'conveniently' – for golden eagles, that is – at regular intervals throughout the winter months, maintaining a constant carrion supply, whereas deer tend to die 'inconveniently', all at once in a hard snap towards the end of winter, making sheep the far more important factor for eagle survival.

What the presence of so much carrion also does is to increase the longevity of the adult eagles, because they are better able to survive the winters – just when carrion is most available – so that they have longer lives during which to produce young, often living up to forty or fifty years. In the dryer east deer and sheep numbers are much lower, so there is far less carrion, but three natural prey species are much stronger – blue mountain hares, ptarmigan and artificially managed red grouse – allowing higher eagle chick production; but it is also much more hazardous. Man the killer raises his ugly head once again. Eagles are shot and poisoned because of conflict with grouse moors and so the average eagle life span in the eastern Highlands is cut to only twenty-five to thirty years.

So I asked Jeff just what is the status of our golden eagle, the apparently cherished (if you read the tourist guides) symbol of wildness, the icon of a pristine environment. He tells me there are currently about a thousand birds, occupying some four hundred and ninety ranges, of which four hundred and twenty contain breeding pairs, the rest immature birds. It appears to be a relatively stable population although it is undoubtedly kept down by illegal persecution. But the underlying threat is land use. In recent years hill sheep farming has been badly hit and flocks have peeled away from the high pastures like snow in spring. Agriculture is changing by the day; there are few certainties in the livestock sector these days. Subsidies are being withdrawn and the days of per capita allowances are a fading memory. There is also mounting pressure to reduce deer numbers and to re-establish native woods, a long-overdue and welcome turnaround for most wildlife, but the removal of both sources of carrion could mean the golden eagle may be in for some tough old winters at the hands of man.

I cannot help being possessive about our eagles. I see them regularly in the neighbouring glens. I fancy I know them and they become old friends, although it is easy to be wrong about individual bird identity. But the very knowledge that they could be here long after I am gone cheers me; it puts me in my place. In the fifty-year span of a healthy eagle's life huge changes could take place across the landscape. Forestry, agriculture, sport, tourism and the patterns of human settlement and transport have all changed dramatically over the past half-century. In the past thirty years the Highlands have opened up in a way few could have predicted. As I walk back down the hill I wonder whether eagles hold memories of the landscapes of their youth? The eagle-eye view of the world could teach mankind a thing or two.

I am heading home. The cold air stings my face and the night flooding up to me from the river valley below seems to lift the air frost with it. Above the pinewood the snow glows like mercury with an inner light of its own. My boots crunch with every step so there is no chance of walking silently. In the wood it is already dusk. It feels as if it hasn't bothered with the brief day at all, and that this twilight never went away, is left over from last night. It is silent, as silent as the frozen loch I can see pale and gleaming through the crow-black pillars of the pines. My breath is the only visible movement. I stand to watch and feel night pool at my feet.

This is my home. Not the gaunt old house or its fireside chair; not the echoing chimes of the grandfather clock in the hall or the creaky board in the landing floor; not my faithful 4×4 truck tucked up in its garage; not the Jack Russell terriers snoring in their box under the kitchen table; not the summer laughter of children at the garden pond, nor the chink of glass and china as we all sit round the family table, although, dear God, I would miss them all more than I can say if they were not there. No, my long home, the home where I feel at one with myself and with the world as I have known it in my time is the wildness of this beautiful place and the wildness it evokes within my head. It is now and has been for many years like coming home; where I feel I belong.

On my way down to the loch shore I pick my steps slowly and carefully, not wanting the spell to break or the moment to pass. The sun is long gone and although the far western horizon still throbs with a purple afterglow, the moon is taking over. I can't see it yet, but its imminence simmers with a red-brick fringe to the trees in the east. I can wait. It's nearly full, only a few days to go to madness, the old madness of the wolf's howl and the badgers' grumpy refusal to come above ground at full moon. These are nature's rhythms, the biorhythms of the seasons and lunar cycles of every sentient organism on the planet, about which we know so much but seem to comprehend so very little.

We should never underestimate the gravitational pull of the moon. In fish and many marine invertebrates lunar drag is the force around which their entire lives and reproductive systems rotate. Many land mammals react to the phases of the moon. We know for a fact that the female badger's pituitary gland secretes fewer hormones at full moon, detectable in her urine by the twitching nose of the male, so that no mating occurs – in fact badger mating peaks on the darkest nights of the lunar cycle. Is their failure to appear above ground on bright nights a relict protective adaptation to reduce the incidence of predation by predators that no longer exist? It might be.

The work of the eminent Oxford biologist Charles Elton in the 1940s and '50s revealed that the Hudson Bay Company's trapping records for beaver and martens, mink and lynx demonstrated a distinct lull during full moon. Prey animals were not exposing themselves to the high light levels of the full moon – actually some ten thousand times light difference between new moon and full moon – and predators were not wasting energy by hunting prey that wasn't out and about.

Has mankind lost his way because we are out of touch with the biorhythms that controlled our lives long ago? Is it our self-imposed separation from nature that is leading us to an inevitable destruction? Is the process reversible before it's too late? Can we relocate our connection with nature and wildness? Can human behaviour be reversed? Can we pull back from the brink? I have no answers to any of these complex philosophical and emotional conundrums and would not wish to pretend that I had. What I do know, as profoundly and as resolutely as I know myself, is that for those with eyes to see it and the wit to value it, there is exquisite beauty out there: rampant, original, dynamic, persistent and exhilarating beauty. The Garden of Eden has become a terrible and sickening metaphor. Pristine it was, magnificent, majestic and utterly inspirational. We are trading Creation for pieces of fool's gold.

At the water's edge I wait for the moon to take over. A shiver passes through me, leaving a trail of tingling skin. It *is* cold. The freezing air is sliding past me, stinging the rims of my ears, as it toboggans down through the pine trees to settle like dust far out on the surface of the loch. With all the luminous presence of a ripe peach the moon's brazier glow pales to amber and then to bright platinum as it lifts diagonally through the trees. Rags of cloud fall away, dazzled. Stars expectantly spark a secret Morse code of their own, urging it on.

A tawny owl floats effortlessly onto a branch only a few feet away with no sound other than the faint scratching of its talons on the scaly bark of the pine. I shiver again, a shiver of emotion rather than cold. It is a sensation I have often felt when wildlife comes to me – however unwittingly – rather than my having to hide and lurk. I smile inwardly, not daring to move. It is very close. One shrill cry – 'Ki-viiiiik!' – trails from its neatly hooked bill; its whole body lifts with the effort, jetting out the sound from deep inside its breast, the gape widening with the last drawn-out syllable. The cry echoes through the pinewood and bounces off the ice of the loch, still ringing far up the other side. Then it sees me. Its round eyes peer like a short-sighted pensioner with thick, pebble lenses too big for his face, its neck extends and withdraws again twice, uncertain, apprehensive, unsettled. I stand still, watching. I stand still, wondering what it can detect of me with those glowing, infra-red orbs and its night hyper-sentience. I am wondering what it will make of me when I have to blink and it sees the moon reflected in my eyes, when this exquisite, soft-plumed, wild creature of the moonlight realises the awful truth, when it sees me for what I am.

# Postscript

*The Epigraph*  Scotland's golden eagle guru, Dr Jeff Watson, died after a brave fight against cancer in September 2007, aged fifty-four. He will be sorely missed. As a conservationist and ornithologist he was widely respected. At the end of his life he was honoured with the RSPB medal for his outstanding contribution to conservation ornithology.

*Chapter 1: The Lie of the Land*  In these times of super-visibility (the internet, Google et al.), it is impossible to conceal where I live. Actually, I neither want nor need to. In any case I laid it all bare when I wrote the long history of my home in *Song of the Rolling Earth*. The reason I have not given it a name in this book is because I did not want to write specifically about this place, per se, as I did in *Song*; rather I have sought to use my walk through the woods and around the loch as a paradigm for any walk and any loch, anywhere.

People say that I'm immensely fortunate to live in such a beautiful place, as if somehow I have just been set down here by chance, or, better still, by some divine beneficence. Sometimes it is said in a tone that suggests it is also a privilege, curiously out of reach of 'ordinary' people. Fortune I can cope with, at least in so far as I have sometimes had some good luck along with the bad, but as with any situation in life, it ultimately boils down to what you make of it and how determined you are to stick at things when the going gets tough. Being a professional naturalist or a writer of non-fiction during the more than thirty years I have lived here in the Highlands has certainly dished up my fair share of tough, but I honestly believe that the joy I have received from nature in my work and in this place is no greater than that available to anyone in any other wild bit of countryside. The metaphorical excursion in this book does not need a place name. Like birdsong, its joys are often simple and commonplace. This book is about understanding and accessing that joy.

*Chapter 2: Spring at Last*   Most people in Britain experience a three- or four-month winter. March is a spring month in southern England: cherry blossom, daffodils, bluebells, birds nesting like mad. Here, north of Moscow and Churchill on Hudson Bay, our Highland winter closes in during early November and is resolutely with us until nearly May – certainly six, and often seven months. Friends and neighbours who suffer SAD have to escape. Alcoholism raises its ugly head. Like Tantalus, our winter is unkind; it seems to play with us, seeming to let go and then hauling us in again. We long for spring – and just when the daffodils bravely lift their trumpets, down comes the snow again. Year after year peregrine falcons on the cliff lay their eggs and then desert them because they get chilled by the driving sleet. For full leaf we have to wait until well into May. That's why it is 'Spring at Last'.

*Chapter 3: Dreams in a Jar*  In the eighteenth century Gilbert White wrote a very good natural history without having the faintest notion about amino acids. Like most others of his time he held the creative hand of God to be responsible for the wonders of nature he described with such precision in that great book. In our time we have not been so fortunate; poor old God has been seriously undermined. Darwin, Wallace and Huxley saw to that more than a hundred years after White penned his inspirational and seminal work at Selborne. Then the Augustinian abbot Gregor Mendel, tinkering with his sweet peas but still convinced it was God's work, showed us how inheritance works, considerably thickening the plot.

Even now the questions persist: What is life? Where did it come from? And who ordained it? It is a sobering thought that in the twenty-first century two-thirds of the world's population do not accept or acknowledge evolution without God's hand. But for most of us everything changed when Stanley Miller brewed up his flasks in 1953, although he just happened to be the lucky one – others were hard on his heels. Once the cat was out of the bag, all in a rush came Watson and Crick and the DNA spiral, and suddenly the origins of life were being discussed on a new and esoteric level few of us laymen could properly comprehend.

For many of us those same questions have not gone away altogether; but I believe it is vital that we don't permit the astounding intricacies of atomic and organic chemistry to sully the deeply personal experiences nature and wildlife can provide, nor their meaning on a personal level to us as individuals, which is what matters when addressing the fundamental environmental issues of our day and man's long-term future on the planet.

*Chapter 4: King of the Castle*    You could be forgiven for asking: What on earth have my whisky and the Scottish water authorities got to do with that remarkable New World triumvirate Emerson, Whitman and Thoreau? Fair question. But for me, the answer is: Everything. Theirs was essentially a literature of meditative excursions, exploring and expanding a new, alternative and uplifting way of looking at nature for the invigoration and spiritual transcendence of all men. I went to Walden Pond in my twenties, walked the Massachusetts woods, sat and stared out to sea from Cape Cod, and have returned to stay in and near Concord several times since. Thoreau has never really left my consciousness, and it is Walt Whitman's lyrics that most frequently dance through when I sit down to write. For those caught up in the environmental movement they have assumed the stature of a world-changing trio.

I remain in their thrall. If it was OK for them to use nature and a walk to lift them out of man's self-inflicted whirlpool of rushed, profit-chasing routines, market forces, and the consequential disinterest in nature and abuse of wildlife, it certainly is for me. Transcending these 'norms' of everyday human existence, then and now, is a central theme of this book, but I have never sought to idolise or sentimentalise wildlife for its own sake, however central a theme it may have been in my life. So I wanted to emphasise that the apparently malevolent and often egregious behaviour of hooded crows is also a norm – actually a far truer norm than what we have come to think of as normal human behaviour. Facing those truths and acknowledging them openly brings us down to earth with a healthy bump.

*Chapter 5: Dawn*  Waking with the dawn is more of a habit than an obsession. I also think it has a lot to do with our latitude. Above the 57th parallel, dawn comes in extremes: before 2.00 a.m. GMT in the middle of June and after 8.00 a.m. GMT in mid-December. So finding myself wide awake and longing to leap out of bed at 2.00 or 2.30 a.m. in the spring can be highly disruptive of sleep patterns (not to say marriage!), which is barely compensated for in winter when, seeing the driving sleet, I would far rather turn over and go back to sleep.

Shortly after writing this chapter I saw a wildcat at the loch again. I now know that they have bred there, or at least in the vicinity, for several years in a row. This is very encouraging and inclines me to think that Ro Scott is right and that the Mammal Society may be being unduly pessimistic. I hope so. To lose this mammal at a time when, at long last, restoration ecology is becoming a reality and native woodlands – essential habitat for wildcats – are re-establishing themselves throughout the Highlands, would be a tragic irony.

*Chapter 6: Energy and the Big Deal*  Very few of us are conscious of the energy flows that govern our everyday lives. The effulgent Sammy was by no means an exception, so she becomes the metaphor for our collective failure to take environmental education seriously, even when we stand on the very brink of a global ecological crisis that is very likely to change all our lives for the worse. I never knew her full name or anything else about her. If one day she reads this and remembers the wild man of the woods who came to her school to lecture on nature, I should like her to know that she had a far greater impact on me than I suspect I did on her!

*Chapter 7: Wild*  In one of his founding speeches to the Sierra Club, John Muir expressed the belief that 'if people had access to the wilderness' they would fall in love with it and preserve it. He thought that others would automatically share his passion for wildness and be similarly affected by it. He got that one badly wrong. Mankind has always raped and pillaged wilderness for his own ends, and continues to do so. Our principal problem is that there are so many of us. But for all that, Muir was partly responsible for a global environmental movement that has steadily gathered momentum for a century since his death. It is very fitting that his name is now perpetuated in the John Muir Trust, which seeks to preserve Scotland's wilderness for wilderness's sake. Yet Muir was right about one aspect of wildness. If you are so minded, it is a drug: heady, uplifting, compulsive and deeply addictive.

*Chapter 8: The Claim*  Biologists would not acknowledge the term. Their word 'succession' implies that certain species fall into place when the opportunities arise. If the conditions suit it, a food supply is present and if competition from other species permits, a colonising species will occupy a niche and thrive or not according to its ability to exploit whatever natural resources are available. I have used the word 'claim' simply because that is what seems to me to be happening. I also like it because it is explicit that competition is a constant. You don't claim something unless you are pretty sure someone else is after it too. In nature that is always the case, no exceptions.

I cannot think of a situation where organisms are not ready to take over at the least opportunity. Even deep ocean volcanic vents have chemo-synthetic bacteria drawing nutrition from arguably one of the least hospitable habitats on the globe. After the great eruption of Krakatoa in 1883 (in which 36,417 people in 165 coastal villages were killed) and the apparent sterilisation of the island, tiny spiders were found to be floating in on the winds within a few days and establishing territories. 'First come first served' is a nice idea, but it isn't accurate in nature. First come may not be suitably adapted to survive and will quickly give way to another organism that is. What does work is 'first come best suited'. Darwin had it right. Fitness is the abiding quality for survival, but the organism still has to lay claim to its chances.

*Chapter 9: Summer's Green Stain*   In a rare comic aside in *Ring of Bright Water*, Gavin Maxwell observed that his diary informed him that on June 22nd it was the start of the British summer, and then two days later it was Midsummer's day, from which he could only logically conclude that summer was all of four days long. Happily, this is not the case. In the year of writing, 2006, we enjoyed a long and relatively hot summer which stretched over fully four months, becoming an Indian summer in October. Perhaps this is the climate change we shall have to expect in the decades ahead. If it is, not just the badgers but much of our wildlife must adapt very quickly, or be forced out.

*Chapter 10: Pine Martens*   Watching pine martens is easy once you have located them. They will raid litter bins and come to bird tables in broad daylight. We are very fortunate to have them; they are still one of Britain's rarest mammals. Their elegance and cheeky opportunism are fascinating to observe. For those keen to see pine martens at close quarters, check out 'www.aigas.co.uk'.

The stove in the Illicit Still is a conventional, old-fashioned, steel oil drum. The conversion kit of cast-iron legs, door and chimney ring is made by Cole Creek in Canada, very cheap to buy and very easy to rig up – all you need is a drill, a hacksaw and a spanner. But beware! The stove is magnificently efficient. A good fire well stoked will become a furnace, turn the whole oil drum red hot and send you scurrying for cover. These stoves are designed for lumberjacks' camps, not for middle-class living rooms!

*Chapter 11: An Explosion of Flowers*   I was inspired to write this chapter by reading an essay first published *circa* the 1960s entitled 'How Flowers Changed the World', by Dr Loren Eiseley (1907–77). It was one of those pieces of writing that stay with you for years and the credit for my attempt to tell the same story lies entirely with him.

*Chapter 12: The Autumn Stalk*   The woodcock is very good to eat, no denying it. Traditionally each bird is plucked and trussed but not drawn before roasting, each one placed on a slice of bread toasted or fried on one side only, so that, while roasting, the juices of the bird's 'trail' can run out and be absorbed by the soft side of the bread. No one seems to talk about the contents of the 'trail' – a subject conveniently *verboten* in the kitchen. A case of what the eye don't see . . .

Many nature writers have written up a deer stalk: W.H. Hudson, Edwin Way Teale, Richard K. Nelson, Sir Frank Fraser Darling and many more. The deer is symbolic of much more than a convenient-sized prey species good to eat. It is written into our deep psyche as *the* prey species that has sustained mankind in the northern hemisphere for millennia. The medieval world worshipped the deer, weaving him into tapestries and embroidery, in carving, etching and literature, poetry and song. The word for deer meat, venison, comes from the Latin *venere*, to hunt. Ever since the extinction of the elk in prehistoric times, in Britain the red deer, *Cervus elaphus*, has been the biggest and has probably always been the most prized deer species for the hunt and the table. Man, the hunt and the red deer are inseparable. I have stalked many deer in my time, of several different species, but the red deer stag reigns supreme. Stalking him was an act of oblation and a backward glance at our shared origins in the primeval forest and that even more ancient association, the hunter and the hunted.

*Chapter 13: Iceland and the Whoopers*   When I returned from the New Hampshire and Massachusetts woods with the notion of this book ringing in my head, I had no idea that my old friend, the celebrated and much loved journalist, television broadcaster, environmentalist and author, Magnus Magnusson (Icelandic by parentage, Scottish by upbringing), was in trouble. Although he had been dangerously ill with septicaemia, he fought bravely back to health and work – as Mamie, his wife, said to me, 'Magnus was brought up to believe that a man did not limp while his legs were the same length.' (This is actually a quotation from Gunnlaugur Adder-tongue, an Icelandic saga-hero who had a massive boil on his foot, addressing the earl of Norway, who asked him why he wasn't limping.) When, eighteen months later, the news of cancer came, it was devastating. Magnus had been so vital, so vigorous, so enthusiastic about everything we had done together over nearly twenty years, that to imagine him facing his own death was simply gutting.

In October 2006 he came to stay for the last time. We walked to the loch together, talking about old times. He was frail, but impossibly Viking-ish, stoical and chirpy, dismissing his obvious difficulties with a laugh and a cloud of pipe smoke. When he left I wondered if I would ever see him again. That day I resolved to write to him as often and regularly as I could manage, letters about the wildlife and the hills and the stuff we had worked on together over the years. This chapter is a distillation of one of those journal-based letters.

*Chapter 14: The Goshawk*   Although I searched for many weeks I do not believe I ever saw that goshawk again. Several times I have seen a large female, as big as a buzzard, soaring over the pinewood beside the loch, and in recent years I have occasionally seen a goshawk over the river, leading me to believe that they may have bred in the spruce plantation on the far side of the valley, but I never saw a bird well enough or for long enough to catch sight of that eye. The Highlands is big and goshawks are secretive, so it's not really surprising. But it is interesting that even though several years have passed, I still look across to the horizon where he disappeared that day. The bird branded himself on my subconscious and upon the landscape so that for me that view will always be where I last saw the goshawk.

*Chapter 15: Pop Goes the Weasel*   The end of the story of Wilba is both charming and comical. The teenage boy who released him back into the wild had a very heavy heart indeed. He was ready to go, a fine young male weasel that deserved the company of wild weasels rather than that of a schoolboy, however besotted. He went off without looking back, hunting, hot on the trail of some poor vole. I missed him more than I can say; those halcyon days are still an amethyst remembrance to me.

I took him to those same Devon woods where I had first stumbled across his natal nest. It had been raided by a predator and he was the sole survivor, although I never knew what that predator was (most likely a fox or badger). I set him down, as was our daily hunting routine, and waited until he was onto the scent of prey, then, steeling myself, I quietly crept away, also not looking back.

A little more than a year later I took my father to those same woods. It was where I had been surveying a colony of badgers and I was keen to show him the setts. So there we were, my father and I, quietly sitting on a bank enjoying a sandwich together on a late summer afternoon, and quite suddenly a weasel popped out of the long grass and ran straight up to me. It climbed onto my leg, where it paused, looking straight at me for a fleeting second before disappearing again as fast as it had come. I was in no doubt then, nor am I now, that it was Wilba, and I published the tale in *The Countryman* in 1962, clearly saying so. In the next edition some boring old misery wrote to the editor saying that the whole episode was highly unlikely and that, while intent on hunting, weasels often blunder into people. I laughed then, and laugh now. I am sure Wilba would have laughed too.

*Chapter 16: Winter*    It is a fact of hill-country life that foxes are shot all the time. They do take new-born lambs. Crofters on low incomes struggling with poor land have demonised the fox and the hoodie as the last two serious predators of their world; gamekeepers loathe them too. They are also illegally poisoned, often resulting in the deaths of other species either by accident or by secondary poisoning. For all this the fox population is strong and probably unaffected by such measures.

Human population control has always been a very contentious issue much clouded by religion, economics and ideology. There are no quick fixes, but that's not a good reason for not discussing it and encouraging policies that can help achieve environmental sustainability before it is too late. For me as a nature conservationist this issue has been bubbling beneath the surface all my life. For fifty years I have witnessed huge swathes of wildlife habitat and wild land gobbled up for the unrelenting needs of development, housing and industry – of people. The popularity and public awareness of nature conservation have also risen dramatically during that period, but always subordinate to the needs of development – a process of one step forward, two steps back. Most people now expect nature to be in reserves, and for wildlife to be managed there by humans to keep it in its place, under 'control'. So I see the two problems closely inter-related. If we could find the political will and an acceptable means to begin to reduce our populations across the globe and the concomitant human pressure on natural resources, nature conservation and the long-term future for humans would benefit hugely.

# References, Further Reading
# and Bibliography

Alston, C.H., 1912. *Wild Life in the West Highlands*. James Maclehose & Sons. Glasgow.

Alston, E.R., 1880. *Fauna of Scotland*. James Maclehose & Sons. Glasgow.

Baker, J.A., 1967. *The Peregrine*. W. Collins. Glasgow.

Bate, J., 2000. *The Song of the Earth*. Picador. London.

Cocker, M., 2006. *A Tiger in the Sand: Selected Writings on Nature*. Jonathan Cape. London.

Colquhoun, J., 1840. *The Moor and the Loch*. Blackwood. Edinburgh.

Crumley, J., 1997. *The Company of Swans*. The Harvill Press. London.

Darling, F.F., 1937. *A Herd of Red Deer*. Oxford University Press. Oxford.

Darling, F.F., 1947. *Natural History in the Highlands and Islands*. Collins (New Naturalist). London.

Darling, F.F., 1955. *West Highland Survey. An Essay in Human Ecology*. Oxford University Press. Oxford.

Darling, F.F. and Boyd, J.M., 1964. *The Highlands and Islands*. Collins (New Naturalist). London.

Dillard, A., 1982. *Teaching a Stone to Talk*. Harper & Row. New York.

Dillard, A., 1989. *The Writing Life*. Harper & Row. New York.

Eiseley, Loren, 1957. *The Immense Journey*. Vintage (Random House). New York.

Eiseley, L., 1978. *The Star Thrower*. Harvest/HBJ. London & New York.

Emerson, R.W., 1994. *Nature and Other Writings*. Ed. By Peter Turner. Shambhala. Boston & London.

Fairbrother, Nan, 1970. *New Lives, New Landscapes*. Architectural Press. Oxford.

Fiennes, W., 2002. *The Snow Geese*. Picador. London.

Fowles, J., 1979. *The Tree*. Vintage/Random House. London.

Gordon, S., 1937. *Afoot in Wild Places*. Cassell. London.

Gordon, S., 1944. *A Highland Year*. Eyre & Spottiswoode. London.

Grahame, K., 1908. *The Wind in the Willows*. Methuen & Co. London.

Grant, I.F., 1924. *Every-day Life on an Old Highland Farm, 1769–1782*. Longmans, Green & Co. London.

Griffiths, J., 2006. *Wild: An Elemental Journey*. Tarcher/Penguin. London & New York.

Harvie-Brown, J.A., 1887. *A Vertebrate Fauna of Sutherland, Caithness and West Cromarty*. David Douglas. Edinburgh.

Hendry, G., 1989. *Midges in Scotland*. Aberdeen University Press. Aberdeen.

Hughes, T., 1972. *Crow*. Faber & Faber. London.

Hughes, T., 1982. *Selected Poems: 1957–1981*. Faber & Faber. London.

Linn, I., 1962. *Weasels*. Animals of Britain No. 14. Ed. by L.

Harrison Matthews. Sunday Times Publications Ltd. London.

Lister-Kaye, J., 1994. *Ill Fares the Land: A Sustainable Land Ethic for the Sporting Estates of the Highlands and Islands of Scotland*. Scottish Natural Heritage Occasional Paper No. 3. Scottish Natural Heritage. Perth.

Lister-Kaye, J., 2003. *Song of the Rolling Earth: A Highland Odyssey*. Time Warner. London.

Lister-Kaye, J., 2004. *Nature's Child: Encounters with Wonders of the Natural World*. Little, Brown. London.

Mabey, R., 1986. *Gilbert White: A Biography of the Author of 'The Natural History of Selborne'*. Century Hutchinson Ltd. London.

Mabey, R., 2005. *Nature Cure*. Chatto & Windus. London.

Mabey, R., 2007. *Beechcombings: The Narratives of Trees*. Chatto & Windus. London.

Magnusson, S., 2004. *Dreaming of Iceland: The Lure of a Family Legend*. Hodder & Stoughton. London.

Nash, R., 1967. *Wilderness and the American Mind*. Yale University Press. New Haven.

Neal, E., 1948. *The Badger*. Collins (New Naturalist). London.

Oelschlaeger, M., 1991. *The Idea of Wilderness*. Yale University Press. New Haven & London.

Proctor, M. and Yeo, P., 1973. *The Pollination of Flowers*. Collins (New Naturalist). London.

Raine, K., 1965. *The Hollow Hill:* and other poems 1960–1964. Hamish Hamilton. London.

Richmond, K., 1960. *Highland Gathering*. Geoffrey Bles. London.

Snyder, G., 1990. *The Practice of the Wild*. North Point Press. San Francisco.

Steven, H.M. and Carlisle, A., 1959. *The Native Pinewoods of Scotland*. Oliver & Boyd. Edinburgh.

St John, C., 1849. *Short Sketches of the Wild Sports and Natural History of the Highlands*. John Murray. London.

Thompson, F., 1978. *A Scottish Bestiary: The Lore and Literature of Scottish Beasts*. The Molendinar Press. Glasgow.

Thoreau, H.D., 1993 edition. *Walden*. J.M. Dent (Everyman). London.

Thoreau, H.D., 1906. *A Week on the Concord and Merrimack Rivers*. Houghton. Boston.

Turner, J., 1996. *The Abstract Wild*. University of Arizona Press. Tucson.

Watson, J., 1997. *The Golden Eagle*. T. & A.D. Poyser. London.

White, G., 1789. *The Natural History and Antiquities of Selborne*. H.G. Bohn. London.

White, T.H., 1951. *The Goshawk*. Jonathan Cape. London.

# Thanks and Acknowledgements

It would be easy to imagine that all the nature writer needs is a pen and a notebook, that he can park himself under a shady tree where muse and the birdsong will fill his pages. Would that it were so. In fact, of course, the writing process is a long and uplifting journey, but also often frustrating, drawn-out and full of pitfalls. Sitting down and working out just how many people have steered me, proffered a helping arm and sometimes carried me along the way always surprises me.

There are those, for instance, who have willingly done the things I should have been doing and thereby enabled me to write. Heading that list is my son-in-law Ieuan Evans, who shouldered so many of my responsibilities, often at very short notice, so that I could slip away to walk or scribble my notes. In thousands of little ways and many big ones, my loyal secretary, Sheila Kerr, has provided unflagging support throughout, whether keeping me to deadlines or warding off marauders, printing endless drafts and generally organising me, always with that priceless and essentially female intuition about whether it's a good moment to disturb me or not. Kay Douglas and Frances Macleman also gave me valuable back-up and support when I needed it.

Next comes my daughter Amelia Williamson, who

generously agreed to read the earliest drafts of the manuscript when the book was taking shape and jolted me out of complacency by scribbling across the title page, 'Dad, I really enjoyed this, but what is it *about*?' As with previous books, Jessica Findlay and Martha Crewe also read and re-read drafts. For their always positive and constructive criticisms I am extremely grateful.

And then there are the cohorts of Aigas Field Centre naturalists and rangers who have helped me with research or pointed things out to me and checked my findings. I particularly thank Duncan Macdonald, Glen Campbell, Philip Knott, Michael Werndley, Ian Sargent, Donald Sheilds, Davy Still, Morag Smart, Vicki Saint, Jenny Grant, Lindsey Duncan, Ros Codd and Melanie Evans. They probably weren't aware just how valuable their input and enthusiasm were because I didn't always reveal my ulterior motives, but without them I would have missed so much.

I am also extremely lucky to have had the support, advice and friendship of some heavy professionals on whom I was able to test my opinions and who were able to confirm (or dismiss) my observations. To Lesley Cranna, Roy Dennis, Paul Ramsay, David Dixon, Robin Noble, Jonathan Willet, Ro Scott, Chris Smout, John Aitcheson, Jeff Watson, Peter Wortham and Laurie Campbell, my most sincere thanks.

All writers depend upon the toleration and selflessness of their families. When I disappear for days or weeks on end my wife Lucy describes herself as a literary widow. She claims she knows 'that look' in my eyes, which means there's no point talking to me. For that understanding and for her patience, love and support, as always, my deep gratitude.

## Thanks and Acknowledgements

My sincere thanks go to the Canongate team, Publishing Editor Nick Davies, Managing Editors Stephanie Gorton and Norah Perkins, and Copy Editor Helen Bleck and to my long-suffering literary agent Catherine Clarke for their professionalism and faith in my work.

Finally, I salute the wild animals with which I share my home. They tolerate me as much as I extract joy from their presence. Only yesterday a large golden-ringed dragonfly settled on my knee as I sat beside the loch. For several seconds we eyed each other. Then, on rigid wings, he rattled off about his business. I have no idea what he thought of me, but I saw him in total awe and the image of his presence will stay with me for years to come.

Formal acknowledgements are due to The Estate of the Late Magnus Magnusson KBE for permission to print the quotations from his translation of the *Edda* in the dedication and *Egil's Saga* from the Icelandic and to Richard Mabey for permission to quote from *Nature Cure*.